Printed in the United States of America

ISBN: 9781791734008
ISBN-13:

O.R. McKeefe Publishing, Inc.

Book Cover Design, Concept and Layout by Seven Marcus Aurelius and P.M. Siluk

will try several times, but is unable to find the respondent at home or at work.

G. **Temporary Restraining Orders (TROs) From A Judge's Point of View**

When a TRO request crosses my desk, I have to review these petitions without the respondent having received notice. In considering these petitions, I weigh the petitioner's safety and welfare against the respondent's rights and constitutionally guaranteed freedoms, such as the right to free speech, one of the cornerstones of our democracy. If the allegations are true, not issuing the TRO can put the petitioner at serious physical, mental or emotional risk. On the other hand, if the allegations are exaggerated or downright false, issuing a TRO could needlessly and irreparably impinge on the respondent's rights. It's a tightrope act and, frankly, I think most applications should be denied unless they are clear on their face. There is always another side to the story, and unless there is a real threat of violence, I believe the matter can wait until the hearing where everyone can have their say. However, when the decision isn't so clear cut, as judges we have no choice but to err on the side of the petitioner, in favor of their safety. We must grant the TRO even if it means causing another person who might not even be aware of the allegations against them to suffer dire consequences. Hypothetically, a person can fabricate a story about someone, throw in a few half-truths on the form, and then get a TRO issued and served without paying any fees (after checking off that box on the form).

Because of the far-reaching ramifications of restraining orders, as judges we strive to settle as many of these cases as we can, thus refraining from issuing the orders. One case I presided over involved two people on one side and eight on the other, all residents of the same apartment building. The parties were all standing in front of the counsel table accusing one another of all kinds of misconduct, including intolerable noise and blocking one another's access to their apartment units. The parties were yelling at one another and generally acting with belligerence towards one another. Fortunately, we have a mediator available, so I told the parties that I have made a tentative decision to issue restraining orders against all of them unless, with the help of the mediator, they were able to settle their differences. Since the hearing was conducted during the morning court session, I ordered them to return to my courtroom at 3:00 P.M., at which time, I would issue my final order. I also informed them that if they were able to resolve the matter before noon, they would not need to return to my court and that I would not issue any orders. Thankfully, they never returned. One of the benefits of settling is that there is no record kept of the dispute at the court other than the name and case number for future reference.

This dispute, as with many disputes, was all about the ego. One's desire to receive for one's self only is pure ego. By everyone giving up something through compromise, the parties in this case were able to set their egos aside, thus doing something proactive and closing an adversarial chapter in their lives.

Another case in which I avoided issuing a restraining order, and instead came up with a creative solution, centered on a conflict among four, 13-year old girls, who attended the same school. The responding parties were clearly the aggressors and had beaten up the petitioner so badly that she had to be taken to hospital in an ambulance. I could see the physical damage on her face. There wasn't much of a defense as the fight took place on the front porch of the petitioner's house. I gave my usual speech about the seriousness and permanence of a restraining order and its potential impact on their future, including their ability to get a job. Then I told them that if they would transfer to a different school than the one the petitioner attended, and their mothers would give assurances that this would happen, I would deny the injunction. I gave them 30-days to change schools. The girls and their mothers agreed to this solution. It was a way to keep the parties apart without permanently tarnishing the young respondents' record.

One of the many cases I heard in which the petitioner should not have taken up the court's time involved a noisy parrot. The petitioner was annoyed by the constant chatter and screeching of his next-door neighbor's parrot, and sought a restraining order. How would you rule in this case?

I ruled that the neighbor simply had to move the parrot to the other side of the house.

Obviously, many of these restraining order cases concern very grave allegations. I adjudicated a case in which a 13-year old petitioner sought a restraining order against a man who she claimed had been raping her every week for more than a year and a half. She eventually reported it to a school guidance counselor. The respondent was the uncle of her best friend. She said that whenever she visited her friend's house, he would come on to her. He ended up taking her to motels where he exposed her to porn and molested her. At the hearing for the permanent restraining order, the respondent appeared with his lawyer. The young petitioner appeared with her parents and a sibling. After hearing her testimony, I asked the respondent's lawyer if there was a police investigation or criminal case pending against his client. Indeed, there was! Because the wheels of justice grind slowly, the petitioner needed the court to take immediate action to protect her from further contact with the respondent and, therefore, was seeking a restraining order. This was one of the strongest, most meritorious cases I have heard in favor of the issuance of a restraining order. Clearly, if I didn't issue the order to keep this man away from her, the girl would have continued to be at serious risk of harm by him.

The respondent's lawyer said his client wanted to testify at the hearing even though he understood that his testimony, which was being recorded, could be used by the district attorney in a criminal proceeding against him. Having been a deputy district attorney myself, I knew the effect his testimony could have if used against him. He had a Fifth Amendment right to refrain from testifying. Much to my surprise, he chose to waive the privilege. Apparently, he wanted to take the stand to deny the accusations against him.

I granted the restraining order to prevent him from doing anything more to the girl while he was awaiting his criminal trial. She needed protection considering that criminal cases can drag on for years.

Sometimes people ask me if restraining orders work. In a recent case I presided over, a well-known female celebrity attorney Gloria Allred had gone to the police, requesting protection from someone who was bombarding her with harassing emails and text messages. The police department responded by saying that they could not help her until she got a restraining order against the offender. They told her that then, if the offender violated the order, they could arrest him. Ms. Allred did not appear before me, but her partner did. He made her case for the permanent restraining order, which I granted. any months later, I ran into Ms. Allred's attorney, and learned that the harassment had completely ceased as a result of the restraining order. I believe that in most of the cases in which I have granted them, they have effectively kept the respondent away from the petitioner, and given the petitioner a degree of security they didn't have prior to the issuance of the order.

H. **Making The Temporary Order Permanent**

To get a permanent restraining order injunction, you have to appear at a hearing presided over by a judge, present your evidence, and allow the other person to present evidence that contradicts yours. Most courts have a duty judge who is available at all hours to handle emergency situations.

In recognition of the serious nature of a permanent restraining order, the law requires a higher burden of proof to obtain the permanent injunction than necessary for the temporary order. As the petitioner, you will have to present "clear and convincing evidence of a credible threat of violence" as demonstrated by "a course of conduct" that has "no legitimate purpose" or "a pattern of behavior composed of a series of acts over a period of time, however short, evidencing a continuity of purpose." This language comes from the California statute. As a judge, I will not grant the permanent injunction unless this standard has been met.

It's not uncommon for people seeking some sort of relief from a wrong they feel has been done to them to file for a restraining order, even though the restraining order makes absolutely no sense under the circumstances. Here's a case I heard which met none of the criteria for a restraining order. One party was seeking a restraining order against their neighbor whom they claimed had killed their cat and dumped their now deceased beloved pet on their front porch. I asked the party seeking the restraining order if they had an autopsy report for the dead cat. Surprisingly enough, they did, and it showed that the cat was killed by blunt force trauma, probably by an automobile. I then asked the petitioner, "Do you want me to issue a restraining order against your neighbors so that they won't kill your next cat?" There was no "course of conduct" or "pattern of behavior composed of a series of acts." With this sort of case, I suppose the petitioner's best option would have been to file a civil claim against their neighbors for killing the cat.

Under the burden of proof language for restraining orders, "threat" is defined as verbal, written, implied by a pattern of conduct, or a combination of verbal or written statements and conduct, made with the intent and the apparent ability to carry out the threat, so as to cause the person who is the target to reasonably "fear for his or her safety, or the safety of his or her immediate family."

A clear illustration of the "apparent ability to carry out the threat" standard can be seen in the following case I presided over. The petitioner pulled out her phone and displayed an email attachment of a photograph sent by the respondent showing the respondent sitting on the floor with a bottle of beer in one hand and a gun in the other with a threatening caption below the picture. The picture demonstrated that the respondent had the means to act out the threat. I granted the permanent restraining order, which meant that not only did the respondent have to refrain from any contact with the petitioner, but she had to turn over her gun to law enforcement within 24-hours.

Do you have to show intent? Intent is required for the prosecution of certain crimes; however, it isn't imperative to demonstrate the offender's intent when you try to secure a restraining order. The intent in restraining order cases need only be implied. As I mentioned earlier, what matters is if the petitioner reasonably (this is the operative word) has a fear that the threat is real regardless of whether or not the respondent intends to carry it out.

"A course of conduct" that must be shown is a pattern of behavior "composed of a series of acts over a period of time, however short, evidencing a continuity of purpose." Following or stalking an individual or engaging in harassing communications, which includes, but not limited to, "the use of public or private mails, interoffice mail, unreasonable texts, fax or computer email" can be considered a course of conduct. However, one isolated event, such as the killing of a neighbor's cat, is not a continuing "course of conduct." Here is another example. The petitioner was assaulted by the respondent, resulting in the petitioner's hospitalization. The assault took place months before the hearing, and since the attack there had been no further contact between the parties. You be the judge. Should I have granted the restraining order? I didn't. The petitioner had a remedy in the civil court for the damages, and it was an isolated event.

Another case I recently presided over that failed to meet

the burden of proof was one I have seen all too often – a matter of two women fighting over a boyfriend. The current girlfriend was pregnant with her boyfriend's child, and the ex-girlfriend sought a restraining order against her because she had allegedly scratched the ex-girlfriend's face. I denied the order because there was no evidence of a course of conduct on the part of the current girlfriend. It appeared to be a one-time incident.

In the petitions before me, I expect the petitioner to present real evidence. If I'm considering issuing a court order dictating to someone that they must refrain from doing or saying something, I expect the petitioner to persuade me that they are not simply being inconvenienced, but rather feel truly frightened or beleaguered. A clear example of a case with no merit is one in which the petitioner claims that her ex-boyfriend has a new girlfriend who lives in the petitioner's building and with whom her ex has fathered a baby. She claims the new girlfriend is flaunting her relationship with the ex and taunting the petitioner by parading the baby past the petitioner's door. The petitioner wants to put a stop to it. I certainly wouldn't issue a restraining order under these circumstances. Interestingly enough, in these former versus current girlfriend disputes, the boyfriends they are fighting over rarely, if ever, show up at the hearings.

I recall a completely frivolous petition in which the entire complaint was based on the respondent staring at her. When I questioned the petitioner, she said that she just knew that the stares were a portent of future harm. It appears she had x-ray vision and could see inside the respondent's head! Some filings are so ridiculous that they don't even warrant the time and expense of a hearing.

On the other hand, here's a petition I considered that did have merit. It came from a person who claimed that the next-door neighbor was throwing rocks at her house. At the hearing the petitioner offered a large bag of rocks as evidence to support her petition. She had been collecting the rocks and putting the dates and times on each one to indicate when they had been thrown. Because I found the petitioner to be credible, I granted the restraining order, admonishing the respondent not to throw any more rocks at the petitioner's house. It was a smart move on the petitioner's part to collect the rocks as evidence.

In order to limit a valid prior restraint on a respondent's conduct to a reasonable period of time and to avoid permanence, California law provides that the permanent restraining order can be issued only for a period of up to three years. It is subject to a renewal under conditions set forth in the statute and the court can modify the order at any time.

In a majority of restraining order cases, the conduct about which the petitioner complained in the petition has a better legal remedy if brought as a civil suit. Nuisance (the unreasonable, unwarranted and/or unlawful use of property, which causes inconvenience or damage to others, either to individuals and/or to the general public) issues such as those brought up in neighbor disputes, complaints of interference with economic advantage, and actions for intentional infliction of emotional distress, are all better left to litigation in court. This includes Small Claims Court.

The following is an example of a nuisance case, which, in my opinion, should have remained strictly a civil suit, and did not merit the filing of a restraining order petition. One neighbor complained that another neighbor was making too much noise playing basketball. The two neighbors began verbally harassing one another. The complaining neighbor filed a civil complaint, but also filed for a TRO against his basketball playing neighbor, and the respondent neighbor filed a cross-petition. In this case, they both succeeded in obtaining TROs against one another.

In harassment cases, the court must look at the facts to determine if such conduct, "would cause a reasonable person to suffer substantial emotional distress." The court concluded that the basketball playing "was not so outrageous, extreme, intense, or enduring, as to come within the scope of injunctive relief for willful harassment." In terms of whether the neighbor in this case was able to obtain relief for a nuisance cause of action, the court stated that, "Excessive and inappropriate noise may under certain circumstances constitute an interference with the present enjoyment of land amounting to a nuisance." In some instances, these sorts of nuisances can be the basis for a permanent injunction. However, each case must be decided on its own merits. The question for the judge in a nuisance case is not whether the petitioner has been annoyed or disturbed, but whether the complained of conduct would cause a reasonable person to suffer considerable emotional distress. People who live in organized communities will of necessity suffer some inconvenience and annoyance from their neighbors. In the aforementioned basketball-playing case, the petitioner applied for a TRO and permanent injunction probably to avoid the costs in time and money of a civil suit. With the TRO he got immediate relief for what was nothing more than a nuisance matter and, in the end, it was determined that, in any event, the playing of basketball does not constitute a nuisance. This was an example of misuse of the restraining order option and, it is also an example of ego-driven reactive litigants. A much more neighborly, conciliatory, and enlightened approach would have been for the complaining neighbor to simply express his concerns with his basketball-playing neighbor and perhaps work out a compromise that would have satisfied everyone's need.

Only a natural person, as opposed to a corporate entity can obtain a restraining order. A restraining order can only be issued against an individual and not a group.

I. **Dealing With Workplace Violence An All Too Common Occurrence Today**

What if you are an employer and someone enters your place of business, ranting and raving, frightening your employees?

Can you do anything? The answer is yes.

Violent outbursts by disgruntled employees, a former employee or just someone seeking revenge, have unfortunately become an increasingly common phenomenon, leaving tragedy in its wake. There is a law in California that provides relief for employers who are dealing with violence in the workplace. The law requires employers to provide a safe and secure workplace and limits the acts to be enjoined to "unlawful violence" or "a credible threat of violence." An employer may take reasonable steps to seek relief on behalf of any employee who is "credibly threatened." Any individual or employer can petition the court to issue a permanent restraining order injunction against a person they perceive to be displaying threatening behavior, whether or not the respondent openly targets or specifically intends malice toward the individual or employer. The law does not require that the threat of violence be directed at a particular employee. The law's purpose is to prevent workplace violence. Thus, as an employer you can petition for a general retraining order against a person, such as a disgruntled former employee or someone else who has been harassing employees in the workplace.

Some jurisdictions also allow for an employer to file a petition for a protective order on behalf of an employee experiencing harassment or threatening behavior whether or not the employee requests such an order. However, employers should always consult with the victim before seeking a workplace protective order. Taking such action without regard to the victim's wishes could pose safety risks for him or her, and possibly other employees as well. In fact, in some jurisdictions, the law requires an employer to notify or consult with a victimized employee before filing for a protective order on behalf of the employee.

Your act of seeking a restraining order against a threatening and/or potentially violent employee, or another person, can contribute towards preventing the violence from occurring, as a restraining order can keep the respondent from owning or acquiring a gun. When I issue a restraining order at a hearing, I will ask the respondent whether they have a gun. If they do, I advise them of the legal requirement that they surrender the gun and ammunition. In one case, the respondent claimed he was a hunter and asked, "Do I have to surrender my rifle? If I do, then I will not be able to hunt." I told him to get a bow and arrow if he wanted to hunt.

If, in light of the workplace threat, as the employer you take no action, you might be found negligent per se (conduct which can be treated as negligence without any proof as to the particular circumstances because it is in violation of a law meant to protect the public). These types of cases brought against employers can result in wrongful death or personal injury damage awards for the plaintiff. In a typical case, the employer's insurance company is supposed to cover the damages and defend the employer in the lawsuit. There have been many times I have witnessed insurance companies deny the employer coverage. The insurer will claim that the failure on the part of the employer to notify the insurance company of a direct or even indirect knowledge of a potential threat of violence voids the coverage under an exclusion called "the duty to cooperate," or because of a provision in the policy that calls for notice to the insurer. It is typical of an insurance company to look for any excuse to not satisfy a claim, and to not defend their insured in court. Sometimes the damage award is so substantial that it exceeds the employer's insurance policy limits. With these cases, a number of questions should be posed: What knowledge did the employer have of the threat? Was the threat direct or indirect? Was a record made of just what the threatening person said? Did anyone in the workplace suggest that a restraining order be sought? If not, why not? Were there any witnesses to the threat?

As an employer, for your protection, you should keep a written record of any actions, threatening behavior or words used by your employees, which might become relevant down the road if you find yourself defending a discrimination or wrongful termination suit.

Why do some fired employees react the way they do? They often lash out in anger, want to blame somebody for losing their job, they might be seeking revenge, or they feel frustrated and see themselves as the victim. These types of ego driven reactions could drive them to engage in threatening conduct.

If an employer suspects a terminated employee might threaten the workplace, they should immediately consult with the human relations manager at the place of business. It is often possible to determine from the terminated employee's responses to the termination notification whether or not they pose a risk. In a recent case I adjudicated, a person threatened the city attorney in the courtroom in a civil litigation matter between him and the police department, by saying, "This is not going to end here." As a result of this statement, I issued the restraining order. The man was escorted out of the building by security personnel. The case went up to the Court of Appeals, which affirmed my decision, opining (stating as one's opinion, adjudging, concluding) there was sufficient threat from the language and manner to justify the restraining order. A copy of the Court of Appeals opinion, *City of Los Angeles v. Garber*, is in the Appendices.

What happens if someone, who is not an employee or former employee, poses a threat in the workplace? Given that the employer has the obligation to provide a safe and secure workplace, the employer can seek a restraining order against the non-employee individual who is displaying threatening behavior. I recently granted a restraining order in a case in which a patron of a library was threatening the library staff. The order was sought by the City of Los Angeles.

In another case, I granted a permanent restraining order sought by a downtown Los Angeles church against a parishioner who verbally threatened the pastor, the president of the parish council and other church members, and had sent hundreds of threatening text messages to them. He was ordered to stay at least one hundred yards away from the church and the individuals whom he had threatened, and to refrain from sending any further text messages to them. The permanent order was for three years, at the end of which time the petitioner could seek to renew the order. The attorney representing the church requested that the respondent (who did not show up for the hearing, by the way) be kept away from all church members. I rejected this particular request as overly broad. It would be a violation of the respondent's due process right because he would not have notice of the restriction to stay away from all of these church members. I advised the attorney to file a new petition containing the names of these other parishioners who were being threatened by the respondent.

In contrast to the outcome in that case, I recently denied a restraining order in another church case. In this one, the church sought a restraining order against a parishioner who was making nasty comments to other churchgoers and the staff at the church. Although his behavior was annoying, it did not reach the level of being threatening, and thus deserving of a restraining order being issued. I told the church attorney that instead of seeking a restraining order, his client could have brought a civil suit for nuisance, or they could have sought to have the parishioner prosecuted for trespassing.

If you have sustained injuries in your workplace, or on public property and, consequently, are suing your employer, or former employer for failure to provide a safe work environment for you, or you are bringing an action against the government for failure to provide a safe environment for the public, you (or your attorney) should request that the judge give the jury a particular instruction (in California it is Jury Instruction 419, which is also in the Appendices). This instruction addresses the law dealing with negligence per se. As I mentioned earlier, employers and the government are required as a matter of law to provide a safe workplace and safe public areas. Failure to seek a restraining order when the actual or constructive knowledge of a risk from an employee, former employee, or patron at a public place could constitute negligence per se. Again, as I have suggested a number of times in this book about various legal conflicts, these cases should settle.

Gun violence is in the news every day. How do we limit gun ownership to people who have the right to own them, but keep them away from people who should not have them or ammunition?

After eight years of presiding over restraining order cases, including the issuance (or non-issuance) of temporary restraining orders, and conducting hundreds of hearings, I realized that we already have a mechanism in place that could be used to reduce gun violence. Our orders include a prohibition against owning a gun (or ammunition) or acquiring a gun (or ammunition). The mechanism needs to be augmented to address the proliferation of gun violence, whether domestic violence, workplace violence, school violence and general harassment. Provisions need to be added for implementation.

I suggest the following:

1.   The establishment of a national data base of restraining orders. CLETS, which includes restraining orders through CARPOS could easily be expanded to create a national system;

2.   Although there is some due process argument concerning a TRO because it is ex parte without notice, a hearing is provided at which time the petitioner (and this could be an employer) must prove to the court by clear and convincing evidence the entitlement to the order. The burden of proof on domestic violence cases is preponderance of the evidence. This difference needs to be addressed. The respondent is given a wide latitude at the hearing and is afforded total due process. At the end of the hearing, an order is signed

only if the petitioner prevails. Although we are not psychiatrists, psychologists or trained in the mental health community, we are certainly able to tell when a party has mental health issues that pose a risk to the community. Our factual findings become part of the order.

3. Before selling any gun (or ammunition) to a party against whom the restraining order is issued, the seller must consult the national data base. If the proposed buyer is on that list, no sale can take place, and the seller is required to notify law enforcement because it is a crime to violate the order. In this way, law enforcement is put on notice of a potential threat.

4. If the proposed seller does not consult the data base, or ignores a listing and sells the gun or ammunition, he/she is liable both civilly and criminally if a gun is used to cause damage to any person or property. It is akin to the felony murder rule. They become an accessory. This ramification is an incentive to compliance.

5. Current law does not allow for expungement of any record of either the TRO or the permanent order. It is a matter of public record. The existing problem is that the TRO may have been granted without a real basis; it is ex parte without notice. Even if the TRO expires on its own because the petitioner does not pursue it further, or the court denies the petition after a hearing, the record continues to reflect the granting of the TRO. A method needs to be provided for expungement.

J. **Constitutionally Protected Speech vs. Unprotected Speech**

It bears noting that mere screaming and yelling, even if it involves foul language cannot be restrained, unless the speech poses a credible threat to someone, or the conduct is so reprehensible, that it must be enjoined. The First Amendment of the United States Constitution protects the right of free speech, but that right is not absolute. In making a determination about whether or not certain speech falls under the anti-harassment statute, the courts make a distinction between political hyperbole, which is protected, and true threats, which are not. Merely endorsing or encouraging the violent action of others is protected, while threatening a person with violence is not. However, when such advocacy is directed to inciting or producing imminent lawless action, and is likely to incite or produce such action, the speech can be prohibited.

In a seminal case on this issue, the owner of an animal-testing lab sued for trespass and a restraining order against an animal rights organization that held protests in front of the petitioner's house. It was part of a campaign against Europe's largest contract animal-testing laboratory. The case isn't so important to read about here in terms of the outcome for the various parties – it underwent numerous appeals – but rather for the principles the court set forth in rendering its opinion. The court held that teaching about the need to resort to force and violence is not the same as preparing a group for such action. Hence, "spontaneous and emotional" appeals for unity and action do not incite lawless action and cannot be prohibited.

In another significant case involving First Amendment issues, a fifteen-year-old boy wrote threatening and menacing letters to his sixteen-year-old girlfriend, describing his plot to kill her parents, fully knowing her mother would read the messages. The court issued a restraining order. The boy appealed, claiming a violation of his freedoms of speech and association, and right to privacy. He claimed that the letters would not have caused a reasonable person to suffer substantial emotional harm because every parent should expect some emotional distress when they do not like their children's choice of friends. His appeal was denied, and his letters and actions were deemed to be harassment within the meaning of the injunction statute. The court determined the boy's actions constituted a knowing and willful course of conduct used to annoy, ridicule, and threaten the mother and that they served no legitimate purpose and would cause a reasonable person to suffer substantial emotional distress. The court further determined that the right of privacy did not entitle him to interfere with the mother's parental rights to direct and control her daughter's activities. Speech that is of purely private matters receives less First Amendment protection.

In that case, the court further stated, "...fantastical threats that once were taken lightly as fancies of immature youth (and) now cause reasonable persons to pause and even to become fearful" can merit the issuance of an injunction.

The alleged threat must be analyzed in light of the entire context and under all circumstances, including prior violence by third parties. The court must determine whether the speech, or conduct, at issue, would cause a reasonable person to suffer substantial emotional distress. A communication need not specify who would carry out the threat to qualify as a true threat. "The fact that a threat is subtle does not make it less of a threat."

With regard to the protections of freedom of speech under the First Amendment, the court has said, "As speech strays further from the values of persuasion, dialogue and a free exchange of ideas, and moves toward willful threats to perform illegal acts, the state (i.e., the government) has greater latitude to regulate expression. (O)nce a court has found that a specific pattern of speech is unlawful, an injunctive order prohibiting the repetition, perpetuation, or continuation of that practice is not a prohibited 'prior restraint' of speech."

When speech, such as defamation (the making of a false statement about someone, and publishing it to others, causing harm to the victim's reputation or some other type of damage) or the intentional infliction of emotional distress, nuisance or other conduct causes damage, those damages can be recovered in a civil action, including Small Claims Court, instead of injunctive relief. There is no injunction because "there is no threat to the free and robust debate of public issues; there is no potential interference with a meaningful dialogue of ideas concerning self-government; and there is no threat of liability causing a reaction of self-censorship by the press."

Can you seek a restraining order against someone who has disclosed or threatens to disclose confidential information? Because such exposure can potentially violate the right of privacy (protected under the California Constitution and presumably under other state constitutions), prohibiting that speech may be proper under certain compelling or extraordinary circumstances. In determining whether such circumstances exist, courts generally apply a balancing test, weighing the competing privacy and free speech rights. Factors the courts consider include whether the person is a public or private figure, the scope of the prior restraint, the nature of the private information, whether the information is of legitimate public concern, the extent of the potential harm if the information is disclosed, and the strength of the private and governmental interest in preventing publication of the information. There must be a compelling reason for such information to be kept private. An injunction that's issued must clearly define the conduct to be prohibited.

Commenting on a matter of public concern in a public forum such as on a website or on a public street is a classic form of speech protected under the First Amendment. The question for the court in cases in which someone is seeking to restrain certain speech is whether or not the speech is considered in the public interest and not merely an effort by the speaker "to gather ammunition for another round of private controversy." According to the court, "it should be something of concern to a substantial number of people" and in some manner contribute to the public debate. A subject that is "a matter of concern merely to the speakers and a relatively small, specific audience isn't a matter of public interest. The assertion of a broad amorphous public interest is not sufficient."

"The First Amendment permits restrictions on the contents of certain categories of speech when the speech is of such slight social value as a step to truth that any benefit that might be derived from it is clearly outweighed by the social interest in order and morality. These categories include defamatory speech, fighting words, incitement to riot or imminent lawless action, obscenity and child pornography. The threats of violence fall outside the protection of the First Amendment because they coerce by unlawful conduct rather than persuade by expression, and thus play no part in the marketplace of ideas." This means that you have no right to threaten violence because the government has a great interest in protecting people from a fear of violence and the possibility that the violence will occur.

Picketing is a protected speech activity, but a court can stop a party from physically impeding pedestrian or vehicular traffic and can prohibit that person from creating a disturbance or harassing customers uninterested in the message.

An example of an unconstitutional prior restraint on speech is an order prohibiting a party from making or publishing false statements. You may be held responsible for abusing your right to speak freely in subsequent tort (a civil wrong that unfairly causes harm to another resulting in legal liability on the part of the person who commits the act) action, but you do have the initial right to speak freely without censorship. You have this right even if what you are saying isn't true.

To establish a valid prior restraint under the U.S. Constitution, the petitioner has a heavy burden to show that the countervailing interest (such as his or her safety) is compelling, the prior restraint is necessary and would be effective in promoting this interest, and less extreme measures are unavailable. The court's order issuing an injunction must be couched in the narrowest terms that will accomplish the specific "objective permitted by constitutional mandate and the essential needs of the public order." The injunction must be sufficiently precise as to provide "a person of ordinary intelligence fair notice that his contemplated conduct is forbidden." In other words, the injunction cannot be overbroad. A good example of this concept is a case in which a deputy sheriff obtained an injunction against his ex-wife from defaming him on the internet, from publishing confidential personal information on the internet and from contacting his employer. An appeals court found that an injunction issued following a trial that determined that the defendant (the ex-wife in this case) defamed the plaintiff "that does no more than prohibit the defendant from repeating the defamation is not a prior restraint and does not offend the First Amendment." A prior restraint on someone's speech has to clearly define who is protected and the conduct that is prohibited.

K.   **What If You Are The Victim Of Threats, Defamation, Or Hate Speech Online**?

In today's world, conflicts between free speech rights and the right of an individual to privacy and personal safety often arise in the arena of social media. The question is when should, or can, hate speech or defamation in social media be restrained? Because this is a relatively new area of concern, the law regarding the First Amendment and its application to online public forums are evolving. Facebook, Twitter and other media technology companies have inaugurated their own rules regarding content that is and is not permissible to post on their sites. For example, Facebook bans hate speech, and if someone reports it, Facebook will remove any content that violates this policy. On the other hand, Twitter does not regulate hate speech, but rather it forbids direct threats and content that promotes violence on the basis of race, ethnicity, national origin, religion, sexual orientation, gender, gender identity, age or disability. There is a fine line between free speech and hate speech. Deciding whether particular speech is worthy of protection or not, is a slippery slope. Striking a balance between unfettered free speech on the internet and censorship in protecting other worthy values is an extremely challenging task, to say the least.

While freedom of speech is protected in the United States and in the European Union, there are exceptions in these EU countries. Some of these national exceptions are designed to prevent hate speech, defamation and threats, while others target speech, which is considered in other countries as merely the expression of an opinion, offensive maybe, but nonetheless legal. Social media sites offer platforms for the rapid spread around the world of all kinds of speech, whether protected or not.

A large problem with regulating what can and cannot be posted on social media is the fact that there is no standard, worldwide definition of hate speech. It's generally understood to encompass speech that incites violence, hatred or discrimination against other people or groups, particularly referring to their ethnicity, religious belief, gender or sexual orientation, language, national origin, or immigration status. The focus of hate speech generally is to stir up an emotional response through misleading facts.

The other major conundrum with hate speech on social media is how the intermediaries (i.e., Facebook, YouTube, Twitter, etc.) can actually moderate or regulate what users post. It is not feasible in light of the enormous amount of data that is posted on these platforms, and in an effort to abide by the principles of democratic speech, for each and every line of content posted to undergo a particular screening process. Consequently, media platforms rely on users to notify them of hateful content posted.

Also, it is difficult to regulate hate speech online because users can have the protection of anonymity when they post content. Intermediaries, such as Facebook and Twitter give users the freedom to be registered under any name they choose, which enables individuals to appear online under pseudonyms or as different people. Thus, it can be challenging to trace back the posted content to a real person.

So what remedy do you have if you believe you have been defamed on social media?

As I have noted previously, defamation involves the making of a false statement about a person, and the publishing of it to others, resulting in harm to one's reputation or some other kind of damage. Publication has occurred if the statement has been communicated to a third party, but what happens if the statement has been conveyed over the internet? It has certainly met the element of being published, but it may be nearly impossible to determine who has harmed you and who has read the statements. Of course, if the statement is made in a public social forum such as Facebook or Twitter, even when you can determine who made the statement, you may not be able to learn the reach of damaging statements made about you. Who sees the statement initially depends on the speaker's privacy settings for their Facebook or Twitter accounts, but you have no way of knowing the extent to which the statement has been shared with other users.

Bringing a defamation lawsuit becomes particularly tricky when the defamatory statement has appeared in a blog or in an online newspaper or magazine. Bloggers can keep their identities anonymous and, therefore, it may be challenging to identify who has published the statement if it appears on someone's blog. The problem is exacerbated when the defamatory statement is in the form of a comment left by a reader on a blog, or in an online news article. Sites generally do not require people to use their real names or to provide identifying information when they post comments.

If you think you have been defamed on a blog or other online site, your best bet would be to contact the blogger and request that they remove the statement. Bloggers retain control over their site content and have the ability to delete harmful comments. Other internet service providers may also be able to remove defamatory content from their sites, even though the provider is not typically considered legally liable for material published by others on their sites. In addition, they might be able to help you figure out who published it.

You should recognize that once a defamatory statement has been published about you on the internet, the damage has usually been done. Even after the content has been removed, it might be possible for someone to still find it. On the positive side though, proving publication is easy, and a way to offer proof of harm to reputation can be by printing any negative comments left by those who read the defamatory language. Unfortunately, a defamatory statement on a blog or an online publication may be read by a vast number of people, and then shared via email or sites like Facebook, thereby increasing the publication and also the damage exponentially.

Keep in mind that in a defamation case, the statement at issue must be a fact and not an opinion. Therefore, even the most offensive Facebook opinions expressed about someone's appearance or the manner in which they speak are most likely protected under the First Amendment, regardless of how hurtful the comments may be.

If you believe you have been defamed online, you can identify who published the defamatory statement, and the damage done has been significant, quantifiable, and you are able to document it, you just might have a lawsuit for defamation.

The prevalence of the internet in everyday life has made harassment via email and social networking sites commonplace. Referred to as cyber-bullying, the term applies to situations in which someone repeatedly uses technology platforms such as blogs, cell phones, emails, instant messaging and chat rooms, to deliberately threaten, harass, or intimidate another person. Cyber-stalking, sending sexually offensive messages to someone, monitoring the victim's online activities, sharing private or intimate information about the victim with others, and infecting the victim's computer with a virus, are all forms of cyber-bullying.

What, if anything, can you do if you or someone you care

about has been a victim of cyber-bullying? First of all, you can seek help from websites like stopbullying.gov and STOMP Out Bullying. The laws surrounding cyber-bulling vary from state to state. At the Cyber-Bullying Research Center, you can find information about each state's approach to the subject through http://cyberbullying. If you want to pursue legal action, the first thing you or your attorney needs to determine is whether the objectionable behavior fits into a recognized cause of action. In making this determination, you need to ask three questions:

1. **Did the behavior violate a criminal statute**?

It might be possible for you to pursue legal action for cyber-bullying based on the state criminal harassment laws. Many states have amended their criminal harassment statutes to expressly include this sort of online activity. In addition to deterring the perpetrator from engaging in future bullying online, the criminal law may also provide for an order of restitution against a wrongdoer if they are convicted, or as a result of a plea bargain (negotiations during a criminal trial between the defendant and the prosecutor in which the accused agrees to admit to a lesser crime in exchange for the prosecutor agreeing to ask for a more lenient sentence). You should know that as with many crimes, the crime of harassment requires "specific intent," which means the perpetrator intended the specific act with which they are charged. So, in order to prove the crime of harassment, the prosecutor must show that the defendant intended for the communication to annoy or intimidate you or provoke a fight. However, if the online conduct unintentionally causes you distress, this is not considered harassment.

2. **Did the behavior constitute a traditional civil tort**?

In addition to pursuing criminal charges, against someone

engaging in cyber-bullying, you can bring a civil action, including seeking a restraining order to prevent further harassment. With a civil suit for a tort action, monetary damages can be sought. The cyber-bullying may fall under the torts of harassment, defamation, or intentional infliction of emotional distress. The basic elements of these torts are generally the same in all states. Civil harassment involves willful and malicious acts with the intent to cause fear, intimidation or abuse that causes damage. To prove intentional infliction of emotional distress, the courts require you to show that the offensive conduct was so outrageous in character, and so extreme in degree, as to go beyond all possible bounds of decency, and to be regarded as atrocious, and utterly intolerable in a civilized community. You would also need to prove that you suffered financial, physical, or psychological injury due to the harasser's conduct.

The advent of the internet and social media forums has, if not encouraged, at least made it easier for people to violate these common law torts. Also, the worldwide reach of the internet may magnify the degree of damage caused by anonymous online conduct beyond that of any in-person encounter.

3.   Did the behavior involve a student?

The third question you or your attorney should ask is whether or not the bullying involved a student in elementary school, middle school, high school, or even at the college level. Most states in the country have legislated laws regarding cyber-bullying. Many of these statutes require publicly funded schools, including colleges and universities, to have specific policies in place to address and correct behavior that can be characterized as cyber-bullying. Schools are also generally responsible for ensuring that their students remain free from harassment pursuant to local civil rights statutes and state constitutions. The law regarding just how far the school's responsibility goes in protecting their students when the harassment occurs off-campus and online is still developing.

If you believe you are the target of online threats, or the victim of defamation through some form of information technology, it may be worth consulting an attorney about the range of approaches you can take to remedy the situation. Before you take any action, however, you should consider the possibility that, as in all other areas of law and life, this could be a case of "what goes around, comes around." Are you now paying the price for something you did in the past? Can you counteract this negative consequence – the online defamation – by bringing in some light with the doing of good deeds?

K. <u>Someone Is Seeking A Restraining Order Against You: What Can You Do</u>?

Suppose you are the respondent, the person against whom someone is seeking a permanent restraining order. What can you do? It bears repeating that there is nothing you can do to stop a judge from issuing a temporary restraining order against you. Petitions for TROs are heavily weighted in favor of the petitioner. As soon as the judge grants the TRO (probably unbeknownst to you as the respondent), the TRO will already be entered, or otherwise appear in public records. In other words, it is too late to undo this blemish on your public record. This is the case, unfortunately, even if the TRO was issued for something as mundane as a neighbor's complaint that you play basketball on your own property too loudly (a real case discussed earlier). A petitioner who files a frivolous claim against you will most likely suffer no consequences, in court, that is, but their actions will come back to haunt them in the future, no doubt. In the legal arena, at worst, the petitioner might have to endure a dressing down at the hearing, and possibly be required to pay your attorney's fees if, as a respondent, you were represented.

If the court accepts the petitioner's statements of perceived threat or harassment contained in their request and grants the temporary restraining order, as the respondent, you will be given various legal forms. The Temporary Restraining Order, a Request for Civil Harassment Retraining Order and a Notice of Court Hearing. If the Temporary Restraining Order is denied, you will be given the latter two forms and not the TRO.

So, now you have been served notice of a hearing on the petitioner's request for a permanent restraining order. How do you respond? At the hearing you will have an opportunity to defend yourself against the charges and, perhaps, prevent the TRO from becoming a permanent injunction. The court is required to consider all relevant evidence. With the stakes so high, do not have a fool for a client by acting as your own lawyer. Chances are that the petitioner will show up in court with legal counsel who will be prepared to rip your story to shreds. Your constitutional rights are at stake. I strongly urge you to have an attorney in your corner who is well versed in this area of law and can vigorously protect your interests. If you prevail, you can request reimbursement of attorney's fees from the petitioner. When a prevailing respondent asks for attorney's fees, it is mandatory for the court to award reasonable fees. As a judge, I inquire of the respondent's attorney about their hourly rate and what kind of time they put into defending the case. Based on the attorney's responses, I decide if the amount of time they put in was necessary, and if their rates are reasonable. Then I calculate how much to award the respondent.

One possible defense you can mount as the respondent is to demonstrate that your conduct serves a legitimate purpose and is, therefore, outside the scope of the law governing harassment. If your speech or conduct serves a legitimate purpose, the petition for a restraining order will be denied, even if such conduct might ultimately be subject to being enjoined after all the facts and applicable law are brought to light. A good example of conduct serving a legitimate purpose is picketing. However, as noted earlier, you cannot physically impede others. In considering restraining order cases, the court excludes constitutionally protected activity from the definition of a "course of conduct" that must be shown for the order to be granted. Constitutionally protected speech, as discussed above, generally includes comments, criticism, organizing a demonstration and speaking up at a political meeting.

A verbal threat made during a single incident with no prior or subsequent events to indicate that the behavior will continue is not viewed as a credible threat. Also, if you, as the respondent, can show that you have voluntarily discontinued the proscribed conduct (what the TRO restrains you from doing), the court cannot grant the injunction against you.

A significant case in this area of law centered on the behavior of a man who questioned a hospital's decision to discharge his mother, who had undergone cardiac surgery there. He grew frustrated when he was meeting with an administrator about his mother's case. The administrator closed the door to the meeting room and then blocked his way out of the room. He pulled the door open, striking the administrator with the door and shoving her into the wall. A temporary restraining order was issued against him, and a hearing date was set for the permanent injunction. For months afterwards, he stayed away from the hospital and did not threaten anyone who worked there. Nonetheless, at the hearing the court imposed a three-year permanent injunction against him, precluding him from contacting any employee of the hospital, and ordering him to remain 500-yards away from any of that hospital's facilities. On appeal, the court dismissed the permanent injunction, finding no evidence establishing that he was likely to commit further acts of violence against the hospital employees.

At the hearing, as the respondent, you may present your side by offering evidence in the form of declarations, affidavits (written or printed declarations or statements of facts, made voluntarily under oath, taken before a person having authority to administer an oath), reports, or oral testimony. The same forms of evidence can be put forth by the petitioner as well. The court must receive such evidence, subject only to reasonable limitations that are necessary to expedite the harassment procedure. The court may not arbitrarily limit the evidence presented to written testimony when relevant oral testimony is also offered. In restraining order hearings, cross-examination (the examination of a witness at a trial or hearing by a party other than the direct examiner upon a matter that is within the scope of the direct examination of the witness) of witnesses is not only permitted (as in other hearings) but is given wide latitude with the allowance of hearsay evidence. The purpose of cross-examination is to impeach testimony by the other side.

You might get lucky with the petitioner failing to show up for the hearing. When that happens, the TRO expires on the date of the hearing. In my court, when the petitioner neither shows up for the hearing, nor makes a call to the court clerk with an explanation, I will dismiss the case with prejudice, which spells a death knell for the case. Nevertheless, the TRO can be extended or reissued for cause such as an inability to serve the respondent. After several failed attempts to serve the TRO, it will expire, but the petitioner can file for a new TRO if the respondent reappears and resumes the harassing behavior.

If, as the respondent, you want the court to grant a mutual restraining order to prevent the petitioner from saying or doing something as well, you would have to file a counter-petition prior to the hearing. In the absence of such a counter-petition, the court may not grant an oral request at the hearing to make the restraining order mutual. The reason for this is because the petitioner is entitled to due process of the law, which includes an opportunity to present their objections to mutual restraining orders at a hearing.

L. **A Word About Hearsay**

Once again, hearsay evidence is testimony in court of a statement made out of court and is offered to prove the truth of the matter stated. During the TRO process, often hearsay is offered by the petitioner to make their case. Police reports are a prime example of hearsay. When a complaining party files a report with an officer, the complainant will probably refer to other people saying and doing things. Since, as the respondent, you are not present when the complaining party is seeking the TRO, you can do nothing to keep the judge from considering this hearsay. However, at the hearing you can try to diminish the impact of the hearsay by arguing that it should be given very little weight. The courts have determined, however, that if hearsay evidence is relevant in the hearing for injunctive relief, they must receive it.

In one case, a respondent who was the former patient of the petitioner, a psychologist, began harassing the psychologist after their professional relationship was terminated. The respondent tried stopping the psychologist's car, kept her house under surveillance, made phone calls to other professionals to tarnish the psychologist's reputation, and sent her threatening letters. The petitioner claimed she suffered from significant emotional distress, and that the respondent's conduct distracted her from her work. The respondent objected to hearsay declarations and claimed that the petitioner was required to make an appearance to testify about her emotional distress. The court held that the petitioner's direct testimony was not required, and that the circumstantial evidence (testimony not based on actual personal knowledge or observation of the disputed facts, but of other facts from which deductions can be drawn) she presented was sufficient. A court can draw inferences from the circumstantial evidence presented, and also from the demeanor of witnesses. The hearing may be based on affidavits or declarations, which are themselves a form of hearsay evidence.

As I noted, police reports are classic examples of hearsay and, therefore, as a judge I give them very little weight. Just because someone said something to a police officer filing a report does not make it true. In a case I presided over, a woman sought a restraining order against another woman, claiming that the respondent had used pepper spray on her. However, the police report contained no mention of the pepper spray allegation. Under these circumstances, the use of hearsay evidence (i.e., the police report) worked against the petitioner. I figured that if the respondent had really sprayed the petitioner with pepper spray, the petitioner would have mentioned that fact to the police officer who took the report. In addition, the petitioner made no reference to pepper spray in the petition she filed with the court. Consequently, I denied the restraining order petition.

M. **What Happens If A Respondent Violates A Restraining Order**?

If the respondent does whatever the order forbids them from doing, the petitioner can either have the respondent arrested or ask that they be cited for contempt of court. Usually, the petitioner calls the police and has the respondent arrested. In most cases, the arrest is automatic and not something respondent can talk their way out of because violating a court order is a criminal act. The arrest brings a new level of seriousness to the matter, as now the respondent not only has to make bail in order to be released from custody, but he or she also has to answer to the charges filed by the city attorney or district attorney's office. The respondent will need to hire an attorney or rely on a public defender. If convicted, the respondent may have to do time in jail, and the criminal charge will appear on CLETS and in the public record.

N. **Domestic Violence Is Different**

What is domestic violence and how do protections from this abuse differ from a basic restraining order? Domestic violence involves abuse or threats of abuse when the person being abused and the abuser are or have been in an intimate relationship, which can include marriage, domestic partnership, dating, living together, or having a child together. It also occurs when the abused person and the abuser are closely related by blood or marriage.

What kind of behavior against a person in this relationship constitutes abuse? According to the domestic violence laws, abuse consists of physically hurting or trying to hurt the person, intentionally or recklessly, sexual assault, making someone reasonably afraid that they or someone else is about to be seriously hurt, or harassing, stalking, threatening, or hitting a person, disturbing the person's peace, or destroying their personal property.

If you are the victim of domestic violence, what can you do about it? There are several civil and criminal protection or restraining order options available to protect you from further abuse. These orders won't necessarily stop an abuser from stalking or hurting you, but they do allow you to call the police and have the abuser arrested if they violate the order. In many states, when the police respond to a domestic violence situation, one of the parties (hopefully the abuser) is asked to leave the home. Also, in many states, officers are authorized, or even required to remove any guns present at the scene of a domestic violence incident. In some states, the police can issue an Emergency Protection Order (EPO) to protect the person believed to be the victim when the abuser is arrested for domestic violence. The EPO is generally for a limited period, such as several days to a week. Every state has statutes allowing for some sort of protective order. There are different names for these protection orders depending on the state. In California, they are called restraining orders. A protection order for a longer term than an EPO typically lasts for one to five years, and sometimes even indefinitely. A victim can renew the protection order if he or she still feels threatened by the abuser. A protection order may include a variety of provisions, including:

1. Prohibiting the abuser from having any contact with the person seeking the order;
2. Permitting the abuser to peacefully communicate with the victim for limited reasons, such as transfer for visitation of their child;
3. Ordering the abuser to stay at least a certain distance away from the victim, his or her home, job, school and car;
4. Requiring the abuser to move out of a home shared with the victim; and,
5. Ordering the abuser to attend counseling sessions.

Even though the direct harm was to the victim, the protection orders may also cover children, other family members, roommates, or current romantic partners of the victim.

How do you get a protective order? You will have to file the requisite legal papers with your local court, serve the papers on the abuser, and present evidence of the abuse at a hearing. Sometimes the police will serve the papers for you.

At the hearing on the petition for a domestic violence restraining order you will have a lower burden of proof to meet than if you were filing for a restraining order against someone you are not now nor the past have been in an intimate relationship with. To obtain a general restraining order for threatening behavior at the hearing, you will need to provide clear and convincing evidence of the threat. For domestic violence cases, you will need only to show a preponderance of the evidence that the threat or harm has occurred. The evidence can include, for example, photographs of bruises and taped recordings of threats.

For help filing a domestic violence restraining order, you should find a qualified domestic violence attorney, or an appropriate legal aid organization. The court does not provide any sort of physical protection for the victim. They simply issue an order.

O. **Let's Change The System**

In my view, we need a legislative change in the restraining order laws to make them more even-handed. For example, I believe the petitioner should be required to pay the filing fee, just like any other litigant. If the petitioner had to pay the $430 filing fee (the current fee in California) and give notice to the respondent, I suspect that the number of frivolous and malicious restraining order petitions would be greatly reduced. If paying the filing fee is a hardship, the petitioner could appeal to the court to waive the filing and service fees. If the petitioner ends up getting a permanent restraining order injunction, the costs should be recoverable by the petitioner from the respondent, just as in Small Claims Court. If the petitioner loses or fails to show up at the hearing, I believe the court should impose sanctions, requiring that the petitioner pay something to the respondent and/or perform some sort of community service. Failure to pay would constitute contempt. These costs should be assessed by the court unless the court finds there was *prima facie* (on the face of it) merit to the allegations even though the petitioner's case was insufficient to meet the clear and convincing burden. Monetary sanctions and a community service remedy would, in some small way, at least realign the balance in the respondent's and the petitioner's worlds. Being penalized with sanctions is the price petitioners who file frivolous claims must pay.

With sanctions imposed, the court would get the benefit of the additional revenue, the public would gain from the petitioner's community service, and the respondent would be slightly compensated for their costs and the deprivation of rights they suffered. Perhaps, if people knew that sanctions could be imposed, and that they must pay the fees to file for restraining orders, they might think twice before filing when the activity they object to does not rise to the level of harassment that the law was designed to protect against.

An injustice that results from the granting of a TRO, is the lack of mechanism for respondents to expunge (destroy, erase, or remove any reference to the restraining order from the public record) their records. It's my opinion that if the permanent restraining order injunction is denied once the hearing takes place, the entire record of the TRO and hearing should be expunged from all active and inactive files.

Another issue of concern regarding the hearing for a permanent injunction is the permissibility of hearsay. If I were creating the laws, I would make hearsay inadmissible across the board at the restraining order hearings, unless it falls under one of the hearsay exceptions.

P. **The Bigger Picture**

It bears repeating that in deciding general restraining order cases, the judge performs a balancing act. We have to weigh competing interests, such as the reasonableness of the petitioners' fear for their safety, or the destruction of their reputation, versus the potential violation of the respondent's constitutional rights. Although we are all given free choice by our creator – or whatever you choose to call the higher power – this does not mean we can do whatever we want and damn the consequences. There is a rule of the universe, or what some refer to as karma, which says that if a person is caring, compassionate and giving, positive things will come back to him or her. Conversely, if a person's motivation is ego-driven, and fueled by the desire to receive for one's self only, if not immediately, then eventually, they will have to return whatever gains (in other words, pay the price) in a monetary form, or through suffering health-wise, or by ending up with damaged relationships, or even by being subjected to a court order dictating how they can behave or what they can say.

Regardless of what happens in your restraining order case, or any other legal case for that matter, you can reduce your anxiety level by accepting the outcome. If you emerged on the losing side of the case, you might consider that it came out this way because you needed to cleanse something you did in the past. You can also say to yourself, whatever happened could have been a lot worse. You needed to learn a lesson, and going forward, you will know better than to repeat the behavior that got you into this mess in the first place.

I'VE BEEN SUED, OR I'VE SUFFERED SUFFICIENT DAMAGES TO BRING A LAWSUIT – WHAT DO I DO?

3

In thinking about bringing any kind of lawsuit, you should ask yourself the following questions: Why do I want to sue someone? If I am the one being sued, what is my reaction to the suit and to the entity who is suing me? What is motivating me to get involved in this lawsuit as either a defendant or a plaintiff? Is it anger, revenge, hostility, or some other ego-driven desire?

Can you do anything to overcome these negative, ego-feeding desires so that you can approach the lawsuit with positive energy? Absolutely! You can try to resist the impulse to get even and, rather, forgive the other side for whatever you feel they have done to wrong you. You can let go of the anger or hatred you bear for your opponent.

As Dr. Walter Jacobson, the author of *Forgive To Win*, says:

"When people have wronged you, and you feel justified in seeking a legal remedy, I encourage you to do so without the added baggage of anger, harsh judgment and resentment. I encourage you to find a way to forgive them for their bad behavior at the same time that you may be pursuing legal recourse. Forgiving others is simply a process of rising above the emotional battlefield, and freeing yourself from the emotional shackles of anger, bitterness, resentment and victimhood that are a barrier to true joy and inner peace. Consequently, it is my recommendation that: Win, lose or draw, the best way to deal with those who you have engaged in legal battle with is to let go of your anger, your grievances, your resentments, and find a way to forgive them as well as yourself for your own happiness and peace of mind. Anger hurts YOU. Forgiveness heals YOU. Hold that thought and apply acceptance, tolerance, compassion and forgiveness in all aspects of your life as best as you can."

https://www.facebook.com/forgivenessguru/

I recognize this is not so easily done as said, and I am not suggesting you become fast friends with your opponent; only that you suppress your ego and your desire to receive for yourself only and, instead, convert that desire to a willingness to give and to share. In this way, you will connect to the positive energy in the world. This positive energy brings order and fulfillment, as opposed to the chaos and disorder that flow from allowing your ego to drive your actions. As my former client, the late and great composer, Johnny Mercer, wrote, *"You have to accentuate the positive, eliminate the negative, and don't mess with Mister In-Between."*

Perhaps, after asking yourself the questions posed above, and recognizing that lawsuits primarily generate negative energy, you still want to proceed with the legal action. Shedding your negative feelings about your opponent, and showing forgiveness, does not mean that you are throwing in the towel with respect to your lawsuit. You can still pursue the case with the intent to win, but you will be doing so without the chaos that accompanies egocentric activities and, hopefully, with less of an emotional strain.

At this stage, I suggest you ask yourself these additional questions: Who am I? Am I a good client with a case that has merit? Then, you need to take a hard look at who your opponent is. Are you suing a bank or an insurance company?

If so, you might have a leg up. These sorts of defendants are generally not well liked by juries. On the other hand, are you bringing an action against Disneyland? You might have an uphill battle because, in my opinion, most people are very fond of Disneyland. It's like suing Mickey and Minnie Mouse.

As you think about who you are and who your opponent is, consider the answer from a spiritual perspective. Our true enemies are not found in the outside world. Our real enemy is our own desire to receive for ourselves alone, a longing for ego gratification. This enemy is the dark side (as in *Star Wars*). It's the dark side that leads us to blame external circumstances and other people for our problems rather than taking responsibility for them ourselves. If so-called enemies continue to appear in our lives (in the legal realm, they might be our opponents in a lawsuit), it's because we have failed to eliminate their true origin – the enemy within.

A. **Neither Fish Nor Fowl: Filing in Limited Jurisdiction Court**

You have thought about your motivation for getting involved in a lawsuit, and now you are ready to start the process. What's the first step? You have figured out if your case involves some sort of specialized subject matter, and you also need to determine how much money is involved in the controversy. There are courts that have something called limited jurisdiction, meaning that they only have authority over specific type cases or cases involving limited financial recoveries. As we have already discussed, Small Claims Court is one such court of limited jurisdiction. Others include bankruptcy courts, family law courts and labor courts. A very high percentage of cases in this country are processed in courts of limited jurisdiction. Depending on the state, these courts can be called county, magistrate, justice, or municipal courts. In some states, there are courts of general jurisdiction that are designated by statute to hear and decide specific types of cases. For example, in California, a Superior Court is considered a court of general jurisdiction. However, certain of these California superior courts are designated to hear only juvenile matters, thereby becoming courts of limited jurisdiction since they are, in essence, operating as juvenile courts.

If the amount you are fighting over is more than $10,000 (the limit for Small Claims Court), but less than $25,000, you have a limited jurisdiction case. If you are asking for more than $25,000 in damages, the case will be designated as an unlimited jurisdiction case. The idea behind limited jurisdiction cases is that since the amount in controversy is restricted to $25,000 or less, the litigation process should be streamlined to allow for quicker and less expensive dispute resolution. For one thing, the discovery (the pre-trial devices that can be used by one party to obtain facts and information about the case from the other party in order to assist the party in preparation for trial) procedures are limited in these cases in order to save time and costs.

B. **Should I Represent Myself?**

There are good reasons why parties in a lawsuit should seek legal representation. On the defense side for instance, when a plaintiff makes a summary judgment motion (a motion by any party to a civil action seeking a court order ruling that no factual issues remain to be tried, and therefore a cause of action in a complaint can be decided upon certain facts without trial), the defendant may not realize there are technical defenses they can raise to the motion. As lay people, defendants are not trained to raise appropriate objections to evidence presented in court. If the objections are not raised, they will be waived. In other words, if your opponent introduces inadmissible evidence and, as a defendant, you do not object, that evidence can be considered by the court.

In most restraining order cases, respondents tend to represent themselves, but respondents are generally unaware of the burden petitioners must meet in these cases. They probably do not know that the petitioner must demonstrate, among other requirements, that the respondent is engaged in a continuing course of conduct, as I have already discussed in the previous chapter. There are certain "magic words" that the respondent needs to say in his or her defense. If the respondent does not know those "magic words" (i.e., the proper language to use in their defense), they will lose at the hearing. In the *Restraining Order* section of this book, I have already stressed how dire the consequences can be for a respondent, against whom a restraining order is issued. A good lawyer can save the respondent from a lot of grief.

Similarly, in *Unlawful Detainer* cases, as a defendant it behooves you to have an attorney who can protect your rights. An attorney might be able to help you to avoid an eviction from your home. A lawyer familiar with Unlawful Detainer (UD) cases will be in a better position to work out a settlement for you. As the defendant, you probably are not aware that you can have the record sealed after reaching a settlement. UD lawsuits can impair a tenant's credit and ability to rent other rental units. Landlords typically do a search of a tenant's rental history before agreeing to rent a unit to a tenant, and the databases they search may contain information about suits you have been part of. Therefore, whenever you are settling a UD matter, it is a good idea to get a court order to seal the record. By sealing the record, it will be much more difficult for a landlord to discover information about an eviction proceeding. An attorney will know about having the record sealed and other matters involved in UD cases that might come back to haunt you.

Here's a good example of a case that came before me in which the defendant represented himself in a UD case, and could have secured a much better outcome had he been represented by a lawyer. The defendant was a former professional basketball player, who had purchased a seven-million-dollar home in a ritzy area, but eventually could no longer make the mortgage payments. The bank, which was, of course, heavily represented by lawyers, took his house in foreclosure. The basketball player was trying to forestall his eviction. You would think someone with that kind of money would automatically hire a lawyer, but because he was in dire financial straits at that point, he chose to represent himself instead. A question arose as to whether the defendant could have qualified for a loan modification. The bank refused to modify his loan. As the judge in this matter, I knew that the defendant could have offered a defense of wrongful denial of a loan modification. I even granted him a continuance to amend his pleadings (the formal allegations by the parties to a lawsuit of their respective claims and defenses), but when he came back into my courtroom he had not amended his defense properly. In the end, the poor guy was evicted from his house. After the conclusion of the case, the defendant approached me in the hallway and said he wanted to talk to me. I told him that I was forbidden from having *ex parte* communication, but did give him one piece of advice, "Get a lawyer," I told him. If the former basketball player had been represented by a competent lawyer, he might have been able to stay in his home, because his lawyer would have raised an appropriate technical defense. For example, the defense of wrongful denial of a loan modification could have been put forth. The moral of the story is that as a non-lawyer, you most likely do not know what your rights are, so you should talk to someone who does know and who can help protect your rights.

Another example of the value of obtaining counsel can be seen in the context of breach of oral contract cases. If you are a defendant being sued for breach of an oral contract, and more than two years have passed since the breach, if you represent yourself, you most likely would not know that the statute of limitations has run. An attorney would assert this defense to make the case disappear. In civil cases there are all sorts of affirmative defenses that can be raised on your behalf by a lawyer. If you are representing yourself, you would not know what these defenses are, and you cannot raise them on appeal unless they were raised during the initial proceeding.

If you represent yourself in a case, whether civil or criminal, you are acting in *pro per*. *Pro Per* is a term derived from the Latin *in propria persona*, which means "for one's self" and is used to describe a person who handles his or her own case. The adage that a person who represents him or herself in court has a fool for a client is absolutely true. If you knew nothing about electricity, would you undertake the job of rewiring your house? Without medical training, would you perform surgery on yourself? In almost every instance, you can boost your chances for a positive outcome of your case by hiring a competent lawyer.

C. **How Do I Find A Good Lawyer And What Other Steps Can I Take To Better My Situation**?

You have found yourself embroiled in the legal system, on one side or the other of a lawsuit. The first opportunity you have to exercise your free will in order to affect the outcome of your case is by choosing a good lawyer. Once you have carefully chosen an attorney to defend you, or bring a suit on your behalf, if you want to improve your chances for success, you should cooperate fully with your attorney, sharing all pertinent information with them, and following their legal advice whether you like it or not. Make sure not to hide anything from your lawyer.

Not only do you want to engage a competent lawyer, but you also want to be a good client. Especially if you are heading towards a jury trial, it is important that you be a sympathetic party and that you come across as genuine, cooperative and not antagonistic. I recommend that you behave this way in your dealings with your attorney, too.

You can make other choices at this point to help you reach a positive outcome, such as engaging in behavior that will benefit others. In other words, doing good deeds can help

you to control your destiny. Take it from Sophocles, the cele-
brated playwright of ancient Greece, who wrote, "To be doing
good deeds is man's most glorious task." If you follow the
golden rule in your everyday dealings with people, goodness
will reflect back on you as though there is a mirror across the
universe.

It would also serve you well to adjust your attitude towards your opponent in the lawsuit, and to refrain from making negative comments about your opponent. Making negative remarks about others is engaging in "evil tongue." It is
speech that says something negative about a person, is not
previously known to the public and is not seriously intended
to correct or improve a situation. When we speak ill of others,
not only do we potentially do damage to their lives, but our
hurtful words will eventually come back to harm us, as well.
Basically, if I gossip, it is another one of those negative behaviors that will bounce off the universe's mirror and reflect negativity back on you. You should avoid speaking with an evil
tongue, and also listening to the gossip of others.

In seeking an attorney, one wise choice you can make is to
adopt a positive outlook. A client once came to me who was
embroiled in a dispute with his ex-wife over some property. I
listened to his story and afterwards he handed me a retainer
check to take his case. I thanked him, and as he was walking out of my office door, I heard him mumble, "Yeah, with
my luck, I am going to lose this one, too." I then said, "Here's
your check back. If you've already decided to lose, you will
lose. I'm not in the business of losing." I told him he needed
to adjust his attitude (in other words, his consciousness) if he
wanted me to represent him. He would not take the check
back. Instead, he agreed to change his attitude, and I agreed to
take his case. Ultimately, the case settled.

Like most of us, you are probably not going to want to
spend a whole lot of money on an attorney, but what happens
if, in order to save money, you get an inexperienced lawyer?
It might be helpful to keep in mind something my father, who

was a farmer, used to say: "Oats are one dollar a bushel. If you want the oats after they come through the horse, they're a lot cheaper." Going cheap can become expensive.

The best way to find a trustworthy and capable lawyer is through referrals from friends, family and colleagues. Of course, you will want to meet the lawyer in person. Make certain that when you go to your prospective lawyer's office, you meet with the person who will be assigned to your case. Often, the senior partner of a firm will drop into say hello during your meeting. He or she will most likely not be handling your case, but rather you will be assigned to an associate in the firm. The best lawyer to represent you is the one who feels right for you in your gut.

Be conscious of the décor in the office and its location. Is the office well-appointed with spectacular views out the windows, and impressive artwork decorating the walls? Be aware that the firm's clients (one of whom might be you) are paying for those fancy digs. In your search for a lawyer, do not be deceived by a glossy webpage and flashy ads on social media.

If you are not able to get an attorney recommendation from someone you know, and you end up calling a lawyer who advertises on TV, or in a newspaper, or even on the back of a bus, make sure to ask a lot of questions when you call. Often these firms that advertise are merely fishing for clients whom they can then send on to another firm. The firm they send you to will pay a referral fee to the initial firm that advertised. You will receive a phone call from the unknown firm to whom your case has been referred. The first thing you will want to ask is who will be handling your case. It could very well be a paralegal, not a licensed attorney, who will be doing quite a bit of the work on your case. It is typical for large firms to use paralegals to manage much of the paperwork, including filing documents with the court and doing research. Know that they are not lawyers and cannot legally represent you in a lawsuit.

When you are on the phone with the firm, make sure to talk to the specific lawyer who will be representing you. You can research the attorney on the internet. You will want to learn about the attorney's experience. How many cases have they tried? Is the lawyer a member of any associations, such as the American Board of Trial Advocates? Has there been any disciplinary action taken against the lawyer? What is the lawyer's track record of wins and losses? If your case will be assigned to an associate, you should ask what role, if any, a firm partner will play in your case (especially if you came to the firm on the reputation of the partners). You should ask any or all of these questions when you first talk to an attorney whom you might want to represent you.

Many sole practitioners use what is known as a "contract" lawyer. They are not employees, but rather independent contractors who work on an hourly fee basis. This arrangement could be beneficial to you because these lawyers are not on a big firm payroll and, thus, are not required to bill a certain number of hours. In my law practice, I have no in-house lawyers to work on my cases, which greatly reduces my overhead because it means I do not have to pay lawyers' salaries, or pay for their office space. These are costs borne by larger firms, and can be reflected in what the larger firms charge their clients. Over the past thirty years, I have relied on contract lawyers to help me with cases.

Choosing the right lawyer is a personal decision, and sometimes you might just have to rely upon your instincts. If your case is going to wind up in a jury trial, keep in mind that jurors are people with their own biases and gut reactions to the parties in a case before them. You want to improve your chances for a positive outcome by picking a lawyer who is likeable, and whom you think will relate well to a jury. Equally important is to find a lawyer who is experienced with the subject.

Here's an example of an outcome that hinged on the likeability factor. I represented a couple in a case against their insurance company for damages caused by a fungus in their home. My clients were a general contractor and his wife, both extremely personable. Apparently, their insurance policy excluded coverage for mold issues. Despite the law appearing to support the insurance company's defense, the jury found for my clients, and awarded them substantial damages. In talking to the jurors after the verdict, I learned that they thought my clients were wonderful people, and had suffered at the hands of the insurance company. One of the jurors even telephoned me after the trial, wanting to share her written notes from the juror's notebook she kept during the trial. I took her to lunch, and she brought the notebook along. In it, she had mentioned that the defense lawyer was wearing a nice suit, but that she didn't trust him and had hoped for a brisk wind to come along and blow away all the papers he had strewn across the counsel table. Her notes revealed that she thought one of the witnesses was cute, she wondered if he was married and that she had a favorable impression of the judge. She reiterated that the personal appearance and affability of both the clients and the lawyers made all the difference in her decision making.

I was involved in another case in which I learned that the jury decided in favor of my client, who was the plaintiff because, according to a juror I questioned afterwards, the members of the jury "hated" the defense lawyer. This lawyer had objected to every single question I asked the witnesses. Despite the fact that the judge overruled at least 95% of the objections, the lawyer was not deterred. He kept popping up to object and then sitting back down. The jurors resented being stuck there in the first place, and the defense lawyer's antics only extended the time they had to serve. Years later, the jury foreman (jury member who acts as the chairperson and spokesman for the jury, and is elected by the other jurors) actually became a client of mine.

Many lawyers decide to pursue a career in law because it can be a lucrative field. After all, the law business is similar to other businesses in that the object from the lawyer's standpoint is generally to make a handsome profit while providing good service at a reasonable price or, at least, that is what the public would like to see as the goal of all lawyers. Unfortunately, there are a great many lawyers who are simply in it for the money and, sadly, are not the slightest bit interested in providing their services at a decent price. Not all lawyers make a significant amount of money, however. Some pursue the profession for altruistic reasons. Public defenders, district attorneys and public interest lawyers generally fall into this category. The lawyers who work for governmental entities such as the City Attorney's Office, or the Office of the State Public Defender earn a net salary. When you engage a private lawyer to bring a lawsuit on your behalf, there are three different fee arrangements you may be able to make with your attorney.

D. **To Pay Your Lawyer Hourly Or On Contingency: That Is The Question**

1. **Hourly Fees**

You can agree to pay your attorney on an hourly basis. Typically, if a lawsuit has been brought against you, you will pay a lawyer on an hourly basis to defend you since there is no big award at the end for your attorney to take a percentage of. However, if your defense lawyer will be filing a cross-complaint (the written complaint that a defendant may file against the party suing them, or against a third party as long as the subject matter is related to the original complaint) against the person or company suing you, then the lawyer might want to take the case on a contingency because there will be the possibility of collecting some money after all.

The general practice, when you hire an attorney on an hourly fee basis, is to have an executed (a written) retainer agreement with your lawyer. Under California law, a written agreement is required for cases in which the attorney's fees can exceed $1,000. If your lawyer requests an evergreen retainer, this means you will be asked to deposit an agreed upon sum into a trust account. The lawyer's fees are withdrawn from that account as they are earned. For example, if you as the client have agreed to deposit an initial $10,000 into the trust account, and your lawyer earns $5,000 for the month in hourly fees, then you must deposit $5,000 to replenish the account.

You will want to be very clear about your lawyer's billing practices. Do they charge by the hour, or for every quarter hour, or by one-tenth of an hour? Do they bill for time spent on the phone with you? Do they charge for their travel expenses? The more hours the attorney can bill, the more money they will get paid. Unfortunately, with this fee arrangement, it is in the lawyer's best interest to keep a case going for as long as possible. This reality can lead lawyers to introduce frivolous, sure to lose motions (requests that the court provide relief or a ruling directing some act to be done in favor of the applicant) in order to run up the billable hours.

Here's an old joke that pokes fun at this conduct. A lawyer who died at the young age of 35, arrived at the Pearly Gates and asked Saint Peter, "Why am I here, I'm only 35 years old?"

Saint Peter responded, "Not according to your billing records."

A friend of mine, a partner in an insurance defense firm, exemplifies the truth of this joke. The majority of insurance company lawyers are paid less than their counterparts in law firms are paid. In order to earn as much money as other lawyers, the insurance defense lawyers often do unnecessary work to beef up their billing hours. My friend told me a story of how he once billed 26 hours in one day.

"I thought there were only 24 hours in a day," I said. He chuckled and explained how he had achieved this feat. He was set to appear in the same court for four separate motions on behalf of four different clients. He charged each client for the time he spent travelling to the courthouse, waiting in the courtroom, and returning to his office, all part of customary legal fees. Each client ended up paying the lawyer for the identical six-plus hours, never knowing that perhaps their case had been the first on the calendar, that he had to be in that court anyway, and that their lawyer could have returned to his office much earlier, thus spending less time and charging for less hours. No one client knew that he, she or it was paying for the same billable hours as the other clients. With four clients each paying for the same six-plus hours, my friend's firm was able to bill for 26 hours of work in one day! The other two hours came from other work. The lawyers should have been honest and arranged to split the fees charged among the various clients.

You should be aware that one way in which law firms manage to afford expensive trappings and expand their firms, is by hiring young associates whom they bill out to clients at rates far exceeding what their limited experience would dictate. These associates work exceedingly long hours, basically chained to their desks because they are required to work a certain number of billable hours in order to keep their jobs and have a chance at being made a partner eventually. Despite the fact that the associates are doing the work, clients believe they are getting quality representation because of the good name of the firm, but this is not necessarily true. The fees charged for time put in by the principals of the firm and that of the associates, are noted separately on the attorney's bill, however, so you can tell who is doing what. Pay careful attention to what you are being billed for. It is generally advisable to engage an attorney on an hourly fee basis, because it will usually cost you less in the long run than if you hire an attorney on a contingency fee arrangement, and the damages are substantial. However, since some lawyers will overbill their clients by doing unnecessary work, you should ask your lawyer to provide you with a memo itemizing what the lawyer is doing, or plans to do on your behalf, with an explanation as to why they are performing those tasks along with the plusses and minuses of each of those tasks. This way you will have a record that can be used later in the event that you become involved in a fee dispute with your lawyer and, heaven forbid, a possible legal malpractice case.

Here is a perfect example of what I call the "billing machine," and how some firms really take advantage of a client with deep pockets. A well-off company having run into some legal problems, wanted to be represented by a big law firm. Although I was not going to be representing the company, the CEO asked me to accompany him to a meeting with lawyers from a national law firm. The firm had over one thousand lawyers. When we entered the conference room for the meeting, we encountered five lawyers sitting at the table. After listening to the dialogue, I knew exactly what was going to happen. I asked each of the lawyers what their specific role was in the firm, and each one pointed to another attorney who had a different specialty. The CEO only needed one or two of them to help him with the company's legal problems, but clearly this firm saw an opportunity for multiple billings. I told the CEO as we left that he was going to be hosed. In the end, he was.

2.   <u>Contingency Fee Basis</u>

Many clients cannot afford to pay their lawyers hourly, or to pay for their costs of litigation. Instead, they arrange to pay their lawyer on a contingency fee basis, which means that the lawyer will work on the case without charging a fee, but will take a percentage of the recovery if the case wins or settles. In other words, the lawyer's compensation is contingent upon winning the case and getting the money. The rewards for a lawyer can be great, but so can the risk. If you have a winning case resulting in a huge monetary award, it can be quite lucrative for your attorney. Typically, an attorney will be paid between 25% and 50% of the recovery amount. On the other hand, if your case loses, the lawyer receives no compensation for all the hours they put into your case, and is also in the hole for the amount (which can be substantial) of their out-of-pocket costs for the litigation.

The expenses that come directly out of the lawyer's pocket include the costs of expert witnesses. You would be surprised by the variety of experts a lawyer might need to rely upon. Typical examples include forensic accountants and doctors. One time, I needed to bring in a cattle feeder on a case to testify regarding the reduced market value of cattle that were traumatized by an event and, therefore, did not gain sufficient weight. Not surprisingly, fat cows are worth more than skinny ones. For cases involving the quantification of damages, hiring a forensic accountant might prove very helpful.

Personal injury cases, specifically torts, provide the best example of a contingency fee arrangement. As defined previously, a tort is a civil wrong (as opposed to a criminal wrong) that unfairly causes harm to another resulting in legal liability on the part of the person who commits the act. The harm or injury caused by a tort claim can include everything from loss of income and loss of profits to non-economic damages such as pain and suffering, embarrassment and a tarnished reputation. The victim of the harm can recover their loss as damages (money) in a lawsuit. Tort cases run the gamut from automobile accidents to slip and fall accidents to emotional distress to defamation to dog bites and everything in-between. Tort cases are discussed in greater length in Chapter 8.

You should be aware that firms that take cases on a contingency fee basis have a financial incentive to settle as quickly as possible. The longer the case is in litigation, the more expensive it becomes for the firm that must pay the lawyers to work on the case, and pay the discovery costs. It is often in the firm's best interest to settle, even if it means accepting less money than they might recover if the case went to trial. I am fairly certain that over 90% of personal injury cases settle. On the other hand, lawyers being paid by insurance companies to defend lawsuits, want to keep those cases going for as long as possible. For them, once the case is settled, their money stream dries up until another case comes along. Olivia Bissell, an insurance defense lawyer with whom I battled on opposite sides of cases for 25 years said, "You can't bill a closed file." Olivia and I are now very close friends. Our friendship demonstrates that even though lawyers must often become adversaries in the courtroom because they are representing opposing parties, they can still maintain a cordial relationship with one another.

3. **Hybrid Fee Arrangement**

What if you cannot afford the attorney's hourly rate, but you feel confident that you have a winning case and, in the end, you do not want to fork over to your attorney a huge amount of the damages award? It is possible to have a fee arrangement with your lawyer that takes on the characteristics of both hourly fees and contingency fees. In a contingency fee agreement, the lawyer will typically take 40% of the ultimate award. With the hybrid arrangement, the lawyer will agree to take a smaller percentage of the ultimate award, plus charge you an hourly fee at a reduced rate. All the terms are negotiable in this sort of plan.

4. **Negotiating Fees**

As a client, do you have any leverage regarding your attorney's fees? You should not sign a boilerplate engagement letter with your lawyer. You can try to negotiate the fees. During the course of your attorney's representation, carefully review the bill you are given. When you dine in a restaurant, do you always make sure the bill accurately reflects what you ordered? If they charged you for a filet mignon, and all you ordered was a salad, wouldn't you object? When you check your attorney's bill, make sure that the costs are legitimate and necessary. In most cases, if the attorney bills you for a trip to Hawaii to take a deposition (a deposition is part of the pretrial discovery or investigation that an attorney for a party to a lawsuit arranges, in which the attorney takes the sworn testimony of the opposing party, a witness, or an expert for the opposition), you are being taken for a ride (or in this case, a plane flight). Unless, of course, it is necessary to take the deposition of someone involved in the case who actually resides in Hawaii. In some cases though, it makes good sense to take a deposition by videotape, but it is sure much more enjoyable for the lawyer to lie on the beach in Maui than to take a video deposition from an office in Los Angeles.

If your case concludes unsuccessfully, you might be able recoup some of the money you spent on your lawyer. As a general rule, lawyers do not want to take the time and effort to justify all their expenses to you by producing the entire file and all the billings. It is often less expensive for them to settle by returning some money to you, rather than risk having to defend a legal malpractice claim you might bring.

5.   <u>Loans On Personal Injury Cases</u>

In the case of a personal injury lawsuit, if you have settled, or are on the verge of settling your case and in need of money before the insurance company pays your claim, you can take out a loan. This is similar to a Payday loan (also called a payday advance or salary loan) in which the lender loans you money at a high rate of interest to tide you over until your next payday. In the case of a lawsuit, the loan will tide you over until you collect the settlement award. This is not a risky loan for the lender as the legal case has already concluded, and the lender makes its money on the interest the borrower must pay.

6.   <u>Loans To Law Firms Who Have A Large Volume Of Personal Injury Type Cases</u>

You might be wondering how law firms can afford to take on a large number of personal injury cases simultaneously.

After all, these cases are very expensive to prepare and litigate. A number of considerations go into a lender's decision as to whether to make a loan to a law firm. The loan is predicated on the inventory of cases, the nature of the cases, the risk factors and the turnover time. The lender typically charges an interest rate of about 18%, and some even charge more than that. The lenders are banking on the law firm settling or winning a large number of their cases, or at least some of them. These are non-recourse loans. In other words, there is no recourse for the lender if the borrower law firm loses the case. With a recourse loan, the lender could go after the borrower for the loan amount regardless of the outcome of the case.

7. Loans On High End Cases With Significant Damages

These types of loans are generally used for intellectual property cases in which the recovery can be substantial for the prevailing party. For example, you might consider securing this type of loan if you are suing someone over a copyright or trademark infringement, or a patent violation. If your case might result in a significant damage award to you, you can seek to borrow money to pursue your case from an individual money lender or syndicate of people who are willing to invest money in your case. Your attorney will prepare a budget based on the estimated costs of the litigation, and then present that budget to the prospective lender. Once the lender approves the budget, they will lend you, as the borrower, that amount.

Once the case is resolved, the plaintiff borrower pays back the loan anywhere from 2½ to 4 times the amount of the loan. These loans are very expensive. Many of these lenders require that the borrower borrow a minimum of $1 million. If they lend the plaintiff a million dollars, the lender's return will be from 2½ to 4 times that amount in addition to the initial one-million-dollar loan amount. Some of the lenders might require a "kicker" in the form of profit participation. Thus, the lender might require that they also receive a portion of the profits gained from the successful case. On the other hand, if the case is lost, the lenders get nothing. The lawyers who are working on the case get paid out of the loan amount. The costs of the litigation, such as expert witness fees, travel expenses and photocopies of documents, are also paid from the loan proceeds. The loan can be made by a direct deposit into the equivalent of a construction account and is paid out as expenses are incurred. Alternatively, the loan can be made through a line of credit.

8. __The LawFund Program__

Under this program you, as a litigant, would enter into an agreement with LawFund to split the recovery amount so that you would get 50% of the recovery, less the costs of litigation, and LawFund would get 50%. LawFund would pay your lawyer's and advance the costs of the lawsuit. As opposed to in the above example (under Loans on High End Cases), the litigant who makes an agreement with LawFund will fare much better because they will get 50% of a $5 million-dollar settlement (if that is what the case settled for), less out-of-pocket costs. In that example, they will walk away with $2.5 million, less expenses. LawFund only accepts cases with a potential recovery in excess of $5 million dollars. Under the LawFund program, you do not borrow anything, and have no personal liability for repayment.

The ability of a plaintiff to pay for litigation costs is a common problem, and can create a lot of anxiety. Here is an example of how litigation costs can become so prohibitive that a plaintiff might not be able to pursue their case sufficiently because of a lack of funds.

In a case involving two partners in the music recording business in Los Angeles, one partner claimed that his late partner had, unbeknownst to him, sold equipment belonging to both of them, and did not give him his half. The buyer of the equipment was located in Vermont. The problem was that the plaintiff did not have the money to take the deposition and verify the terms of the sale, although he did have sales records showing the purported sale price and payments.

In a non-jury trial, the judge found some of the terms ambiguous and limited the amount of damages accordingly. The judge, about whom I have nothing good to say, so I will not say it, had no real basis other than what he had been doing throughout the trial. He just did not like the plaintiff, and it was obvious from the way he treated him. The purpose of this story is that if you are experiencing the same problem, you need to do something about it before it is too late. If you cannot afford to do appropriate discovery, and your lawyer will not advance the costs, you need to do something then, not later. The first thing to do if no lawyer will put up the expenses, is to find one that will. If you really believe in your case, and you have been advised that you have a good chance of winning with enough damages to justify the costs, then borrow the money. Just make sure to tell the absolute truth to someone loaning the money to you. Do not diminish the value of your case by not doing what you should do to maximize the likelihood of success. The abusive practices of the "haves" is a reason why the "haves" often beat the "have nots." They will purposely force you to pay for travel and other expenses, they will make numerous motions, or they will compel you to run up the costs with the "experts." Often, the expert fees are the most significant and can be dramatic. I had a case where the forensic accountants billed almost $300,000.

In any event, the purpose of this example is to stress how important it is for you, as a plaintiff, to find a way to fund proper discovery in your case. If you cannot afford to cover the costs of the necessary discovery, you can request that your attorney advance the costs which, hopefully, they will recoup once you have won your case. Finding a lawyer who is willing to advance these costs is a good idea. If you cannot find a lawyer to cover the discovery expenses, but have been advised that you have a good chance of winning your case and recovering sufficient damages to justify the costs, borrow the money from someone. Of course, make sure to fully disclose the facts of the case to the lender. The bottom line is, if you have a strong case, do what is necessary to maximize the likelihood of success.

Sometimes the opposing party will file frivolous motions to run up your costs. For example, they might file a motion for summary judgment. If such a motion is granted, it can end the case. Therefore, once the defendant brings in all kinds of evidence to attempt to demonstrate that there are no unresolved factual issues in the case you, as a plaintiff, are left with no choice but to refute their evidence by gathering your own evidence, which can be quite costly. One remedy available to you when the other side files this sort of frivolous motion to compel you to do something is sanctions. The court can punish a litigant making such motions by imposing sanctions on the party who engages in this kind of conduct. The court-imposed sanctions generally take the form of requiring that the party bringing the motions reimburse you for your attorney fees and other costs associated with your having to defend the motion.

When you anticipate that the other side will be filing frivolous motions, or they have already filed such motions, make sure your attorney drafts a letter to send to the other side, threatening to ask the court for sanctions in the event that they do file a frivolous motion. It is critically important that you (through your attorneys) establish a paper trail demonstrating why the motion is frivolous. Often judges will not take any action to reprimand or sanction a party for running up the costs of litigation. This is yet another reason for you to settle your case.

E. **I Can't Afford A Lawyer: Lawsuit Financing To The Res-**

cue!

If you are not able to pay an attorney to represent you, nor do you have the money to fund a lawsuit, you do have options. One such option is a lawsuit-financing program sponsored by LawFund Management Group, LLC (LFMG – see my earlier discussion). It is a program I developed as a way to help people like the wonderful clients I represented in the following case:

The case revolved around a fig product company that suffered a devastating fire to their warehouse. The second largest producer of fig products such as the fig paste used in Fig Newtons, the company controlled the growing of figs, the fig drying process, and the packaging and selling of the end product. As a result of fire damage to the warehouse, damage to the equipment, the loss of inventory and the interruption of business loss, they filed a claim with their insurance company. At the time of the loss, the fig company was turning a healthy profit and its two principals, Richard and Jim, were doing very well financially. With fancy cars, private planes, grand homes and country club memberships, they were living the good life. They also happened to be very nice guys.

After the fire, their insurance company hired a local independent adjuster rather than using in-house adjusters to assess the damages. The independent adjuster contacted Richard and told him that if he handed him $100,000 in an unmarked envelope, the claim would sail through the insurance company, and that if Richard refused, there would be a problem with the claim. Understandably, Richard was outraged and rejected the demand. Within a few weeks, it was announced in the press that the fire had been caused by arson, and that two local guys had confessed to setting it. After that announcement, the insurance company denied the claim in its entirety. The company argued that our clients engaged in insurance fraud by seeking damages from a fire intentionally caused by them. The estimated damages from the fire were between eight and ten million dollars. It turned out that the insurance agent had sold the company owners a policy that included a substantial penalty for being underinsured, and which excluded a major portion of the business interruption claim.

The truth of the matter is that the fire was not caused by arson. It was accidentally caused by homeless people camped alongside the fig product plant, who were in the habit of lighting small fires to keep warm. On a particular cold evening, one of those fires got out of hand and caused the building to catch fire. The guys confessed to setting the fire and claimed that they had been paid by Richard's brother to do so. Distraught over this turn of events, Richard and Jim engaged my services. Both the court-appointed lawyer assigned to represent one of the confessor defendants and I knew that the story he told was bogus. We hired an investigator to look into the inconsistencies in the two defendants' stories. When we interviewed the two men, they told us that they were being paid by the lawyer for the insurance company, then admitted to fabricating the story about setting an arson fire. The defendants' attorney convinced the deputy district attorney to drop the charges against the defendants. Despite the disappearance of the arson case, the insurance company still would not agree to satisfy the fig company owners' coverage claims. This is another glaring example of what I discussed earlier – the all-too-common refusal of insurance companies to satisfy the claims of their policy holders.

Since the company's principals could afford to pay our fees, we were initially retained on an hourly fee basis. It was a complicated case because of the insurance coverage issues, the negligence of the insurance agent, the bad faith of the insurance company, the independent adjuster's shady conduct and the damages suffered by the company. We filed a lawsuit against the insurance company, the agent, the independent adjusters, the law firm representing the insurance company and an individual involved in the salvage. This led to five different defense lawyers being retained. The ongoing battle became very expensive. More than 150 depositions were taken, and two trips to the East Coast from California and several trips to Southern California were necessary. In the course of this contentious lawsuit, the independent adjusters even threatened my life, and I had to carry a gun for self-protection. It turned out that an admission by one of the adjusters to the extortion attempt had been tape-recorded and, because of the threats, certain depositions were held in the courtroom. Although this procedure was unusual, the judge required it in order to better monitor the case. Whenever any objections were raised, he emerged from his chambers and made a ruling on the objection. Eventually elevated to serve on the Court of Appeals, the judge confided in us that the best part of getting the new position was that he would no longer have to deal with this particular case.

The court reporter assigned by the court to keep track of the documents in the case, had to rent a warehouse to hold the hundreds of boxes of documents that needed to be catalogued for use by any of the parties. He made so much money on this case that he was able to add another wing to his house. In the end, the fig company was forced to go out of business. Richard and Jim, individually, ran out of money. Fortunately, they both had personal insurance. When the independent adjuster (who earlier had tried to extort money from Richard) sued them for defamation, their private insurance carrier agreed to provide a defense, but at its usual rates and with certain restrictions. Although this offered them some relief, ultimately, they both filed for bankruptcy, their wives left them and they could no longer afford their legal expenses. There was no one to pay our fees, so we had to withdraw. Richard and Jim were left to find new counsel to represent them. Eventually, they found someone to take the case on contingency who settled for so little (in order to get himself paid) that there was nothing left for Richard and Jim. Only the banks got paid.

After the case concluded and our firm walked away without getting paid our outstanding fees, I was determined to find a way to secure legal help in the future for companies and individuals like Richard and Jim. They were upstanding, decent businessmen and pillars of the community, who certainly did not deserve the financial ruin and upheaval in their lives that this case caused.

LFMG was formed to expand the legal options available to businessmen and individuals who have suffered substantial monetary damages based on solid legal positions, and either do not have the resources to finance a lawsuit, or who would choose to forego filing a lawsuit to recover those damages because of the cost involved. One of those costs, to a business at least, includes the use of personnel to manage the suit, thus taking staff away from the day-to-day operation of the business. For businesses and individuals who have been sued or threatened with a lawsuit and their insurance company has declined to provide a defense, or has claimed coverage exclusions, the legal costs can be daunting.

LFMG's program is designed to allow those businesses and individuals the option of employing LFMG's management experience, skills and its financial resources to recover their damages rather than relying on their own financial resources and management time. In this way, the aggrieved party can avoid expending its own cash or assets for what could be a protracted period. It also obviates the need to use the time and efforts of management personnel to oversee extensive litigation, allowing them to devote their time to the operations of the business instead.

LFMG offers a case review and, whenever necessary, engages the support of consultants, which can include economists, accountants, engineers and any other essential experts who can assess liability issues and damage claims. When LFMG agrees to take a case, LFMG will:

       1.   Manage and oversee the case to its conclusion, drawing on its own consultants' experience and in-

volvement in litigation to maximize the likelihood of success;

    2.   Monitor the attorneys' activities, providing expert management and oversight to ensure the best outcome for the aggrieved party; and,

    3.   Participate in all settlement negotiations, including the management, supervision and distribution of settlement and judgment proceeds among the participants.

For more information on LFMG and how to sign up for their services, you can visit their website: lfmg.net.

F. Insurance Coverage Issues

A word about the nature of insurance and the companies that provide it might be helpful here. The purpose of insurance is to provide financial protection against events that could cause physical injury or a loss of property. That protection includes providing you, as the insured, with a defense against a lawsuit filed against you or your company.

Insurance coverage is a complicated subject in which most lawyers are not well-schooled. If you find that your insurance company is not responsive to your claim, your first step before approaching a lawyer might be to engage a public adjuster if it is a property claim against your own insurance company. Public adjusters work exclusively on property claims and are well worth their fees, which are a percentage of the claim. The public adjusters compile inventories, value the property, review the coverage and communicate with the insurance company's in-house adjuster, or an independent adjuster if the company does not have its own. The public adjuster's job is to document the extent of the loss and/or replacement costs, and to present that information to the insurance company in support of a claim. Hopefully, the amount claimed will not be contested, but that is rarely the case.

The recent wildfires will generate many claims. Just a few words to give you some specifics on what you might expect to happen and a few provisions to consider.

Be wary of something known as a "co-insurance" provision. It means you needed to insure your property up to its value. If not, and you suffer a partial loss, you can end up paying a portion of the loss because you were under insured. These provisions are not found in homeowner policies, but often appear in commercial policies. They often affect inventories and the fair market value of a building. They can present some potentially daunting issues, so be careful.

What if you are under insured? Can you sue your insurance agent (someone who acts on behalf of an insurance company) or insurance broker? The answer is that it is very difficult, although there are certain circumstances that could make the agent or broker liable for your damages.

As part of the typical homeowners policy (and possible renters policies) you are entitled to something known as "additional living expense." It means that the insurance company must reimburse you for costs of housing, food (if you generally ate at home), mileage and other expenses. It does not mean that you can move into the Ritz Carlton, or eat in the fanciest of restaurants. It is what is called an "incurred expense," so you need to spend it and there is usually a time limitation pegged to a return of the property to its pre-loss condition. I had a case where the insured tried to collect a sum representing rent at an apartment he was not living in. It was considered a fraud, resulting in the insurance company not paying any part of the claim.

Most policies provide that in the event of a covered loss of your home, you can either replace the home with another of "like kind and quality," or repair the damage, subject to limitations provided by the policy. You can "cash out," meaning you can take the money representing the fair market value and do nothing more. Maybe you were thinking of downsizing anyway.

Often you will need to turn to an attorney for help in a dispute with your insurance company and, certainly, if your case involves something other than property damage. In property cases sometimes, the attorney will reduce their fee, considering that the public adjuster must also be paid. The public adjusters take about 10% of the recovery amount. Public adjusters can only be used when you are pursuing a claim against your own insurance company. On contingency, the attorney will earn between 33-1/3% and 40% of the recovered amount, plus reimbursement of their costs.

I once gave a talk before the California Bar Association on the subject of insurance company practices. My presentation was entitled, *"The Only Float in Town Isn't at the Rose Parade."* Insurance companies are notorious for engaging in all kinds of stalling tactics to reduce or avoid paying altogether on the claims filed by their policyholders. In this way, they are able to hold on to and use the money paid in premiums for as long as possible, generally by investing it. In other words, insurance companies play the float. Of course, they are not so thrilled about paying out a claim because this reduces their investment money and increases their costs. The longer they can hold on to the money you pay in as premiums, the more money they can potentially earn.

In a case I handled years ago for an insured party who was denied coverage by their insurance company, I wanted to obtain the records of the company's claims practices, including their statistics regarding paying out claims, and I also wanted to take the deposition of the most senior person in the claims department. The insurance company fought vigorously to keep me from doing so. They gave me the run-around with lines like, "Such and such is no longer at that office," etc. I finally obtained a court order permitting the deposition and flew to the Midwest to take the deposition of a senior claims person.

During the deposition, I asked, "If you have one hundred claims, how many of these would be denied, how many would end up in litigation, and how many would be dismissed for any variety of reasons, such as the death of a plaintiff, or their lawyer backing out of the case, or their inability to secure a lawyer to represent them so they had to go it alone?" I also asked, "Of these one hundred cases, how many actually went to trial, giving the plaintiff a win?" The senior claims person provided all these statistics. It turned out that the company paid the full value of only about 10% of the legitimate claims. The company had figured out that only very occasionally did a plaintiff remain in the case for the long haul, going to trial and winning an amount greater than the initial claim. Because this was a rarity, it was not particularly risky for the insurance company to deny most claims.

If you have the perseverance to stay in the game, can weather the economic pressures, and trust the competence of your attorney, you just might beat the insurance company, especially if you know how they play the game. As you can see, they tend to stall, dodge, delay, create expenses for you (what it costs you in lawyers' fees), and then offer you very little on a claim. When the jury gets a glimpse of the insurance company's bad faith in practice, this can allow you to recover all the attorney's fees you have had to pay, and if you can show that the insurance company's practices were malicious, intentional and in conscious disregard of your rights, you might even be awarded punitive damage (damages awarded to punish or make an example of a wrongdoer who has acted willfully, maliciously, or fraudulently). This is your best leverage, and the insurance company knows it. If you can stay in the game long enough to get the insurance company to the courthouse steps, you have a chance of beating them or settling for a meaningful amount.

In the case I cited, after the deposition the insurance company made an overture to settle, conditioned on my client agreeing not to disclose the records of the case and the deposition testimony. The settlement was huge because the insurance company was fearful that the disclosure of the information that we obtained in the deposition would be tremendously damaging for the company in the future.

In another case, I tried to take the deposition of an underwriter (an insurance person who assesses the risk of enrolling an applicant for coverage or a policy). I was told he no longer worked at the company. I was suspicious, so I had someone call the insurance company office and ask for him. We were told he was out to lunch, thus exposing the lie that he no longer worked there. I obtained a court order to take his deposition. His responses in the deposition proved disastrous for the company. The case went to trial at a Federal Court in Las Vegas. After we rested the case at the end of the day on a Friday, the jury was to begin deliberating on Monday morning. I returned to Los Angeles for the weekend and arrived back at the courtroom in Vegas at 9:00 AM, exactly on time. Trial lawyers have their little routines, and one of mine was to always be standing by the door when the jury arrived in the courtroom. It shows my interest in the jury. Once the jury retired to the jury room, I began to take things out of my briefcase and place them on the counsel table. At 9:17 AM, the jury buzzed. I assumed they had a question. I was wrong. They had reached a verdict! Not only that, but they awarded my client the amount we were seeking. The whole process, including the selection of the foreperson only took them 17 minutes. It was the quickest jury deliberation in my entire career.

There are attorneys who are engaged by the insurance company specifically to support the denial of a claim, and to provide some legal basis for it. Consequently, the insurance company can claim they denied the claim "on advice of counsel." This is a risky practice because it waives the insurance company's attorney-client privilege, thus enabling you to take their attorney's deposition along with the claims representative's deposition, and to gain access to all their communications with their attorney.

There are laws on the books to help an insured recover for a loss when the insurance company either refuses to pay in a timely manner on a legitimate claim, or the insurance company fails to provide the insured with a defense when it has the duty to do so.

Here's an example of a case I handled in my practice in which my client won a far greater sum of money than he was initially willing to accept, only because of an insurance company's refusal to provide a defense to its insured. I represented Five Star Dye House, which had purchased two commercial dryers for drying wet-dyed jeans. The seller of the dryers had engaged a delivery service to deliver the dryers. Because one of the dryers was damaged en route, Five Star refused to accept delivery of the dryers, which had been purchased to replace old dryers that already had been removed in anticipation of delivery of the new, more efficient units. The dryer seller would not fix the damaged unit until it received payment from the mover. My client sued the mover for negligence, and for delaying paying the machine seller for the repair. Five Star filed a lawsuit against the mover for over $1 million in damages based on a loss of business, since Five Star would be without dryer capability for three months. The mover turned the claim over to its insurance carrier, Essex Insurance Company, and requested Essex to provide a defense to the suit. Essex refused, maintaining there were no coverage for anything involving an auto or a truck, and this was a truckman's policy! In fact, when this case went up to the California Supreme Court, one of the justices asked, "What does this insurance policy cover if not truck accidents?" The lawyer for Essex responded that it covers "slip and fall at the office." The panel looked very skeptical. If you are interested in learning more about this case, and what the California Supreme Court opinion looks like, a copy of the opinion can be found in the Appendices.

Because the mover had little money, it was not able to

mount much of a defense to its own suit. It retained an in-experienced, newly-licensed lawyer, and could not afford to hire any experts on accounting matters, or garment production. Not surprisingly, the judge decided in Five Star's favor, and awarded $1.35 million in damages. Of course, the mover did not have the money to pay the judgment, nor to appeal the verdict. However, it had the right to sue Essex for not providing the defense to which they were entitled. After the judgment, I approached the mover and offered to defer any collection action on the judgment if they would assign whatever rights they had against Essex to my client, Five Star. The California Supreme Court opinion also talks about what rights are assignable to a judgment creditor (in this case, Five Star), which may allow the defendant to avoid paying the judgment itself. Certain rights are assignable, and others are not.

The mover agreed to my proposal, and Five Star then claimed the damages from Essex Insurance based on the latter's failure to provide the defense it was obligated to provide. The judge ultimately found in favor of Five Star. He concluded that the incident involving the mover was, indeed, covered by its insurance carrier, and that Essex had committed bad faith by rejecting the mover's claim for coverage, and by refusing to defend it from the lawsuit, and although insurance policies have coverage limits, the bad faith in this case negated the limits of the policy.

This decision allowed Five Star to recover more than $3 million, because over the course of ten years this case was ongoing, interest had accrued on the judgment. Essex sought relief from the California Supreme Court over the issue of attorney's fees, arguing that according to California law, attorney's fees were only recoverable by the policyholder. Five Star was the assignee with a right to recover on the judgment, but it was not the insured party. The California Supreme Court rendered a decision in favor of Five Star's right to collect attorney's fees, thus changing the law in California to allow for assignees of a judgment to recover attorney's fees from an insurance company if the latter was found to have acted in bad faith. The law firm representing Essex, which was presumably being paid on an hourly basis, must have made a bundle in billings, considering how many years this case dragged on.

I have been known to advise clients to pay me an hourly fee despite their plea that they are unable to pay, and would prefer making a contingency fee arrangement with me. One such case involved the destruction of a homeowner's house by fire. The insurance company attorneys lowballed my client, maintaining that the dollar amount of damages was far below what it really was. I knew the opposing attorneys for the insurance company, and anticipated a very large settlement. I pleaded with my clients to engage me on an hourly basis, knowing that given the amount of work necessary, they would end up spending less money paying me hourly than the percentage of the settlement they would have to pay me. When I met with the clients, I discovered that although they did not have the necessary funds to pay me hourly, they were able to borrow money from their parents.

After some preliminary discovery, it became apparent that my clients would prevail, so the insurance company offered to settle for $700,000. I consulted with my clients telling them that I was confident we could get more, and they agreed to find a way to continue paying my hourly fees. I negotiated further with the insurance company's attorneys and the final settlement far exceeded the $700,000 offer. It settled for more than $900,000. By paying me on an hourly basis, the clients ended up owing me 10% of what they would have had to pay me in a contingency fee arrangement. By following my advice, they saved themselves a lot of money.

Sometimes when an insurance company refuses to pay on a claim, you can sue the company for "bad faith." Any party to a contract has an implied obligation to act in good faith. If a court finds that a party acted in bad faith, they can award consequential damages for emotional distress, loss of income and loss of a good credit rating. The insurance company will always argue the "genuine dispute doctrine," claiming that there is a valid dispute in order to avoid a bad faith judgment against them. In an insurance bad faith case, the damage amount is not limited to the amount of the insurance policy provisions.

I represented a plaintiff in a bad faith case involving water damage to the marble floor tiles in his home. There is a rule called the "line of sight," which states that if there is damage covered by insurance, an insured is entitled to have everything repaired that is connected to that damaged area within the line of sight. Consequently, my client requested his insurance company replace all the tiles in the three rooms that were within the line of sight of the damaged tiles. These were unique tiles, and he could not find replacements that would match the other tiles within the line of sight. The insurance company refused to pay for the tile replacement. They hired a tile expert who claimed that the damage was caused by something not covered by insurance and, furthermore, he maintained that the tiles could be easily replaced. This insurance company was in the habit of not paying on claims, making lowball offers to their insureds, and stalling them to the point where they were forced to settle with the insurance company, because they simply could not afford to pay a lawyer to pursue their claims. When you sue for bad faith, if you win, you are awarded attorney's fees. In that case, which was a jury trial, the case settled for $250,000 on the third day of trial. I was not inclined to settle, because I thought we could win on the bad faith claim, but my client wanted to take the money that was offered. The original damages were about $65,000, so the insurance company lost money on this case. In retrospect, it was probably a good call on my client's part. As I have mentioned previously, it is better to compromise and walk away with something rather than walk away empty-handed.

What else can you do when you have suffered damage to your property, and your insurance company refuses to pay the value of your claim? You can hire an appraiser to assess the value of the insurance claim. They will be able to figure out for you the cost of your property damages. For an in-depth look at the appraisal procedure as a helpful tool to use when an insurance company is undervaluing the costs of your damages and acting in bad faith, take a look at my article in the Appendices entitled, *"Using The Appraisal Process to Resolve Insurance Disputes"* (*Los Angeles Lawyer Magazine, July-Aug. 2002*). Minimal changes or interpretations have occurred since 2002. It is recommended that you update by researching the authorities if you want to use this procedure.

G. Let's Change The System Some More

If I were in charge of the judicial system, I would institute some changes to make it more equitable. As I mentioned a number of times in this book, I would like to see a much greater emphasis placed on avoiding trials altogether and settling cases.

Unfortunately, as a general principle, the outcome of legal cases favors the haves over the have-nots. Those with resources can use various legal tactics to stretch out a case, making it too expensive for the have-nots to continue paying their lawyers. The remedy for this unlevel playing field would be to adopt the British legal system in which the loser pays the legal fees of the winner. Today, in the United States, attorney's fees are only recoverable by the prevailing party if it is part of the contractual agreement, or there is an element of bad faith in an insurance company's conduct. The have-nots have a better chance of succeeding if they can find a lawyer to take their case on a contingency. When your opponent is convinced you are in it for the long haul, they are more inclined to settle.

Another way to level the playing field would be to increase the maximum recovery amount allowed in Small Claims Court to $25,000. If we could do that, it would increase the number of people who could bring their claims in Small Claims Court, and not be penalized by their inability to afford a lawyer, since lawyers are not allowed in Small Claims Court. Small Claims Court is a quick (generally it only takes about 90-days from filing until the trial), inexpensive and fair way to recover damages when you feel you have been wronged. I'll bet lawyers would not be in favor of my proposed expansion of the dollar amount recoverable in Small Claims Court. They would be deprived of the cases that would previously have been brought to them because they were worth too much to take to Small Claims Court. The point to emphasize is that the haves cannot use lawyers to bludgeon the have-nots, there is no discovery other than subpoenas, and almost no motions so that they cannot run up the bill and force the have-nots out of the game by creating expenses for them. In small claims, everyone just tells their story and the judge decides. It is real justice.

H. How Can I Avoid Trial? Mediation Or Arbitration – What's The Difference?

Mediation and arbitration are very different animals. Mediation is non-binding. The parties select a person, often a retired judge, to act as a go-between. The mediator reads the briefs submitted by the opposing sides and assembles the group of litigants with the goal of helping them settle the case. Arbitration, on the other hand, is almost always binding, and is conducted like a trial.

Whether you choose to go the route of mediation or arbitration, it is best to be represented by a lawyer. In either case, you want to be able to put forth the strongest case possible, and an expert (i.e., a lawyer), will in all likelihood be much better equipped to argue the merits of your case than you will.

You would seek mediation generally when your opponent is being unreasonable, and you believe that if you bring a neutral third party or mediator, will recognize that the other side is being unreasonable, and will point that out to them and suggest ways to compromise.

How do you find a mediator? There are dispute resolution companies that have lists of mediators for hire, most of whom are retired judges and lawyers. Sometimes it is possible to get three free hours of mediation from volunteer mediators. Because a mediator does not render a decision, the parties will often accept someone known to the parties or, at least to the lawyers. A personal acquaintance with the mediator makes it more likely that the parties will be receptive to the mediator's suggestions for settling the dispute. These days, mediation has become a cottage industry with many judges retiring from the bench to become mediators, a more lucrative job with flexible hours and calendars.

Different mediators have different styles. Some talk to all parties together right off the bat, in the same room. Others begin by speaking to each party separately, promising not to divulge to the other side anything they have been told in confidence. They will point out the strengths in your case to the other side, and inform you of the weaknesses in your case, hoping to draw all involved into a compromise. Good mediators are paid very high fees, as much as $1,000 per hour. I actually am a mediator, having taken a course at Pepperdine University and received my certification.

Arbitration is conducted much like a trial, although it is designed to be faster than a court proceeding, and less costly because of a very limited right to appeal. Arbitrators can be found in the same manner as mediators, from lists put out by dispute resolution companies. Many of them maintain lists of both arbitrators and mediators. Usually in arbitration, there is a single arbitrator, although the parties can agree to use three arbitrators, with two of the three required to be in agreement for an award. The primary problem with arbitration is that there is almost no right of appeal. Unless you can prove fraud in the proceedings, or that the arbitrator failed to disclose a prior relationship with one of the parties, or a personal interest in the outcome, you are stuck with the arbitrator's decision. This points to the necessity of choosing your arbitrator very carefully. It might be more of a gamble to appear before a biased arbitrator, than to present your case before a jury of your peers. Sometimes arbitrators gain a reputation for favoring one side over another in certain types of cases. As an example, once an arbitrator acquires a reputation for being too generous with plaintiffs in health insurance cases, the health insurance companies will be unlikely to engage that arbitrator again.

If you have a contract with the other parties containing a provision for mandatory arbitration, you must take your dispute to an arbitrator. When you and the other parties cannot agree on an arbitrator, you can petition the court to compel arbitration, and to assign an arbitrator to your case. Courts generally grant these petitions. A quick hearing will take place in which the court will appoint an arbitrator from a list of retired judges looking for work. This process presents another problem, which is that the assigning judge will often choose a retired judge with whom he or she is friendly. So, you end up with whomever the judge likes.

In some parts of the country, you can be sorely disadvantaged if you are coming from outside the area. There can be a real hometown advantage for local attorneys who know the arbitrators. They tend to be part of "the good ole boys' network." When I represented a client in an arbitration in Texas, someone had told me in advance, "Take care of the judge." They were referring to the arbitrator who was a retired judge. I was not willing to pay off the arbitrator/retired judge, so our opponent, who was represented by a local attorney, won this $10 million lawsuit. These judges often favor the local attorney in their rulings because this is where their repeat business comes from.

As I am sure you have guessed by now, I am not a big fan of arbitration. Yet another problem with this forum is that the arbitrators generally want to be fair and make a good impression on everyone involved, so they tend to pull a King Solomon trick, and determine that the baby should be cut in half, something not good for anyone, especially the baby.

I'VE FOUND A GOOD LAWYER; NOW WHAT?

4

A. ## What To Expect At The Initial Interview With The Lawyer

At your initial interview with an attorney, even though you might have already decided that you want this attorney to take your case, the attorney still has to decide whether or not they want to represent you. You should bring along any evidence you have to support your claim, including correspondence, photographs, emails, a print-out of text messages, any reviews by experts, such as accountants and statements from prospective witnesses. In short, bring anything that you think will help your case. Most lawyers will not accept a case until they are satisfied that there are documents to support the client's position. Once the attorney has agreed to take your case, they will draw up an agreement for you to sign, spelling out the terms of the attorney's engagement, including the fee arrangement. Is the attorney going to bill you hourly, or take the case on a contingency basis? Hourly fee attorneys are more likely to take marginal cases because they will get paid, win, lose, or draw. Contingency lawyers are gambling on the outcome, and are hopeful that the case will ultimately settle for a large amount of money in a short time period. Find out if the lawyers at the firm settle cases quickly in order to get themselves paid.

B. ## How To Be A Good Client

When you share your story with a potential lawyer, you must be perfectly candid and not hide anything that might be relevant to your case. In my numerous years of practice, I have learned that, as a general rule, we win cases we are supposed to win, because those cases have merit and involve a deserving client, and we lose the ones we are supposed to lose when the case lacks merit. Too often, the parties choose not to disclose things they believe will be detrimental to their case, or they simply lie about certain details, believing if they are truthful it will affect how their lawyer will think about them and represent them. Hiding facts from your attorney can have devastating consequences. For a lawyer, there is nothing worse than being surprised at a trial by something your client neglected to tell you.

Sometimes clients can be their own worst enemies. Here is an example. I had a criminal case in which my client was accused of insurance fraud. I was told it was the biggest theft case in Orange County, and it received an abundance of news coverage. I remember precisely when I tried the case because my son was born during this 5½ month trial. My client, Tony, did something so stupid that he turned a hung jury (a slang term for a hopelessly deadlocked jury in a criminal case in which a decision on guilt or innocence cannot be made), which would have been a win for him as the defendant, into a conviction.

Tony owned a company that stored gold and other precious metals for customers in vaults they maintained in Santa Ana. To cover the cost of the storage, they offered a service to their customers, which entailed selling the customers' gold to outside parties, paying interest to the customers on the value of the gold, and then returning the gold to its customers on 24-hour's notice. Tony banked on there always being some amount of gold from customers stored in the vault at any given time that he could give to a customer who requested the return of their gold. In a worst-case scenario, Tony figured he could replenish a customer's gold by buying gold on the open market.

Unfortunately, Tony and his partner, a co-defendant in the case, sold all of their customers' gold at once to raise money to invest with some guy, who had a gold-mining venture in New Mexico. He claimed to be able to turn lead into gold. That should have been the first clue. Unexpectedly, two separate customers came in on the same day demanding their gold from the vault. Tony and his partner had 24-hours to return the gold to these two customers, but there was no gold available in the vaults, and they did not have the money to buy it back for their customers. Tony testified at trial that on a Saturday, he received a call from a prospective customer who wanted to meet him at the vault. Tony agreed and went to the vault. He claimed that after a few minutes, the doorbell rang. Upon opening the door, he was confronted by two guys wielding guns, who tied him to a chair and supposedly cleaned out all the gold in the vaults. Then, according to his testimony, he tipped himself over and was able to reach the alarm. The cops came and found him on the floor still tied up. When Tony filed an insurance claim, it was denied on the grounds that the robbery was a setup by Tony to cover up for the missing gold that he had sold to give money to the goldmining guy. Tony was arrested for the crime of insurance fraud.

We were able to bring in a former FBI agent, who testified that he had been in the vault the day before the robbery and saw that the vault was full. What is interesting is that I found out, years later, that Tony had been an FBI informant and, in this way, they were paying him back for his previous help. I did not know it at the time. Also, Tony provided me with a new witness, Karl, who was prepared to testify that he, too, was at the vaults the day before the supposed robbery, and saw that the vaults were full. Of course, I had to interview this new potential witness. I did so, and was left with a funny feeling that something was amiss with Karl. After consulting with co-counsel and defendants, I reluctantly called Karl as a witness. He turned out to be very convincing.

After a 5½-month trial, both sides rested. The judge gave the lawyers a week to prepare for final arguments and jury instructions. Suddenly, on Easter weekend before the conclusion of the trial, I received a call that Karl had been arrested. It turned out a friend of his had seen the television coverage of this case, and had invited him to his office for a glass of wine. During the course of their conversation, the friend mentioned the testimony and asked Karl if it was really true. Karl admitted the whole story was made up to support Tony's argument that the vault was full before the so-called robbery. Karl told his friend that he owed Tony a favor. The friend asked if the lawyers knew about this fabrication and, thankfully, Karl said, "No." Suddenly, the friend's office door burst open, and the police rushed in and cuffed Karl. They had been in the adjacent room, videotaping the entire conversation through a hole they had drilled behind the desk.

As a result of the recording, the District Attorney requested the case be reopened to consider this new evidence. The request was granted. After the trial, I spoke to several of the jurors, who said that without this videotape of Karl discrediting Tony's defense, they would have ended up in a hung jury, meaning no verdict against the defendants. The judge granted our request for bail pending an appeal. Wouldn't you know it? Tony skipped bail and fled to Costa Rica! My client destroyed his own case. The lesson to take away here is that it is crucial for you, as a client, to leave the handling of your case to your lawyer, and that it is in your best interests as a client to always tell the whole truth and nothing but the truth. Tony made up his crazy story because he thought it would strengthen his defense. If I had known he was concocting this story, I would never have let him do it.

You might be wondering if I would have taken this case if Tony had told me the truth about his activities at the outset. As a general rule, attorneys in criminal cases do not ask their client if they did what they are accused of. If the attorney intends to put them on the witness stand, there is an ethical problem for the attorney if they ask their client if they committed the crime, and the client says they did, and then the attorney wants to put him on the stand to claim their innocence. Attorneys cannot have their client testify if the attorney knows they will lie in court and say something other than what they had previously told their attorney.

C.   Preparing The Complaint

Once the attorney reviews all the documents you provided and speaks to all available favorable witnesses, they will begin to research the legal issues and analyze the facts of your case vis-à-vis the relevant law. Based on the research and what the client has shared with the attorney, a complaint is prepared. The complaint sets forth the facts of the case, the identities of the parties, the relationship between them, evidence that the jurisdictional requirements have been met (i.e., why the case is filed where it is), the legal basis for the claims and the damages allegedly caused by the defendant. Often multiple defendants are named. A good complaint anticipates defenses that will be raised by the defendant. For simple cases, there are form complaints in which one only need check the proper boxes.

1.   Types Of Damage Claims

There are two classes of claims you can make for damages. One type, called the First Party claim, is brought against your insurance company or any party that has wronged you directly. The other type is called the Third-Party claim. In the latter type of cases, you are seeking relief from the party responsible for causing the damages, but they are represented by an insurance company that will be providing their defense and, possibly, indemnity (the insurance company will pay for any damage award issued by the court). If the case is brought against an uninsured party, or if the insurance would not apply to the nature of the claim, the uninsured party will have to engage attorneys and pay them on an hourly fee basis, since there are no contingency fees to be awarded if the attorneys successfully defend their client.

2.   Venue: Where To File The Complaint

Generally, complaints are filed where the defendant lives, is engaged in business, or where the property is located in a property dispute. When a case is filed before a court, the court decides whether it has personal and subject matter jurisdiction and, if so, whether it is the most appropriate forum or venue. There is a doctrine called *forum non conveniens* (Latin for "inappropriate forum"), which allows a judge to transfer a case if the court chosen by the plaintiff is not the most convenient one. If courts in two different states will accept jurisdiction in a case, the plaintiff has to show that justice requires the trial to occur in the forum suggested by the plaintiff. Later, I explain a bit more about why attorneys might try to get a case transferred to a court in a different jurisdiction.

Some litigants engage in what is called "forum shopping," in which they try to have their case heard in the court most likely to provide a favorable judgment. From personal experience, I know that if you are a plaintiff in Los Angeles, it is generally better to have your case heard in a downtown courtroom than in a more local courtroom such as Santa Monica. In general, the downtown juries are more liberally disposed towards plaintiffs. Also, when I am considering the venue in which to file a case, I try hard to stay out of Federal Court because those judges are appointed for life and tend to be rather dictatorial. There was one judge in particular who had been a decent Superior Court judge, and was eventually appointed to the federal bench in Los Angeles. Unfortunately, I had a case before him, when he was on the federal bench, which lingered for nine whole years! During that time, the opposing counsel on the case and I even tried jointly to get the judge to rule on a motion, or at least schedule a trial. He completely ignored us. The only reason the case ever concluded was because the judge died. After his death, his clerk called and informed us that he had found the case on the judge's desk and asked what we wanted done with the case. We took it to arbitration. That experience soured me on having cases go to a Federal Court.

Certain states have even acquired a reputation as plaintiff-friendly jurisdictions and, so, many cases are filed in those states even though there is little connection between the legal issues and that jurisdiction. Another reason that a plaintiff might choose a particular forum in which to file a case is because that forum happens to be inconvenient for the defendant or their witnesses. Having to defend the case in that forum might cause the defendant hardships in terms of travel expenses, health issues, or visa problems. It is leverage.

The defendant, however, can seek a change of venue. They can petition the forum court to reject the jurisdiction and petition it to transfer the case to a more convenient forum for the defendant. As judges, we must balance the interests of the parties, since injustice can occur when a plaintiff is allowed to pursue the action in a forum that is clearly inconvenient for the defendant, but also when a plaintiff is deprived of their right to a timely trial. In any event, there must be a real and significant connection between the venue and the cause of action in order to protect defendants against being pursued in jurisdictions that have little or no connection with the parties, or the subject matter of the case.

3.   **Filing On Time**

A competent attorney will be aware of the applicable statutes, and make sure pleadings (the claim and defenses formally submitted by parties at the beginning stage of a lawsuit) are filed on a timely basis. All states and the federal judicial system have statutes of limitations. As defined earlier in this book, the statute of limitations bars a lawsuit unless it is filed within the statutory time frame, usually two years for personal injury cases, two years for breach of an oral agreement, four years for breach of a written agreement and a certain period of time that runs from discovery of a fraud. These statutes of limitations can be found in the Civil Code (in many states, the name for the collection of statutes and laws, which deal with business and negligence lawsuits and practices). In some cases, for example, those involving a minor, the statute of limitations is tolled, meaning that a minor is given until the age of majority (usually 18), to file a suit, plus a reasonable time period afterwards. The statute is also tolled in insurance cases from the date the claim is made to the insurance company (not from when the event takes place allowing for the making of a claim), until the insurance company denies the benefits under the insurance policy. It is best to put everything in writing, and if there is an exchange of emails, keep them, so in the event of a dispute as to the time a claim is made and when the insurance company denied the claim, there will be a written record.

4. Should The Complaint Be Signed

Once the complaint is completed, depending on the type of complaint, it might need to be signed by the plaintiff. A complaint signed under penalty of perjury, claiming the truth of the facts alleged, is called a Verified Complaint. Sometimes, it is a good tactical decision to verify the complaint because it forces the defendant to file a Verified Answer. If the defendant files a Verified Answer, it means that the defendant swears under penalty of perjury that their denials of any allegations in the complaint are truthful. They may not be able to do that. There are statutes that require certain types of causes of action to be verified. For example, Unlawful Detainer – UD – actions (attempts by landlords to evict tenants, or attempts by a property buyer to obtain possession of the purchased property). For an in-depth discussion of UD, see Chapter 6. Property title disputes must be verified. Suing someone for basic negligence does not require a verified complaint. With verified complaints and answers, if the matter ends up going to trial, the defendant's answers to the complaint can be used to discredit the defendant if it turns out the answers were false. The plaintiff, too, can get themselves in hot water at trial if they alleged something in the complaint that turned out not to be true.

In a recent case in which I represented the defendant, a general contractor, the homeowner plaintiffs alleged in a verified complaint, certain facts that their attorneys included in order to bolster their case. Unfortunately for the plaintiffs, the alleged "facts" did not hold up. I spent about half an hour in front of the jury going over all the allegations in the verified complaint, for which there was no proof, or where the facts that came out in trial were contrary to what the plaintiffs had claimed in the complaint. It was not a surprise that there was a verdict in my client's favor. It was clear to me that the jury did not like the plaintiff, who came across as arrogant and argumentative. During the trial, the judge had to admonish them to stop arguing with me and just answer the questions I posed.

5. **Helping Your Cause**

As a general rule, if the jury does not like you, or your lawyer, they will find a way to decide in favor of your opponent. Even if you have a strong case, if you do not behave like a decent human being, you will have to pay the price. If you lose your solid case, this is yet another message from a higher power that you need to "fix" or correct your behavior or attitude. The outcome of your lawsuit is the "effect." It is all about transformation. You have the ability to change the outcome by changing your attitude, by giving, rather than always taking, and by sharing what you have.

D.   Attacking The Complaint

How can you fight a lawsuit before it goes to trial? There are procedural devices you can use to attack the complaint at various stages in the legal process, starting from the filing of the complaint, during the discovery phase and all the way through to the actual trial.

As a defendant, your lawyer may recommend filing a motion called a demurrer (a formal objection to the legal sufficiency of an opponent's pleading). This is a way to get the case against you dismissed for technical reasons, i.e., the statute of limitations has run (in order words, the plaintiff waited too long to file the complaint). If the demurrer is sustained, it means that the plaintiff cannot prevail, even if the facts stated in the complaint are true. Generally, the court will sustain the demurrer (dismiss the case) with leave to amend to fix the deficiency. As a defendant, using this device is often a waste of time and money. The demurrer educates the other party about deficiencies in their complaint, and if it is dismissed with leave to amend, gives that party an opportunity to fix the deficiency. As a defendant, you should ask your attorney why a demurrer, or similar motion is being filed, and what the likelihood of success is. The filing of a demurrer is often times used to create more billable hours. There are costs involved on both sides – the plaintiff will either have to fight the demurrer, or spend time filing an amended complaint. The cost to the plaintiff can be used by the defense as leverage. Watch for the use of the demurrer and question its necessity.

E.   Filing An Answer

After a plaintiff files a complaint, and the defense does not demur, or make some other motion to get the case dismissed, the defendant will file an Answer and possibly, a Cross-Complaint. The answer will generally deny each of the

allegations in the complaint, and put forth affirmative defenses. Examples of affirmative defenses include a claim that
the statute of limitations has run; that the complaint does
not state a legally recognizable cause of action; that the facts,
as alleged, fail to support a cause of action, failure of performance on the part of the plaintiff, and estoppel (reliance
on something the plaintiff did). The answer is usually filed
within 30-days after the complaint has been served. However,
a demurrer delays the response period. The same applies to a
cross-complaint.

Whether as a defendant or plaintiff, if your case can
possibly be filed in either federal court or state court, you
should discuss the issue of jurisdiction with your attorney.
Sometimes a defendant will want to remove a case from state
court and transfer it to federal court where the costs are usually far greater, the system is more rigid and there are fewer
jurors required to deliberate. For instance, it is a matter of
diversity, meaning that the parties in the case are located in
different states, the case will be heard in federal court. Also,
copyright matters and cases revolving around other federal
questions belong in federal court. On the other hand, sometimes cases are filed in federal court, and one of the parties
moves to remand (to send back) to state court. The bottom
line is that the party with the stronger financial position can
use these methods to string out the other party, requiring
them to spend extra money on changing jurisdictions. If you
are the plaintiff, stay out of federal court if you can.

F.   **Cross-Complaints**

What if you are slapped with a lawsuit, and you want
to sue the plaintiff for something they did to harm you? As a
defendant, you may file a cross-complaint setting forth either
or both of the following: (1) a cause of action against any of
the parties who filed the complaint against you; and, (2) any
cause of action you have against a person you claim is liable,

whether or not that person is already a party to the action, if the cause of action you assert arises out of the same transaction, or occurrence, as the one from the original claim against you.

When you, as the defendant, file a cross-complaint, you are called a cross-complainant, and the party you sue is called a cross-defendant. You still must file an answer to the original complaint, or demurrer. If your cross-complaint is against the original plaintiff, then you can serve it on the plaintiff's attorney by mail, but if you file a cross-complaint against a third party, you must serve that party in person, or substitute service, and a new summons must be issued by the clerk of the court. The cross-defendants must then file their answers, or other responses.

Is it a good idea for you, as a defendant, to file a cross-complaint? Not necessarily. Cross-complaints detract from the primary case, making the case more complicated. It is a means of extending the trial time-wise, which can cut either way for you as the defendant. The jury will be unhappy because it means they will have to serve longer. Remember, as the cross-complainant, you have the burden of proof in order to prevail on your cross-complaint. If you lose your cross-complaint, you will be exposed to additional costs, including attorney's fees. Sometimes, defense lawyers will cross-complain because it allows them to run up their bills. When the plaintiff's lawyer must defend against the cross-complaint, it becomes an additional expense for the plaintiff if your attorney is being paid hourly. Defense of a cross-complaint is not covered by a contingency fee, so you will have to pay your attorney hourly to defend the cross-complaint.

In small claims, a defendant can file the equivalent of a cross-complaint. Not so for UD cases (see Chapter 6). In those cases, the defendant must file a separate action against the landlord or property owner.

Once the complaint and cross-complaint have survived the attacks on the pleadings, and the parties have filed answers to them, this marks the end of the pleading phase of the case. How much the pleadings will cost you as a party to a lawsuit depends on what was done. Therefore, you should find out whether the specific pleadings and motions filed were reasonably necessary. Ask your attorney.

G.   The Christopher Columbus Phase

The discovery (or investigation) process is where the legal bills start to mount. Each side tries to discover what they can about the other side's case. Some methods are more expensive than others. The following discovery methods are essential, fact-finding tools, that you should be aware of because, as the client, you are going to be billed for them. In UD cases, discovery is permitted, but there is a narrow time frame in which it must be completed. All discovery in these cases must be completed five days before trial.

1.   Interrogatories

Interrogatories are questions asked by one party of the other. In simple cases, there are form interrogatories, meaning the attorney sends a form to the other side, which requests basic information, including the identity of witnesses, a listing of pertinent documents, and whether there are photographs, emails and reports. In this way, each side can flush out the other side's case.

However, the form "rogs" (as interrogatories are referred to by attorneys), are not specific enough, and so attorneys might need to design their own rogs, which are called "Special Interrogatories." Often the special rogs ask for information that is privileged, overbroad, burdensome and oppressive, or provide some other basis for the party to whom they are directed, not to answer. When the party refuses to answer, the attorney posing the questions can seek a court order to compel a response. However, if the request for the court order is unreasonable, an attorney representing the party to whom the questions are directed, can make a motion for a protective order. If granted, the protective order prevents the other side from abusing the discovery process by requesting certain information. Prior to making a motion to compel a response to the rogs, the parties must meet and confer (a requirement of courts that before a judge will hear certain types of motions and petitions, the lawyers, sometimes along with their clients, must meet and confer to attempt to resolve the issue, or at least identify the matters in conflict). If you make a motion to compel a response to the rogs, as the judge, I will ask if you have met and conferred before I will hear the motion. Sometimes lawyers will advise their clients to refuse to answer the interrogatories, or they will make frivolous objections to the rogs in order to trigger a meet and confer, simply to run up their bill.

2.   **Requests For Admissions**

This discovery method is used to get the responding party to admit or deny the facts in the request. If they do not deny a fact, it is deemed admitted, so the opposing party does not have to prove these facts in court. An admission by a respondent is supposed to put that particular issue to rest. Most often, the request for the respondent to admit to something is denied, or the respondent's answer is that there is insufficient information to either admit or deny the request. There is a penalty called sanctions for denying a fact that is later proven in court, but in all my years of law practice, I cannot remember ever getting sanctioned when the denied fact is then proven at trial.

3.   **Requests For Production Of Documents**

This is, undoubtedly, the most burdensome and expensive aspect of discovery. Imagine having hundreds, or maybe thousands of documents, or records, that you are required to produce, some of which can prove very harmful to your case or, maybe, you are the one requesting that the other side turn over a boatload of documents that they are refusing to produce. When you are on the receiving end, digging up all your records and poring over them is very time-consuming, and can create problems if the requested documents cannot be found. Sometimes disputes arise over what exactly the request entails. The parties often fight over production of the documents with one party claiming that the other side has not produced, or will not produce documents that are responsive to the request. Before court intervention is sought to compel the production of documents, the parties are required to meet and confer (just as they must do with other discovery requests) to try to resolve the issues. If they cannot resolve their issues, a motion to compel production is made in which the court is asked to order the non-responding party to produce the requested documents. The non-responding party files an opposition to the motion, and the requesting party files a response. After all the briefs are submitted, the motion is set for a hearing.

If the other side appears to be simply playing this game (i.e., the back and forth over document production) in order to run up their billable hours, your lawyer can respond by writing letters to the lawyers representing the other side, pointing out that they are creating big problems for their client which, in my experience, is often an insurance company. The purpose of sending the letters is twofold. First, it is to ensure that the insurance company, or whoever the party is on the other side, sees that their lawyer is running up the bill. Secondly, the letter will end up as an attachment to some kind of motion, which will allow the court to see what is going on.

Must tax returns by produced as part of a document request? Generally, tax returns are privileged, which means you do not have to produce them. An exception to this rule is if you have already produced them to other parties, such as your bank, in that case you have waived your privilege. So, be careful who you give your tax returns to, especially banks.

If a party elects to claim a privilege in order to avoid producing certain documents, they must provide what is called a "privilege log" to the other side. In this log, you must identify any documents that you are not going to produce, and you need to supply the reason for withholding those documents. Then the requesting party can make a motion for production in which they question the privilege status of the requested documents. For instance, they might argue that the requested documents are not privileged because the privilege was waived.

Sometimes you will find a "smoking gun" (a critical piece of evidence that is dispositive of the case) in the documents produced, and which the party offering them up probably was not aware of. I remember going through a file in a hotel room in Philadelphia, where I had traveled to take the deposition of an executive at the offices of an insurance company. The dispute involved whether or not my client had earthquake coverage for a claim made after the 1994 Northridge earthquake. The insurance company maintained that my client, the insured, had not purchased earthquake insurance. I was pleasantly surprised when, going through the file, to discover a document reflecting a conversation between the insurance adjuster and the insurance agent confirming that my client did, indeed, order earthquake coverage. Upon cross-examining the insurance executive about the document, he had to acknowledge its authenticity. This was a perfect example of a case in which the defendant produced documents that unbeknownst to them, contained the smoking gun. The case ultimately settled.

4. **Depositions**

A deposition is the taking of testimony under oath before a certified court reporter and attorneys. A party to a lawsuit can take the deposition of the other party, or of any witness. The deposition takes place outside of the courtroom and is intended to be used in a trial. The testimony is recorded, and often videotaped. The transcript is then read and signed by the person who was deposed.

This discovery tool is an opportunity for both sides to find out what evidence the other side has to support its case, to examine and cross-examine witnesses, as well as the parties to the case. Depositions are taken to preserve evidence, such as when a witness is out of state and not subject to the court's jurisdiction and in order to memorialize testimony that might not be available at trial but, the true purpose of taking depositions is to attach those who are being deposed to a specific position, so that you will know what to expect if they are asked to testify at trial. If the person who was deposed says something at trial contrary to what they had testified to in thier deposition, as trial the deposition transcript is read aloud to them, so as to impeach their testimony in front of the judge or jury.

Here's an example of how a deposition can be used to impeach someone's testimony at trial:

Q: Do you recall having your deposition taken?

A: Yes.

Q: Do you remember being told that you can change whatever testimony you give if you realize that you made a mistake, or it was recorded incorrectly by the court reporter, but that if you do, we could call that change to the attention of the jury? Further, do you remember being told that if you said something on one occasion, before you talked to your lawyer, and then changed your sworn testimony after speaking with your lawyer, this can also be brought to the attention of the jury?

A: Yes.

Q: You just testified that when you approached the intersection the traffic light facing you was green. Isn't it true that when your deposition was taken, you testified that the light was red?

You can ask the witness to look at the transcript to refresh their recollection. Then you can ask if the deposition transcript refreshed their recollection. If they respond no, you read aloud their transcript testimony. You can also read the deposition transcript in court without asking the witness to read it, and see if it refreshes their memory. You can play around with this sort of questioning until you have shown that the witness is not credible.

Often witnesses respond to questions by saying, "I don't recall." This can backfire on them when the only thing they claim to recall happens to be a fact that supports their side of the case. I had a case in which I took the deposition of an attorney who responded, "I don't recall" to seventy-five of my questions, but did respond to the one question that dealt directly with the subject. At trial I stood in front of the jury for 45-minutes and read the repeated "I don't recall" responses to each of the deposition questions. I apologized to the jury for subjecting them to this ordeal, and went on to make the point that this attorney witness was not to be believed. It worked, because they jury found in my client's favor, awarding a substantial sum.

H.   Motions (And Not The Waving Of Your Hands Kind)

A motion is a formal request to the judge for an order or judgment in a case. Motions may be made at any point in administrative, criminal or civil proceedings, although the right is regulated by court rules that vary depending on the jurisdiction. Motions are made for many purposes: To postpone a trial to a later date, to get a modification of an order; for a judgment; for a dismissal of the opposing party's case; for a rehearing; for sanctions; and any number of other reasons. Most motions require the filing of points and authorities, setting forth the legal reasons for granting the motion or opposing it, and written notice to the attorney for the opposing party.

Oral motions may be permitted during a trial or hearing. A competent attorney will be schooled in the rules of court and, thus, they will know which type of motion may be oral, instead of written, and when to object.

While the case is in the discovery phase, the defendants, cross-complainants, or plaintiffs, may make a motion called a Motion for Summary Judgment. In this motion, the moving party claims that all necessary factual issues are resolved, or need not be tried because they are so one-sided. The granting of this motion can end the case. A Motion for Summary Judgment is a favorite motion for defense attorneys because they are often times very complicated, involve substantial research on issues of law, weaving in of the facts and, consequently, can generate large hourly fees. It is like hitting the mother lode, but the problem with this motion is that if there is a factual dispute, the motion cannot be granted if the fact is material to the case. Nonetheless, sometimes judges want to get rid of cases clogging up their calendars, and this is an easy way to do so. Aside from generating fees for the attorney filing the motion, there is a consequence for the party that has to oppose the motion. Opposing the motion can be a burdensome and expensive proposition. In many instances in which the lawyer has been engaged on an hourly fee basis, and their client is not paying their fees for this complicated response to the summary judgment motion, the lawyer will seek to withdraw as counsel to avoid doing work for which they might not get paid.

Since the motion for summary judgment (or defending against the motion) almost always requires attachments in the form of documents, the process of assembling the documents can involve hundreds of hours of time copying exhibits, creating schedules, taking declarations, etc. The motion includes a statement of disputed and undisputed facts, which entails quoting from depositions, or other documents, and identifying the specific page and line in those documents that will be introduced into evidence. This is a mammoth project.

I have seen lawyers hauling banker boxes chock full of exhibits into court to accompany their motions. There is always the question of whether these motions are necessary given the amount of work involved in filing them. A good attorney will know the answer to that question. Ask your attorney whether it is worthwhile to file a motion for summary judgment and what the likelihood of success is.

JURY OR JUDGE: WHICH WAY TO GO?

5

You are fully invested in your case now. The question is, is it going to be decided by a jury of your peers, or a judge? You have the choice of having your case decided by a judge only – called a bench trial – or by a jury. A good attorney will choose wisely as part of their trial strategy.

Bench trials are usually geared towards cases that present only questions of law or equity. Examples include property foreclosures, divorce and child custody matters, contract breaches and various disputes over money and all matters that fall short of being criminal acts. In the bench trial, the judge acts as both a finder of fact and ruler on matters of law and procedure. In other words, the judge weighs all the evidence presented at trial, decides on its credibility, and also makes rulings on the admissibility of the evidence. Bench trials are usually quicker than jury trials because the attorneys need not spend time on jury selection and jury instructions. They are also usually a bit less formal than jury trials. It is helpful to have a bench trial for particularly complex cases that might be confusing to a jury. Also, bench trials can be a good choice for what are often considered by the general public as unlikeable parties, such as homeowners' associations, insurance companies and unpopular political organizations. This is because juries often decide cases based on how much they like or sympathize with one party or the other. Bench trials tend to result in outcomes more favorable to defendants because of the burden of proof and, thus, defense attorneys (particularly insurance defense attorneys) often recommend bench trials to their clients to avoid the enormous verdicts juries sometimes award to the plaintiffs, who are sympathetic injury victims.

Trial by jury is usually a better option in cases in which the ultimate goal is monetary compensation for injuries or damages. In a jury trial, the jury is comprised of members of the community, who serve as the finders of fact at the trial. They hear the evidence presented by each side, and render a verdict based on how persuasive each party's evidence is. The judge presides over the questions of law and procedure that arise during a jury trial, including ruling on attorneys' objections to questions asked or evidence offered. The judge also rules on motions the attorneys make. Jury trials tend to be time-consuming. Another drawback to jury trials is that jurors might not follow the law, but instead reach their conclusions based on emotions.

A trial by jury is often preferable for plaintiffs. While judges have a solid understanding of the burden of proof, and how that burden can shift based on proofs and defenses made throughout the course of a case, juries often do not. The burden juries understand the best is the basic burden of proof that a plaintiff must meet – to demonstrate by a preponderance of the evidence (in civil cases) that the plaintiff's claim is true. Thus, most juries will find that the plaintiffs have, indeed, put forth a preponderance of the evidence in favor of their position in any case that has made it as far as trial. This makes a plaintiff's job that much easier when making their case before a jury, and allows them to focus on recovering the maximum damages rather than having to respond at trial to all sorts of defenses that might need to be surmounted.

Juries tend to take great interest in the human story that is being presented at trial. They are swayed by emotions, and often decide cases on which party they believe should prevail under the circumstances, and their decision is frequently based on whom they like, and don't like in the case, including the lawyers and the witnesses. On the other hand, judges are much less influenced by their feelings about the parties and, instead, decide based on legal nuances and their deeper understandings of the law than an average juror would have. Since jurors so often rule with their hearts, much more than a judge would, a significant advantage to a jury trial is the amount of money that juries award. A particularly compelling sympathy-inducing story about great suffering of a victim at the hands of a defendant can lead to a much more generous award than a dispassionate judge would grant. It should come as no surprise that the heftiest awards historically have all resulted from jury trials.

When arguing your case before a jury, there are a couple of important factors you (really, your lawyer) should keep in mind. First of all, in general, the members of the jury do not want to be in that courtroom, and tend to resent any delaying tactics that keep them there longer than necessary. Secondly, you need to keep the jury interested, which includes not making the case so complicated that they will throw up their hands and say, "A pox on both your houses!" Then they end up awarding next to nothing for either side. When presenting a case to the jury, you should follow the acronym KISS – Keep It Simple Stupid. Since you will hopefully be represented by counsel at this point, the above advice is most relevant for your attorney and for you to make sure they follow this advice. Lawyers should be themselves at trial, and so should you. If you pretend to be different than you are, most likely the jury will see through your deception. I find that informal, down-to-earth demeanor works well. Think how effective Peter Falk's bungling detective in the television show *Columbo* was in getting at the truth.

As a party in the case that will come before a jury, you should not underestimate the value of being likeable. So often the jury favors one side over the other primarily because they simply like the people on that side better. Later, I will write about a slip and fall case we won, not only because the expert witness was so convincing, but also because the jurors very much liked my client, who was a nice elderly lady.

A. **A Short Primer On Jury Selection**

The process of questioning prospective jurors is called *voir dire*. This phrase comes form the French words "to see, to say." The stated purpose of *voir dire* is to determine if a juror is biased and, therefore, cannot render an impartial decision, and to determine if there is cause to not allow a juror to serve. Reasons for dismissing a juror based on cause include the juror's previous knowledge of the facts in the case; acquaintance with the parties, witnesses or attorneys; an occupation which might lead to bias; (in a criminal case) prejudice against the death penalty; or previous experiences such as having been sued in a similar type case. The unstated reason for *voir dire* is to allow the attorneys to get a feel for the personalities and particular bents of the people on the jury panel, and to help them in deciding which jurors to keep in the hopes that those jurors will decide in favor of their client.

In state court, the lawyers are given the opportunity to ask questions of the prospective jurors. In federal court, the judge questions the jurors, usually after requesting that the lawyers provide him or her with questions to ask. I prefer trials in state court so that I have a chance to size up the juror by questioning him or her directly. While the judge is asking general questions regarding family, where they live, type of work they do, their prior jury experience, etc., I memorize the names of the jurors. Later during *voir dire,* I use the juror's name when questioning him or her. Once, after a trial, I spoke to a juror who told me that he was so impressed that I remembered his name that from the very beginning of the trial he had a good feeling about me.

Once the lawyers for each side have asked questions of the prospective jurors, the judge will ask if each juror "passes for cause," meaning that there is no legal reason (such as the reasons enumerated above) to discharge that prospective juror. If there is a dispute over whether a juror should be dismissed for cause, the judge makes the decision.

Next, each party is given the right to exercise *peremptory challenges*, meaning that the lawyer can dismiss the prospective juror without providing a reason. These calls are totally speculative. I have kept jurors that I should have rejected, and I have kept jurors about whom I had my doubts, but who ultimately found in my favor. Each side is allowed a limited number of peremptory challenges. As each juror is excused, another name is called, and that juror replaces the excused juror in the jury box. As the client, you can provide input to your attorney during this process. If you have a feeling, either positive or negative, about a prospective juror, you should share that with your attorney. Your attorney should always make a motion to disqualify a juror for cause outside the presence of the jury. Many jurors are itching to find a way to get out of serving on the jury. The most common reason given is to say they could not be fair in their deliberations.

One of the things I take note of when questioning prospective jurors is their body language. If the juror is sitting with their arms tightly crossed while you are asking questions, but keep them unfolded while being questioned by the opposing side, this is a juror I would consider excusing. According to psychologists, crossing the arms could indicate resistance to your questioning, or a way of protecting oneself. On the other hand, an open position could mean that the juror is receptive to your questioning and/or your position.

Certain types of professionals tend to be biased or more difficult to convince of a position. For instance, accountants are typically skeptical and have a "show me" attitude, so they might not be the best jurors for a plaintiff seeking lost profits or lost income. Social workers, in contrast, tend to be more liberal and want to make plaintiffs whole again by awarding them damages.

An example of a case in which the jury based their award, to a great extent on the jurors' feelings towards the parties, can be found in the following case involving my brother-in-law and a collection agency. It is also a good example of a case in which a punitive damages award was wholly appropriate.

He was a tile maker who leased a tile press for his business. The contract with the equipment leasing company stated that he could purchase the press for one dollar at the end of his lease period. He tried to buy the press when his lease was up for the one-dollar price specified in the contract. The company refused to sell him the press and claimed he owed the company $3,500. The company owner turned the matter over to a collection agency, which sent him a nasty collection letter threatening to foreclose on his house and put his children out on the street. When he objected to paying the $3,500 demanded by the equipment leasing company, the company sued him for the money. In representing him, I filed a cross-complaint against the leasing company for breach of contract and for unlawful debt collection practices. I also brought a cross-complaint against the collection agency for breach of the Fair Debt Collection Practices Act. In the cross-complaint, I emphasized how both cross-defendants had ruined his credit. He had built up exemplary credit over many years, and now, suddenly, because of what they had put him through, he was not able to purchase more equipment for his business. It was a direct result of the conduct of the collection agency and leasing company that his credit suffered. I even offered into evidence a giant blow-up of the nasty collection letter. I asked for $935,000 in damages, both general and punitive, because the conduct of the company and collection agency was willful, malicious and oppressive. Although the financial damages were marginal, most of what I was seeking were punitive damages. In court, I pointed out that he was living with his wife and four children in a one-bedroom apartment. In response, the collection agency lawyer dismissed his predicament as "no big deal," and made the callous comment, "Living together like that was good for them. It made them a closer family." I could feel the room grow icy cold when he said this. The jury ultimately awarded us $935,000 of which about $600,000 was punitive.

After the trial, the foreperson confided in me that the jurors emphasized with his plight, and despised the defense and the collection agency for their callousness and, thus, chose to punish them by awarding exactly what we had requested.

This case illustrates how punitive damages are sometimes justified, it also demonstrates how critical the jury is in a case, and how important it can be to appeal to the jurors' sense of humanity. You just never know who is going to show up in a jury box.

While the previous case was successful because of a very sympathetic jury, I have had my share of cases in which the jury has been ill-disposed toward my client, and demonstrated those feelings through their verdict. According to universal spiritual principles, the right jury will always show up. You, as a client, will get the jury you deserve. So, in a sense, it does not matter how much time your attorney devotes to trying to ensure that you will have the perfect composition of jurors to hear your case. No matter how careful your attorney is in selecting the jurors who will consider your fate, you cannot know for sure what decision they will reach.

In a case I later describe in great detail, we filed a motion for a new trial after learning that the bailiff had told the jury that a less than a 2-hour deliberation would be "plenty." The jury, wanting to be released before the upcoming three-day holiday weekend, followed the bailiff's advice and reached a quick decision. Given the jurors we had chosen, that was a wholly unexpected result, but something had happened during the trial that changed the jury composition. A juror, whom we very much wanted, had a family emergency, and had to be excused during the trial. There were two possible alternates to replace him. We liked one, but not the other.

Unfortunately, the one we did not want was chosen to replace the juror we liked. The result was a 6-2 verdict against giving my client the damages award he sought. Six jurors were needed to reach a verdict. If the other alternate had been selected, the result could have been different. Also, one of the jurors we chose to keep was covered in tattoos and was working at a minimum wage job. We kept her, thinking that she would have no sympathy for the big corporate defendant in our case. I later learned that she had said to the other jurors, "Let's get out of here. Who cares about this case?" It just goes to show that jurors are unpredictable, and no matter what we as attorneys do, the right jury will show up. We lost our case in terms of the amount of the verdict, so I ask myself why. It was a strong case, and because time separates the cause from effect, I will never really know why we got the jury we did. Was the client having to pay back an old debt? Was I?

Regardless of who takes their seats in that jury box, your attorney's performance before a jury can make all the difference in your case. Your attorney should know not only how to select a jury panel, but also how to address a jury, and how to avoid various procedural pitfalls that jury trials are subject to. In essence, to successfully navigate before a jury, the lawyer must tell your story in a captivating and convincing way, while effectively employing all the legal means at their disposal. It is like a stage production with everyone playing their respective roles.

Anyone who tells you they know how to pick the right jurors is mistaken. It is by no means an absolute science. Sure, there are certain telltale signs that would cause you to excuse a juror but, even then, there is no guarantee that that particular juror would not have found in your favor. On many occasions, I have questioned why I kept a juror who ultimately decided against my client. Like the tattooed lady in the aforementioned case, and just as many times, I have kept a juror who did not fit the profile of the type of juror I was looking for, but turned out to have been a good decision. Even if I believe that I have done the best job I could in selecting a jury, sometimes the jurors simply do not do the right thing, and they come out with a completely unexpected conclusion. You can never be certain what you will get with a jury. As Forrest Gump's mother said to her son, "Life is like a box of chocolates, you never know what you are going to get."

In the case referred to above in which the jury reached a swift conclusion after the bailiff's mention that less than two hours of deliberation would be sufficient, what happened during *voir dire* explains the outcome. During *voir dire*, a prospective juror had informed the court he had a vacation planned for three weeks from the start of the trial. Another juror was a biology teacher and said she could not miss another week of teaching if the case lasted longer than three weeks. The case ended up being submitted to the jury on a Friday afternoon. In order to avoid returning to court the following week, these jurors found for neither party, thus disregarding their obligations to the court. This was a clear example of a miscarriage of justice. The jurors' behavior in this case exemplifies conduct driven solely by ego with no thought of giving of themselves in terms of time and civic duty. Somewhere down the road, these jurors will have to pay the price for their selfish, ego-driven behavior (i.e., experience the effect of). If you are called upon to serve as a juror, it would be wise to fulfill your civic duty by taking the responsibility seriously. Jurors should (as should everyone on the planet) always follow the golden rule, do unto others as you would have them do unto you. Thus, when one sits on a jury, they should remind themselves that down the road if they are involved in a lawsuit themselves, their own fate might just be in the hands of a jury. Therefore, as a juror, they should make every effort to give the case their full attention and ensure that the parties involved receive a fair trial.

With jury trials, it is important that the case be tried in the right jurisdiction. In certain instances, such as for particularly lengthy cases (called "long cause" cases), will be sent to other courts in the county. This happens where I practice in Los Angeles County. In Los Angeles, there is a court in another district known as the "plaintiff's bank," because the jurors there tend to be very liberal in their awards. Sometimes, plaintiffs' attorneys will try to get their cases transferred to that court. It is all about knowing the judicial environment. As a client, you should be able to trust your attorney to be savvy regarding these jurisdictional matters. Ask your attorney about it.

How can you, as a party to the suit, help the jury reach a verdict in your favor? You must play your role as your attorney instructs you. The most important thing you can do is to try to be likeable. When you are on the witness stand, do not cry, do not be arrogant, and do not play the victim. Generally, jurors will sympathize with you if they like you, not because they feel sorry for you.

I had a case once in which I instructed my client not to wear a lot of jewelry, as he was prone to do, and not to brag about having dinner with President Bill Clinton. He ignored my advice and boasted about hobnobbing with the President. The jury, who seemingly had no love for this guy because of how he presented himself, and because of the evidence, ultimately found against him.

Once all the lawyers' challenges of the jurors have been exercised, and the parties agree to accept the jury "as presently constituted," the jury is ready to hear your case.

B.   What's The Quickest Way To Get Through This Jury Trial?

You and your lawyer decide you want to move your case through the trial stage in as short of time as possible. You are in luck! If certain conditions are met, you can get what is called an expedited jury trial. At any time leading up to the trial, such as during a trial-setting conference, or a status conference, the parties can request an expedited jury trial. All the parties have to agree to participate, however, and if they are represented by lawyers, their lawyers have to sign a proposed consent order granting an expedited jury trial. There are a few exceptions but, for the most part, the results of this speeded-up trial are binding upon the parties. The court must approve the use of an expedited jury trial for litigants who represent themselves, for minors and for an incompetent person. So, what does an expedited jury trial entail? Here is what you gain from one:

1. All the parties waive the right to an appeal or to make most post-trial motions;

2. Each side gets up to five hours to complete *voir dire* and to present its case;

3. The jury is composed of eight or fewer jurors with no alternatives;

4. Each side is limited to three peremptory challenges, but the parties may request one additional peremptory challenge, which it is up the court to decide whether to grant;

5. The jury can still deliberate as long as needed;

6. The rules of evidence still apply unless the parties stipulate otherwise;

7. The verdict is binding;

8. A vote of six of the eight jurors is required for a verdict; and,

9. The statutes and rules covering costs and attorney's fees still apply unless the parties agree otherwise in the consent order.

C.   Here Comes The Judge

Where do judges come from? Do they inherit the job from their parents like a family business? Of course not! The answer depends on which type of court the judge sits in. Federal court judges gain their position differently than state court judges. Depending upon which category of federal court, they are either nominated by the President, and confirmed by the Senate, or appointed by the Senate. Appointments by the President are for life.

The selection of state court judges varies by state. They are chosen either by appointment by the governor or legislature, by a legislative committee based on their merit, or through partisan elections in which they run as part of a political party's slate of candidates. Some judicial candidates run for a position in states with non-partisan elections and, thus, they do not list their party affiliation on the ballot.

In California, there are two different systems for selecting state court judges. The state's appellate judges are appointed by the Governor, or are elected by popular non-partisan vote. Since I serve as a *judge pro tem* (one appointed on a temporary basis during which time he or she exercises all the functions of a regular judge), my appointment took a different route, which I discuss below in the section "My Journey To The Bench."

Are all judges knowledgeable and bright individuals? People like to think that judges are not only fair-minded, but also brilliant professionals, but this is just not true. Some are not very bright. Some judges are completely inexperienced in civil matters, as they arose directly from the district attorney's or public defender's office. Other judges, although highly intelligent, are simply not nice people. For example, I was sitting in the courtroom during a "law and motion" session (this is the time when a judge will hear pre-trial motions for many cases) at which there were about forty lawyers in the room. The judge called a case, and a very young lawyer appeared before him. Just as the young lawyer began to speak, the judge interrupted him and asked, "Do you have your Bar card?"

The young man was taken aback and asked, "Why, your honor?"

The judge's response was, "You are incompetent. I can't believe the Bar would give you a license."

Can you imagine how that young lawyer, at the beginning of his career, must have felt? Why was it necessary for the judge to humiliate the young man in front of a roomful of lawyers? It is judges like this one who give the profession a bad name. Think about it – you could end up with this judge, or another judge with a similarly unpleasant disposition.

Does my desire for one side to prevail make a difference in how I rule when I am presiding over a case? I cannot speak for all judges, but in my case, the answer is no. Here is an example – I adjudicated a case in which a lender was charging 99% interest on a loan. The defendant borrower claimed it was usurious (charging illegal or exorbitant interest rates). This lender was operating under a particular statute in California allowing a lender, who is licensed under the state financial code, to charge whatever amount of interest they want without being limited by the usury laws. The defendant argued that the statute was unconstitutional. Wanting to find the statute unconstitutional, because I thought the interest the lender was charging was unconscionable, I asked my research attorney to find support for the claim that the statute was unconstitutional. Unfortunately, he was only able to find a case where the statute had been found constitutional. So, despite how I would have liked to rule, I had to follow the law, and thus found the statute to be constitutional.

Can judges make a difference in a case? We certainly have an impact on the outcome of the cases we hear. We decide how to rule on the various pre-trial motions made by attorneys, whether to dismiss a case altogether, what to admit into evidence, whether to sustain or overrule objections, what instructions are to be given to the jury, and overall how to conduct the trial. We are even able to exercise power after the trial has concluded by setting aside a judgment. Although we have many opportunities to exercise our discretion, at the end of the day, as judges, we must follow the law.

As impartial as we try to be, obviously judges are human beings who bring to the bench our own backgrounds and inevitable biases. In some of the cases I have argued, it is clear that the judge's ruling reflects their dislike of one side or the other, or even a dislike for one of the lawyers. There are judges who have been known to render their decisions for convenience sake or some other unsupportable reason. This happened with an insurance case I worked on as an attorney. The client owned a warehouse in which he stored electronic parts. the warehouse suffered flood damage after a landscaper neglected to cap off an outside water source. The client claimed he could not sell the damaged parts because they were exposed to moisture, but his insurance company told him to sell them anyway. Accordingly, his company tried to sell them, but a customer came to inspect the parts, and upon discovering that they had been exposed to moisture, refused to buy them. The insurance company claimed the parts were in good condition and would not test them, so my client hired an independent expert to test the parts for damage. The defendants made a motion for summary judgment claiming nothing was in dispute which, of course, was untrue. The judge threw out the case simply because (according to her) this expert witness's report was not legible. That was nonsense because the documents had been filed electronically, and the other side had no problem reading them. Apparently, this judge would regularly grant summary judgment motions simply to keep her caseload down. Her rulings were frequently overturned on appeal. Her decision in the above case was reversed, but it took two years. Fortunately, this case eventually settled with the insurance company finally paying out $2.5 million in damages.

Also, I can cite examples of cases in which the judges have been fickle in their decisions, far too readily changing their minds. I had a traffic accident case in which my client's car was rammed by another car, causing him to hit and kill a teenage girl, who had been a pedestrian. My client and his wife, a passenger, sued the other driver for causing the accident and injuring them. I tried to get the evidence about the girl's fatality excluded. My client was suing the driver who caused the accident for damage to my client's car and for significant injuries that he and his wife suffered. The driver who caused the accident, had been on her cell phone, was distracted and made a left turn across multiple traffic lanes, hitting my client's car and causing it to spin out of control. Initially, the judge disallowed evidence of the girl's death, but later changed his mind and permitted the defense to bring it up. Once the judge changed his mind, the dynamics changed. The jury found in favor of the defendant, and against my client. The finding came about even though in a prior criminal case for manslaughter, my client had been found not guilty.

In another case, I was faced with a power-obsessed judge, who rendered a completely irrational decision. It was a fire insurance matter that included an allegation of arson. The policyholder was accused of setting his own home on fire to collect the insurance money. The judge simply did not like the way I conducted my cross-examination of a witness, and he told me so. The judge seemed to be drunk on power and thought he could do whatever he pleased in his judicial capacity. When my client won the case, the judge took the verdict away from him. You might think that once a jury decides a matter, the decision stands unless it is overturned on appeal. In reality, a judge has the discretion to set aside a jury verdict that he or she does not agree with. In this case, the judge said, "Your client is a liar and a thief, and he's not going to get any money." This is the same judge who had berated the young lawyer asking to see his Bar card. The judge signed a court order setting aside the judgment, citing as his reason that the evidence did not support the verdict. He only awarded my client enough money to pay off the home mortgage to the bank. I appealed the case on behalf of my client, and it eventually settled.

What happens if your case is assigned to a judge whose reputation precedes him or her (like the judge who tries to arbitrarily clear her calendar), and whom you would prefer not to hear your case? There are procedures to enable a party to "challenge" a judge, and have the case assigned to another judge. The challenge must be made within a short, specific period of time after the case is assigned. Each side has the right to only one challenge of the judge without having to state a reason. If they want to challenge the next judge, it has to be for "cause," which must be established. There is no challenge to a federal judge. You should be cautious in challenging your assigned judge because the next judge assigned to your case could be worse. Attorneys who regularly litigate in a particular jurisdiction are familiar with the proclivities of the judges, whether they tend to be pro-plaintiff or more defense oriented. The attorneys should be astute at knowing when to challenge a judge and when to stick with the one you get.

What if you end up with a judge who is presiding while drunk? I had a case against an insurance company (suing insurance companies was a very large part of my practice for many years) in which the presiding judge assigned our case to a substitute judge, instead of to one of the regular judges sitting on that court. The presiding judge had been an insurance defense lawyer before becoming a judge. I guess I should not have been surprised when he assigned our case to a retired judge, who had also previously been an insurance defense lawyer. During the trial, the judge kept dozing off. When we had to approach the bench for a conference, I observed that the judge reeked of alcohol. After I rested our case, the defense made a motion for a non-suit (meaning that the plaintiff has not proven enough of their case to require the defense to put on their case). The judge dismissed the case. In speaking with the jurors afterwards, I learned that they would have liked to have awarded my client $2 million, based on what they knew of our case from the opening statement alone, and the evidence we introduced.

Claiming that the judge had been inebriated, I moved for a new trial. I even obtained declarations from the clerk and the court reporter, confirming my contention. Unfortunately, the new trial motion was required to be heard before the very same judge. Arguing to another judge, I stated that the only way we could get a fair hearing was to have it presented before a different judge. My request was granted and given the overwhelming evidence concerning the trial judge's impaired condition, this later judge granted us a new trial. It seemed justice had been served, but my excitement was short-lived because the defense appealed, and the 4th District Court of Appeal reversed the judge who had granted us a new trial. That court was affronted by our impugning the reputation of the trial judge (by pointing out his affinity for the bottle) with whom several justices had a personal relationship. The moral of this story is that, as a litigant, you have very little control over who will be deciding your case and what the outcome will be. It is a crapshoot, which leads to my oft-repeated advice that you find a way to settle your case.

You cannot determine who will decide your case, but you can have an effect on your trial. The bottom line is that for either a jury trial or a bench trial, as a client, you want to come off as likeable as possible. The same goes for your attorney. As I have pointed out previously, if you can leave your ego behind and approach your case with the mindset of someone who wants to give, rather than take, to compromise rather than to avenge what you perceive as a wrong, you will endear yourself to the judge and the jury. The case will result in the outcome that was meant to be.

1.   **My Journey To The Bench**

It all happened quite fortuitously. The law business had been good to me financially. For a long time, I had been searching for a way to use my many years of experience as a trial lawyer to do something to give back to the community.

When I was in Van Nuys, part of the San Fernando Valley in Los Angeles, I would get together for lunch with my good friend, Superior Court Judge James Kaddo. Over our deli sandwiches one day, Jimmy was bemoaning the shortage of Civil Court judges in Van Nuys, and because of budgetary restraints, despite the shortage, they could not bring in additional judges. The court calendars were overcrowded, causing the judges to be overworked and unable to devote enough time to their cases. Plus, the litigants were suffering from long delays before getting their day in court.

I asked Jimmy if I could help in some way. He lit up and began to tell me about a program in which volunteers could become temporary judges. Applicants for the position had to meet certain State Bar standards, take courses and test for certification, and then pass a rigid vetting process. He told me that these temporary judges would receive assignments in a variety of courts, depending upon the subjects in which they had received certification. He also said that these judges would have choices in the types of cases they would hear, which appealed to me. I was not interested in Traffic Court, Family Court, or juvenile cases, which left civil litigation, small claims and civil harassment (i.e., restraining orders). I had time, and being a volunteer judge would not conflict with my practice. It was a good deal for the county since I would not be paid. The only perk was free parking. After attending the classes, taking the tests and passing the vetting process, I was appointed a Superior Court *Judge Pro Tem* in 2008, a position which I still occupy today. Jimmy has been my mentor since then. At our weekly lunches together, I often pepper him with questions regarding my work as a judge. I have learned more from him than I could have ever learned from any book or seminar, and for this I owe him much gratitude.

I am often asked if serving as a temporary judge is any different from the job of the judges who are appointed by the governor, or elected. There are very few differences. Once the litigants stipulate (i.e., agree) to my hearing their case, I have the same authority as any other judge. As volunteer judges, however, we cannot preside over adoption proceedings, or issue search warrants. Our role is to cover for judges who were ill, on vacation, out on disability, attending continuing education classes, or unavailable to sit for some other reason. One time, I filled a judge's seat while the judge was out-of-town to attend basketball playoffs. In terms of courtrooms, I simply sit in the court of the judge I am replacing. We also have use of that judge's clerk and bailiff.

The most gratifying part for me is when I have been able to use the discretion afforded us, as judges, to do acts of kindness. One example is the case I describe in the Unlawful Detainers section, in which I did what I could to help a single mother, who was being evicted, by giving her an extra two weeks to stay in her home. Discretionary rulings of this sort rarely result in a reversal on appeal.

Another type of case in which I have been able to exercise my discretion as a judge to help a defendant who is in dire financial straits, involves garnishment of wages. I will look at the financial condition of the defendant and find a way to structure a deal in which the defendant can pay off the judgment over time, but still be able to take home enough pay to live off. The creditor will get paid interest on the outstanding judgment, but will simply get paid back at a slower rate. This type of restructuring of awards often takes place in Small Claims Court.

I've asked myself why I wanted to be assigned to adjudicate restraining order cases specifically. In these cases, we restrain people from acting in ways that negatively affect the lives of others. These cases give me a chance to intervene, and try to facilitate a peaceful solution to the conflict. Admittedly, there was an element of ego that initially drove me to serve on the bench. The title of judge confers a certain respectability on the bearer. The first few times people addressed me as "Your Honor," I felt important. I no longer even hear it.

One of the reasons I decided to write this book was because having been on both sides of the bench, I thought I could help the public understand not only how the legal system works for litigants, but also give an insider view of what happens from the bench side of the courtroom.

When I was initially appointed, I assumed I would be biased against insurance companies. For more than 25 years, I made a very nice living suing insurance companies, primarily over property damage insurance coverage issues in which the insurers stalled in paying their claims, undervalued the claims, or downright denied them. Sometimes, to avoid paying a legitimate claim, the insurance companies leveled accusations against the insured of arson or fraud. Somehow, these insurance companies always found a reason to stall or avoid paying the claims until they reached the courthouse steps, but once I took the bench, I knew I had to be fair and impartial. So, I listened to these cases with an open mind, sublimating my prior experiences. From the bench, I discovered, much to my surprise, that in many instances, the insurance companies were right, and I found myself ruling more often in their favor than against them.

Particularly in many of the personal injury cases I have heard, I have ruled in favor of the insurance company, because I found that the plaintiff's claim was weak or without merit. The following is one example: The case involved a husband and wife suing an individual, whom they claimed had backed into their car, damaging the vehicle and causing them injuries. I looked at the photographs of the two cars that were taken by the defendant, who had anticipated a possible conflict down the road. The defendant's act of taking the pictures was wise and contains a lesson for all of us. That lesson is – Follow the Boy Scout's motto – "Be Prepared."

I listened intently to both the defendant's and plaintiff's stories, and read the separate medical reports submitted by both the husband and wife. Many personal injury cases involve the claimant going to see a chiropractor referred by their lawyer. These lawyers are often the ones who claimants consult with after seeing their names advertised on the back of a bus or bench. My description of this case is not meant to be an indictment of chiropractic as a whole, especially because I have been going to a chiropractor for more than 40 years. I merely want to point out that a cottage industry has evolved around chiropractic diagnosis in personal injury cases. I have read probably in excess of a thousand chiropractic reports submitted in support of injuries. In the car accident case I am referring to above, the chiropractor had entered an identical diagnosis for both the husband and the wife. Both reports referred to "him" and "his" injuries, despite the fact that one of them was for the wife. The completely generic nature of the reports was a "red flag" to me in considering the validity of the claim. The impact of the one car backing into the other was so minimal that it did not appear to me that the husband and wife could possibly have suffered the injuries they claimed, and which were supported by the doctor. This doctor was well-known and referred to by the insurance company as "the notorious Dr. X." Not surprisingly, the plaintiffs had found the doctor through their attorney. He was one of those chiropractors who exploited opportunities to make money by servicing the personal injury business. The lawyer, of course, was responsible for steering business his way.

Since this case was in Small Claims Court, the couple's lawyer could not appear with them. The record in the file showed that the lawyer had initially written to the insurance company, trying to settle the case by making a demand. Apparently, when the lawyer received a response that the insurance company adjuster was not willing to accede to his demands, and that the case had very little financial value, the lawyer bailed on the couple. Unfortunately, I have seen far too many bogus cases like this one, which explains why I have become more sympathetic to the insurance company defendants that I ever thought would be the case when I first took the bench.

Serving as a judge has been a very fulfilling endeavor. It allows me to do something good and meaningful for the community without any financial agenda. It is also a way for me to set aside my ego and do something altruistic, something solely for the benefit of others.

2.   **A Team Effort**

There is a common misperception that judges handle everything related to a case before them. In actuality, there are two other individuals who perform most of the administrative and operational tasks of the court, the court clerk and the bailiff. The court clerk, or judicial assistant, as they are currently called, really runs the court, including the overseeing of all communications with the judge. For litigants and their attorneys, making friends with the judicial assistant is very important because they are the only ones who can grant or deny access to the judge. When the complaints are first filed, they find their way to the judicial assistant, and the record begins. Every date on which action is taken is recorded, so that there is a chronological record of the history of the case. The judicial assistant makes sure filing fees are paid before papers are submitted to the court. The judicial assistant keeps the calendar, scheduling all the hearings. To be perfectly candid, I learned more about small claim procedures from my clerk than from the training manual. Occasionally, when I was on the bench, the clerk would lean over to me and say things like, "You can't do that." When I preside over restraining order cases, my clerk advises me on all sorts of technical issues.

In cases other than those in small claims, or restraining

order court, as judges, we are provided with a research attorney. These attorneys read all the court documents, and then make a recommendation to the judge as to what should be done. Especially on technical matters, such as time limits and statutory applications, we generally follow our research attorney's recommendation. On occasion, however, when there is a question as to the applicability of certain laws to certain cases, or conflicting theories about the case, we do our own follow-up research. I have presided over cases in which I did not agree with the recommendation of the research attorney, and have been known to look up the prior case law, do my own analysis, and come up with a different conclusion. Probably, but more often than not, because of the heavy load of cases that judges are burdened with, we simply do not have the time to delve more thoroughly into the matters before us and, therefore, we abide by the advice of our research attorneys. On average, I preside over anything from 15 to 55 cases each day that I sit on the bench. The well-trained bailiff will respond instantly, preventing the litigant from getting any closer to the judge. When I sit in night court, the bailiff, who does carry a gun, in case you are wondering, walks me to my car and waits until I leave the parking lot.

Here's a little story to illustrate how protective the bailiffs are of their judges. One time I thought I had pressed the button under my desk in chambers to alert the clerk that I was about to enter the courtroom. As I was putting on my judge's robe, my chamber doors flew open, and I came face-to-face with several deputy sheriffs with their hands on their holsters. I later found out that they thought I was in danger because I had mistakenly pressed the panic button under the desk, instead of the button I thought I had pressed.

LANDLORDS AND TENANTS AND BREACHES

6

Since the bulk of the cases I preside over are small claims cases and those that involve either landlord/tenant disputes or restraining order matters, I have devoted a separate chapter.

A.   The Lowdown on Unlawful Detainer Cases

A variety of disagreements can arise between landlord and tenants, but in this section, I primarily address the issue of who had the right to live or conduct business at the property. These matters fall under the Unlawful Detainer statutes. Unlawful Detainer is a statutory cause of action that allows a person or entity wrongfully deprived of the possession of his, her, or its real property by a tenant or former owner to regain possession of it, along with unpaid rent or money owed to the owner, if appropriate. This separate section of the book is devoted to UD cases because they are so prevalent in the courts. The statutes were designed to protect the interests of the landlords and lenders (such as banks) by providing an expeditious procedure for them to evict someone from the place where they live, or where business is being conducted. Although there are cases where there has been a foreclosure, and the buyer wants to evict the previous owner, I am only going to discuss the landlord/tenant matters here. Landlords usually file actions when a tenant stays beyond the term of the lease, the tenant has not paid rent, has broken a provision of the lease, or engaged in illegal conduct. The landlord must first serve advanced notice to the tenant before filing an action in the Superior Court. In the action, the landlord is the plaintiff and the tenant is the defendant. UD cases can also be brought against occupants who refuse to vacate a property that has been sold in foreclosure. These cases might involve a previous owner of a property who refuses to leave after the sale of the property in foreclosure. Employers who provide a residence rent-free as part of the terms of employment, may also take advantage of the provisions to evict an employee from the residence upon termination of the employment. The landlord has only to give a three-day notice to terminate the tenancy.

As judges, we have discretion to delay an eviction. Here is the case I previously mentioned that illustrates what we can do. On the day before Christmas, a single mother of two came into my courtroom asking for a couple of more weeks to stay in her apartment. She had no defense to the action. The landlord had provided her with proper notice and the writ of possession had already been issued. The writ of possession is served on the tenant by the sheriff, and it states that the tenant must leave the property by a certain time period, or the sheriff will forcibly remove the tenant. The woman in this case had recently lost her job, and had nowhere to move to. I thought about what I should do. Who would be harmed by my giving her the two extra weeks she requested? The landlord would not be selling the property or leasing it to anyone else during that time. When I realized that I could help this woman without harming the other party, and still act within the confines of the law, I allowed her to stay in the apartment for two additional weeks. However, I did remind her that if she did not move out after those two weeks, the sheriff would be forced to evict her. After I gave the woman my decision, my clerk said to me, "You're a softy. Our regular judge wouldn't have given her an extension."

I marvel regularly at the good fortune I have as a judge to be able to use my accumulated experience and discretion to change someone's life. There's no reason why we cannot do the right thing as judges, and approach our rulings with a conscience, so long as we adhere to the dictates of the law.

When I was first assigned to the UD calendar, I assumed I would have a bias in favor of the tenants in these cases, naturally being reluctant to toss someone out of their home or business. However, I quickly discovered that many tenants had figured out the system, and had learned to employ all sorts of delaying tactics in order to stay in their homes or businesses rent-free, causing great financial loss to the landlords. On the other hand, I also encountered landlords who abused the system, including those who rented out places that were completely uninhabitable. So, it turns out that I am truly impartial when hearing UD cases.

The chief benefit of these UD cases to the plaintiffs is that they are afforded priority on the calendar. We must hear disputes involving possession of property first before all other cases. The time frames for filing claims and responses in these cases are much shorter in length than in other litigation matters. In California, it is required that cases come to trial within 45-days. The same lawyers appear before us in these cases repeatedly, and they are primarily representing the plaintiffs. The landlords and lender banks almost always are represented by lawyers, whereas the tenant defendants, or homeowner defendants, most often are not. The underlying goal in most of these cases brought by landlords is to get their property back, and many recognize that they will not ever collect the past rent due. These cases are complicated, and the best advice I can give tenants is to engage a lawyer to make sure your rights are protected.

A typical case involves a tenant who is either not paying rent or creating problems in their use of the property. An example of the latter can be found in a case I had in which the landlord was claiming that the tenant was selling drugs on the premises. The landlord sent the tenant a three-day notice to quit. Once the three days had passed, he served the tenant with a complaint asking to terminate the tenancy. The tenant defendant answered the complaint, denying the allegations, thus necessitating a trial. The evidence presented at trial was flimsy – a bunch of statements from people who claimed they had seen certain things, but there were no photographs, tape recordings, or text messages supporting the allegations. The defendant argued that the landlord was simply making these unfounded allegations because he wanted to get the defendant out so he could rent to someone who would pay higher rent. Because the landlord had not met his burden of proof showing by a preponderance of the evidence that the defendant was, indeed, selling drugs on the property, I found for the defendant and awarded costs and attorney's fees to the defendant.

About 90% of these landlord/tenant cases are settled on the courthouse steps by stipulation (an agreement between attorneys or parties that concerns business before a court, and is designed to simplify or shorten litigation and save costs). Generally, all the landlord or the buyer of the property wants is for the tenant or former owner to simply vacate the property as soon as possible. The landlord usually offers to allow the tenant to stay on the property until a certain date, either on condition that the tenant pay something, or that the tenant agrees to not oppose the action and to move out. This saves the landlord the fees, costs and additional time of a legal battle. Often, the tenant can get the landlord or purchaser to agree to a "sealing order" so that only the parties in the dispute and the court can view the file. This is a way to protect the record, and keep it from showing up on the defendant's credit report. Earlier, in my discussion of the importance of being represented by a lawyer, so that your rights can be protected, I mentioned that a lawyer could see to it that as part of a settlement the record of your case is sealed. If the defendant does not move out by the specified date, however, the record gets unsealed. I tell the defendants in my courtroom that this is a good incentive to abide by the move out date, and honor any other obligations they agreed to.

Another stipulated agreement is known as a "pay and stay." In this situation, there is a schedule set by stipulation that as long as the tenant or other occupier makes timely payments, they are allowed to stay on the property. As the tenant, you would want this stipulation to be "lodged," which means that it is not a judgment. In other words, so long as the payments are made according to the agreement, the case will be over. On the other hand, if you, as the tenant, default on the payments, the landlord or purchaser can appear in court *ex parte* (generally a legal proceeding brought by one person in the absence of and without representation or notification of other parties), and the stipulation then becomes the judgment and is enforceable by a writ of possession.

The court must approve these stipulations, which it routinely does, so long as both parties understand the stipulated terms. I had an interesting case in which I asked the tenant if he understood the stipulated terms, and he responded that he suffered from dementia, and was not sure. Cases like these must go to a special court to rule on the party's competency before the settlement can be approved.

Sometimes the tenant is in court requesting additional time to pay the rent. They have lost a job, someone they support is sick, or they have become disabled and just cannot afford to pay the rent. These cases begin with the owner of the property, or in cases of foreclosure, the purchaser at the foreclosure sale, serving notice on the tenant. Typically, the tenant is given a three-day notice to quit, or to pay rent. The notice is served by delivering it to the tenant, and if the tenant is not physically present, it can be left with a responsible person at the rented premises, or posted on the tenant's front door, and a copy of the notice must then also be mailed to the tenant. This gives the tenant an opportunity to cure any default before the plaintiff (the landlord or property owner) files a complaint for possession. Notices to quit extending over a longer time period may be required under federal or local laws for certain low-income housing.

B. **As A Landlord How Do I Evict Someone**?

Usually, you would begin an action when one of the following scenarios occurs:

- The tenant refuses to leave after the lease agreement expires.
- There is a month-to-month lease and the tenant does not move out after a 30-day, 60-day, or 90-day notice to quit is served on them.
- The tenant does not pay rent, nor do they move out after receiving a 3-day notice to pay rent or quit.

- The tenant does not move out after breaking a part of the lease agreement, and they do not comply with the 3-day notice that says to either fix the violation, or move out.
- The tenant receives a 3-day notice to move out for committing waste or a nuisance, or using the property to do something illegal, and does not move out.
- The landlord accepts the tenant's offer to vacate the premises, but the tenant refuses to leave.

UD actions cannot be used to resolve disputes over damages to the property, or over the withholding of security deposits. Consider filing these claims in a separate action in Small Claims Court. You also cannot use UD to regain possession of a storage unit. Rented storage units are commercial property, and a different action is required to get them back. The court in UD cases cannot award you damages for rent you lost after the judgment. In other words, once a judgment is entered against the defendant, it takes the sheriff a week to evict the defendant and, you, as a landlord, would need to file a separate action for the rent you lost during that week if you want to recover that loss. You could file an action for lost rent in Small Claims Court if it does not exceed the monetary limit for Small Claims Court. Otherwise, you could file in a court of higher jurisdiction.

After you have served a 3-day notice on the tenant (you can serve this notice yourself, although you cannot serve the Summons and Complaint yourself) to quit or to pay rent, the next step is the complaint. It is far better to have a registered and bonded process server serve both the notice and the complaint, as this is a person who had no stake in the outcome, and is presumed to be honest with regard to the time, date and method of service.

If the tenant has neither left the property, nor paid the rent by the end of the notice period (or any of the other scenarios listed above have occurred), you can begin an action. The first step is to file documents at the proper courthouse – (in the county where the property is located) – or to file them online. You can determine the proper courthouse in which to file by looking on the court website for the filing court locator. The document you need to prepare and serve on the tenants is called a Summons and Complaint. First, you will complete the summons, which gives the defendant the date by which they need to file a response. You will serve the summons with the complaint.

If you do not have an attorney to help you, you can often get assistance at a non-profit legal help center, or find the proper forms to file online at most public libraries and law libraries. In California, all sorts of court information, including general resources and information on special topics, can be obtained online from the Judicial Council of California. You should bear in mind that UD cases are very technical and rule-oriented. You want to make sure that your paperwork is completed properly and that all information you provide is accurate. You will have to pay a filing fee unless you qualify for a fee waiver.

Next, you will have to arrange for service of the summons and complaint on the defendant. You cannot serve your own claim on the defendant, but rather service must be performed by someone not involved in the case, who is at least 18 years old, or the local sheriff, or a licensed process server. You can find a process server by perusing the web, or checking the *Yellow Pages*.

Again, as the landlord, you can serve the 3-day notice on the tenant yourself, but you cannot serve the summon and complaint yourself. The three common ways to serve the summons and complaint on the tenant are:

1.   **Personal Service** - A process server hands a copy of the summons and complaint to each defendant in person. If the defendant refuses to take the summons and complaint, service is sufficient so long as the server states they are a process server, informs the defendant that they are being served, and then leaves the papers as close to the defendant as possible. The court looks most favorably on this type of service.

2.   **Substitute Service** - If personal service is unsuccessful after several attempts, the process server may serve the defendant by substitute service. This requires the server to give a copy of the summons and complaint to an adult, who is in charge where the defendant lives, and also to mail a copy of the documents to the defendant at the same location. The server must complete a declaration affirming the efforts made to perform personal service first.

3.   **Posting and Mailing** (Also called "Nail and Mail") - If the process server is unsuccessful in serving the summons and complaint after making diligent efforts to do so, you may ask the court for permission to perform service by posting and mailing. There are specific forms that

you must complete, and they need to be accompanie by a declaration affirming the server's attempts to serve th summons and complaint through personal service and subs itute service first. If the court grants you permission, the p ocess server posts a copy of the summons and complaint t the property in a way that the tenants are most likely to see it (which might necessitate nailing it on the door), and n the same day, sends a copy by certified mail to the last pla e the defendant lived.

A Proof of Service of Summons must be complet d for every defendant. The registered process server and/ r the sheriff will complete this form and mail it to you after s rvice has been performed.

It bears repeating that an attorney, or at least a non rofit legal help center can save your bacon in UD cases. The roper filing of the complaint is imperative. You can run the isk of losing your court case if the judge determines that yo r service on the defendants is defective, and keep in mind, tl it the cost of a lawyer might be cheaper than the cost to you i additional loss of rent and damages you will suffer if yot case is delayed or dismissed for a legal defect. Also, if you o not state a cause of action in the complaint, the complaint ill be found defective, and thus the court will not have jurisd ction over the defendant.

There are a number of delay tactics defendants use o buy more time to remain on the property. These defense t ictics are discussed in the next section, "As A Tenant How D I Defend Against An Unlawful Detainer Action?" Generally if the tenant has not been paying the rent, there is no defens . Not being able to afford to pay rent is not a legal excuse. A written response in which the tenant tries to explain his r her situation, or offer a defense, is due from the defendant ithin 5-days from the personal service of the complaint, inc ding Saturdays and Sundays.

After substitute service and/or service by postin ; and mailing, the response time for the tenant is longer t y five days. Next, a trial will be scheduled. As I said before, UD cases (which determine if a landlord can take a property back) are given priority over other types of cases. Normally, a judge will hear and decide the case within 20-days after the tenant or landlord files a request to set the case for trial. A defendant is not permitted to file a cross-complaint. If the defendant moves out before the trial, the UD case is dismissed. If the landlord seeks monetary damages in the form of past rent due, or "holdover damages," it becomes a regular civil case for damages, and is put on the regular calendar, which may take a year to go to trial. Practically speaking if the amount is not significant enough to justify the expenditure of fees and costs, especially if the tenant seems unable to pay it the landlords will most probably not pursue it.

If you are the tenant, you should be aware that it is important to convey the impression that you are unable to pay the damages. You should consider asking the landlord to dismiss the case once you have moved out, and they have regained possession. You should refrain from major purchases, such as new cars and expensive jewelry. If the landlord chooses to go to trial anyway, and they are successful in their claim for holdover damages, they can use the collection methods listed earlier, which could include going after your possessions to satisfy the judgment they were awarded.

At the hearing, both the landlord and tenant can testify, present evidence and be represented by attorneys. If the court rules in favor of the tenant, no eviction takes place, and the landlord may be ordered to pay the tenant's legal costs and expenses. If you, as the landlord, win the case, the court will issue you a writ of possession upon submission of an application and after you have paid the necessary fees. The writ of possession gives the tenant five days from the date that the writ is served to leave voluntarily. If the tenant refuses to leave by the end of the fifth day, the writ of possession authorizes the sheriff to physically remove and lock the tenant out, and seize the tenant's personal belongings that we e left in the property. The landlord is not entitled to posses: on of the property until after the sheriff has removed the ter nt or prior owner.

You cannot evict someone yourself. Only the sheriff c n enforce this judgment by physically ejecting the tenant frc n the property and locking him or her out. Thus, even if the t :nant is many months behind in rent, or has no right to remai after foreclosure, you cannot do any of the following:

- Evict the tenant.
- Dispose of the tenant's possessions.
- Lock the tenant out.
- Cut off the electricity, or water.
- Remove outside doors or windows.

Leave enforcement of the judgment to the sheriff. f you regain your property, then it was meant to be. You can c loose to view any financial loss you suffered along the way a your repayment of a debt owed for some past misconduct o your part and, hopefully, this whole experience, includin; your loss of rental income, has impelled you to change you : way of thinking, i.e., your consciousness. Maybe you will ac with greater generosity and kindness going forward.

C. __As A Tenant How Do I Defend Against A UD Case__

First of all, prior to filing an eviction action, the la: dlord must give you proper notice asking you to move out or x the problem, such as paying rent owed. They must serve nis 3-day notice through one of the methods listed in the pri r section. If you do not do what the notice asks before the otice time runs out, then the landlord may file a UD compla nt to evict you. The landlord who files the complaint is call d the plaintiff, and the tenants are the defendants.

The first thing you should do when you receive the otice is to try to make some sort of deal with your landlord (r purchaser of the property that you are occupying. Maybe you can avoid all the grief that comes with having to defend a court action against you. Landlords, for the most part, also want to avoid the aggravation and expense of filing an action against you. Most likely, all the landlord really wants is to get you out of the property as soon as possible.

If you cannot work something out with your landlord, or the purchaser, chances are that you will be served with a summons and complaint. In your defense, you must file an answer or motion in response to the lawsuit. The response must be in the proper legal form, which speaks in favor of engaging an attorney, whether private or from a public legal aid office, to assist you. It is not sufficient to call or send the landlord a letter, or send a letter to the court explaining your situation. You have five days to file your response if you were personally served. The five-day period begins with the day after you were served the complaint. If the fifth day falls on a court holiday or weekend, you have until the following day to file. For example, if you were served on a Monday, then the fifth day is considered the next Monday because the actual fifth day falls on a Saturday. If another person was served on your behalf, a copy of the summons and complaint must be mailed to you, as well. With this substitute service you have 15-days to respond to the postmarked date. The date of service does not count towards the 15 days. If there are multiple defendants in the case, each one who wants to present a defense, must respond. You can also try to settle the case out of court (see the discussion about stipulated agreements in the previous section).

If you believe you have an action against your landlord, you can file a separate complaint. If warranted, you can file a Notice of Related Case to advise the court that the UD case and the complaint you are filing are related. You can even attempt to get the cases "consolidated" so that your civil case will stop the UD case from proceedings, pending resolution of the issues in the civil case.

Under certain circumstances, as judges, we can stay the UD case until the civil case is concluded, as long as the tenant or former owner pays a reasonable amount of rent while the UD case is still pending. If the tenant defaults on the rent payments, the UD case goes right back on the court's priority calendar. Again, since these cases are typically complicated, especially with respect to lawsuits over the refusal of banks to grant loan modifications, I strongly urge you to seek help of an experienced UD lawyer.

Generally, defendants will respond to a UD summons and complaint by filing what is called an Answer. An answer is a formal written statement that admits or denies the allegations in the complaint, and sets forth all available affirmative defenses, but if you believe that the plaintiff's eviction notice, or the summons and complaint, or service of the complaint is defective, you may file a Motion to Quash. This motion asks the judge for an order setting aside or nullifying an action, such as a request that service of a summons be quashed when the wrong person was served.

A motion to quash service challenges whether the service has been proper. This motion must be filed no later than the last day on which the tenant must plead (i.e., file a response), or within any additional time the court may allow for good cause. If you win, the plaintiff must re-serve the summons and complaint, thus buying you more time on the property. Our decision on these motions, as judges, comes down to looking at who served the notice or complaint. If the process server is registered, there is a presumption of proper service. You can also file a motion to quash to dismiss the action on the grounds that it is in an inconvenient forum (the place where legal disputes are decided). The appropriate forum depends upon which court has jurisdiction over the parties and the subject of the case, a matter governed mainly by statutes and court rules. If the property is in another jurisdiction, the case is either transferred there or is dismissed, forcing the landlord or property purchaser to start over. Again, this buys time.

Another defense tactic you, as the tenant, can employ is a demurrer (defined earlier as a formal objection to the legal sufficiency of an opponent' pleading). You can file this motion if you believe that the plaintiff did not include enough information in the eviction notice or the complaint to justify an eviction. The demurrer must be filed within five days of service of the summons and complaint. The landlord will oppose it, and this takes time. Along with the demurrer, you must file and serve a notice of hearing. It must specify a hearing date, which is obtained from the court clerk. The date depends upon the court's calendar, but it must be set for a hearing not more than 35 days after it is filed, or on the first available date thereafter. In this way, you might be able to delay the eviction for a month or more.

As the tenant, will you benefit from declaring bankruptcy? Filing for bankruptcy will buy you additional time in the property, but is it worth it? The bankruptcy automatically stays all court actions, including the landlord's UD action against you. Time will pass while the landlord goes to the Bankruptcy Court to get relief from stay, and the Bankruptcy Court then dissolves the stay. It is a process, which will give you some more months perhaps in the property, but at what cost to you? Before you go that route, think about the fact that once you declare bankruptcy (with all the hassles that entails), all your non-exempt property will be subject to the control of the trustee.

You should consult with an attorney, or someone in a legal aid office to assist you in filing a response most suited to your situation. Most plaintiffs use standard complaint forms, and these forms are designed to withstand attacks on their adequacy. Thus, demurrers are usually overruled. Many landlords' attorneys will make *ex parte* applications to the court to advance the date of the hearing on the demurrer or other motions on the grounds that UD cases are entitled to a priority spot on the calendar. Keep in mind that the filing of these motions increases the amount of attorney's fees and costs the landlord will seek from you if the landlord prevails in opposing your motion(s) or demurrer. I always grant these *ex parte* applications. The reason for the demurrer, which seldom has merit, is to buy time since the hearing on the demurrer is often scheduled for many weeks later. The landlord's *ex parte* application puts the case back onto the quick track.

Once the demurrer is overruled, the tenant has five days to answer the complaint, the five days begin on the date the notice of the court's decision on the demurrer is served. If you fail to answer within the five days, a default judgment can be entered against you upon application by the landlord. The court clerk records the default, and the judge enters judgment for restitution of the property and a writ of execution on the judgment. The judgment can apply to tenants, sub-tenants and any other occupants of the premises.

When you, as the defendant, plan to answer the complaint, make sure you file the proper forms on a timely basis, and that you fill out the answer forms completely. Begin by reading the complaint carefully, and making sure that you clearly state in the answer anything you do not agree with, or find to be untrue in the complaint. Include everything you want to convey to the judge in your defense in as much detail as possible. For example, if you disagree with the amount of rent the plaintiff claims you owe, mention that in the answer and explain why you do not owe that amount. If the property is in bad condition (maybe even infested with rats or other pests), say so and state whether or not you asked the plaintiff to fix the problem, and what the plaintiff did, or did not do, in response to your request. If you believe the property needs many repairs, include that. If you believe the landlord is retaliating against you for something you did, such as complain about the unacceptable conditions of the property, also explain that too.

Typically, the best thing to do is to document in writing all defective conditions of the property. Documenting the defects with photos is optimal. If the landlord will not fix the problems, you may use what is called a "deduct and repair" provision to correct the defects yourself, and then deduct the amount you spent from the rent. Most laws require you to give the landlord notice within a certain number of days of your intent to deduct and repair before you start doing any repairs or taking any rent deductions. As a tenant, you should also call the local housing department to lodge complaints if the property is under rent control. Doing so, establishes a record in the event that violations are found. This record can be used in court as a defense to the UD case. Know that the rules, including timelines for notices, are going to be different in each jurisdiction. You, or your lawyer, will need to refer to them before acting.

After you fill out your form Answer, you are required to serve the plaintiff with a copy, and then file it with the court before the deadline. Here are the steps you need to take.

1.   Make two copies of the completed Answer form;

2.   Have someone at least 18 years old, who is not involved in the lawsuit in any way, mail one of the copies to the plaintiff, or to the plaintiff's lawyer.

3.   Have this person (the server) complete and sign a Proof of Service.

4.   Retain the original of the Answer and the completed Proof of Service to file with the court. You will have to pay a fee for filing an Answer, and if you cannot afford the filing fees, you can fill out a request to waive the fees. After you file your Answer, a trial will be scheduled within 20 days from the date the plaintiff requests a trial date.

If there is a judgment against you at the hearing, meaning you are going to be evicted, the judge will issue a writ of possession to the plaintiff/landlord, which orders the sheriff to carry out the eviction. You will have five days from the service of the writ to vacate the property.

When you have lost your case at the hearing, and your eviction is imminent, you can apply for a stay of the eviction (a temporary hold on the eviction process issued by a court). This motion must go back to the same judge who entered the judgment. California law provides that a stay must be granted if the trier of fact (judge or jury) finds that the moving party will suffer "extreme hardship" if no stay is granted, and a stay will not irreparably injure the non-moving party (i.e., the landlord in this type of case). While the stay is being considered we, as judges, need to set certain conditions, such as a requirement that the tenant pay some rent. Sometimes, we require the tenant to pay the reasonable value to the court on a monthly basis in advance.

D.   **What About Occupants Not Named In The Summons and Complaint?**

In a UD action, normally only the tenant needs to be served, however, in order to evict a subtenant, or other person claiming the right to possession, the subtenant or such person needs to be served and given an opportunity to present a defense. When the process server goes to the premises, they are obligated to ascertain if there are other adult occupants living there who are not named in the summons and complaint. The server needs to inquire of the person being personally served, or any person of suitable age, who appears to reside at the residence, whether there are other occupants. If the identity of other occupants is disclosed, and those occupants are present, the officer or process server must serve these occupants with the complaint.

What tends to happen more often than I would like to admit, is that any occupant not named in the court judgment may delay the eviction process simply by presenting a completed claim of right to possession to the officer seeking to enforce the judgment. Once the occupants are property served, if they choose to claim the right to possession, they must file their claim within ten days. I have seen many cases in which a lease between the tenant, or prior owner, and the unnamed occupants, are created after the fact to stall the proceedings, and cause the landlord, or new property owner, to negotiate a deal with the claimant (the unnamed occupant) rather than incurring the expense and hassle of trying to evict them. Often these occupants not named in the complaint, maintain they have a lease arrangement with the tenant (i.e., a sublease) or prior owner, oral or in writing, and they can provide evidence that they have been living on the property in question. There are people who take advantage of landlords by bringing in water bills and receipts in their name, in order to prove that they have the right of possession of a property, even when they know that they do not. They concoct an unfounded claim for possession because they know that it is cheaper for landlords to pay them to leave the property than to fight a court battle. They are right. Often, the landlord does pay them off. Lawyers who make regular appearances in the UD court have dubbed this scenario "cash for keys."

When unnamed occupants make a claim objecting to enforcement of the judgment, the court must hold a hearing. The court determines when to schedule the hearing and decides at the hearing whether or not the unnamed occupant(s) (the claimant) has a valid claim of possession. If the court determines that the claimant's contention is valid, the claimant can then be added to the landlord's UD complaint. A crowded court calendar helps the occupant because while the clock is running and they are waiting for the hearing, they are not paying rent. When an unnamed occupant is added as a party to a case, as the judge, I tend to require them to pay full, or partial rent, until the case is resolved.

As a landlord, you can file a motion to have possession of the premises immediately restored to you on the grounds that the defendant resides out of state, has left the state, can-

not be found within the state after due diligence, or he con-
cealed themselves to avoid service of the summons.

If the complaint is based on a curable breach (som thing
the tenant can fix, such as non-payment of rent), and t e defendant was not previously served with proper notice then
the notice may be served at or after the hearing. If t e defendant does not cure the breach within the requisite time,
the plaintiff/landlord may file and serve a supplementa complaint.

This type of situation arises when people move into place
as squatters, and once the sheriff shows up with a writ c f possession, the squatters claim they have a right to be the e. As
a judge, I have learned that it is common in these situ tions
for landlords to pay these people to leave because it is c eaper
than litigation, which has an uncertain outcome. The otice
and supplemental complaint may be served by mail. T e de-
fendant/claimant has ten days from the mailing to re pond
with an Answer.

As judges, we determine whether the defendant/cla mant
has a valid claim of possession by considering all the ev lence
produced at the hearing. If someone is planning this rt of
scheme, they should have a gas or phone bill, or some other
evidence to show they are actually living on the proper y.

E. **Retaliatory Eviction**

Tenants often accuse landlords of retaliatory evi tion,
meaning the landlords want the tenant out of the bu lding
for reasons unrelated to rent. A retaliatory eviction ccurs
when the landlord has improperly increased the rent b cause
of some legal behavior on the part of the tenant tha they
object to. Often it is because the tenant has complaine l to a
regulatory agency about the condition of the leased pre aises,
or the tenant has participated in a tenant's association or organization advocating tenants' rights. If they are not c rrent
on their rental payment, the tenant may not raise retal atory

eviction as a defense, even if the tenant has complained about the habitability of the property. Since these are usually factual disputes, and can often become emotional, the court makes a finding after holding a trial. A key consideration is whether the landlord acted in good faith in raising the rent, or in doing any of the things about which the tenant has complained. Motive is generally an issue of fact.

Many tenants suing for damages based on a retaliatory action by the landlord will choose to have a jury trial. It is common knowledge that jurors generally do not like landlords, and will probably sympathize with the tenant. Tenants often do better in jury trials when they defend themselves against a landlord represented by a lawyer, because it is also known that juries are not in love with lawyers. As the defendant/tenant, if you cannot afford the court fees, you can file for a fee and cost waiver. It is up to the judge's discretion whether to grant it. Most often, I grant the fee and cost waiver because I believe that cases should be tried on their merits, and that waiving the fees and costs hurts neither of the parties.

As judges, we make an initial determination as to whether the tenant is in default regarding the rent. Some tenants who are aware of this process, and are claiming breach of the warranty of habitability, will deposit their withheld rent into a special account. If they have done this, I would not find the tenant in default.

An understanding of who carries the burden of proof in these cases is essential. If the tenant raises retaliatory eviction as a defense, the tenant has the burden of proving by a preponderance of the evidence that the eviction was in retaliation for some legal act on the part of the tenant. Once again, the burden means that it is "more probable than not" (some interpret this as meaning that there is a 51% probability).

If the defense of retaliatory eviction is successfully established, judgment in the case is entered in favor of the defendant/tenant, and the tenant remains in possession of the property. In effect, the landlord loses, and the landlord may not recover possession of the property. When the tenant prevails in their retaliatory eviction defense, the landlor may be held liable for compensatory damages, as well as pu itive damages, with the amounts determined by statute and within the judge's discretion.

It is mandatory for judges to award reasonable atto ney's fees to the prevailing party if either party has request ed attorney's fee in their initial pleadings, and if it is in th lease agreement. If you believe there is a chance you will w n, include a request for attorney's fees. As a general rule, udges are not in favor of granting punitive damages, and the a ount of the damage awards sought are often reduced by the udge. In my view, a small damage award against a giant corpo ation is nothing more than a footnote on its financial state nent. However, if the corporation, or other landlord, is no in a state of good financial health, collecting damages might reak them altogether. The object is to make it hurt (for the landlords), but not to destroy them. Some jurisdictions r quire the attorneys to file a separate Memorandum of Costs and a Motion for Attorney's Fees in order to collect them.

F. **Constructive Evictions**

Often defendants in non-payment of rent cases, clai that the property is uninhabitable. Since this is an affirmat ve defense, the defendant has the burden of proof. On the A swer, the defendant/tenant fills out the items that render the property uninhabitable. They must be identified.

I presided over a case in San Pedro, California, in whi h the tenant brought in pictures of his maggot-infested apar ment that his landlord was trying to evict him from for not aying his rent. Clearly, the only reason the tenant continued o live in this disgusting place was because he did not have e ough money to rent somewhere else. He was willing to live wi h the maggots as long as he was not paying rent. You be the udge. Should I have evicted him or not? Was there another sol tion?

I found for the defendant, concluding that the apartment was, indeed, uninhabitable. I entered what is called a conditional judgment. In the judgment I rendered for the tenant, I specified that he was not obligated to pay rent until the situation was rectified. I told the landlord that once he cleaned up the place and brought me proof of such, he could request another hearing. If he corrected everything, then the judgment would be in his favor, and the tenant would have to pay the full rent or risk eviction. At that second hearing, the tenant argued that the landlord had not fixed the problem. The landlord brought a report from a pest abatement company indicating that the repairs had been made. This certification of repair aroused my suspicion and I questioned its authenticity. I ordered the landlord to bring me a report from the city confirming that the pest problem had been eradicated. He never complied with my request and, therefore, I did not change my previous ruling in favor of the tenant. It certainly did not hurt that the tenant had brought in current pictures of the disgusting condition of the premises, even after the landlord claimed he had made the repairs.

The only time a tenant can raise an inhabitability defense is when the landlord's complaint is based on non-payment of rent. Often a tenant will continue to pay rent while they are trying to get their landlord to make repairs and fix problems with the property. If the landlord files a UD action to regain possession of their property for reasons other than non-payment of rent, the tenant cannot use the inhabitability defense. There is a remedy for the tenant, however. The tenant can send a notice to the landlord requesting him or her to fix the problem. If the landlord is unresponsive, the tenant may have the right to make the repairs and deduct the costs from the rent, or to vacate the premises without being liable for further rent, so long as the tenant has given written or oral (written is preferable) notice to the landlord of the condition of the property which renders it uninhabitable, and the tenant has allowed the landlord a reasonable time to make the necessary repairs. As the tenant, you may not exercise repair and deduct rights exceeding the value of one month's rent, and may not exercise such rights more than two times in any 12-month period.

A landlord of residential properties must maintain those premises in a condition fit for human occupancy, and must repair all subsequent dilapidation of the property that renders it unfit for habitation. The landlord owes a duty to the tenant to provide habitable premises. It does not mean that the landlord must ensure that the premises are in a perfect, aesthetically pleasing condition. If the tenant raises this defense, as judges, we must determine whether a substantial breach of the landlord's duty has occurred, not simply a trivial violation. If we find a substantial breach, we reduce the rent, and give the tenant the right to continued possession conditioned on the tenant's payment of the reduced rent. We order the landlord to make the repairs and correct the conditions that constitute the breach, and to accept the reduced rent until the repairs are made. Also, we can award costs and attorney's fees to the tenant if the statute allows for it, or the parties' rental agreement provides for it.

A judgment for the tenant with a reduction in the monthly rent, especially in cases of rodent infestation, broken utilities, or other unsanitary conditions, usually motivates the landlords to rectify the problems so they can collect the full rent. Once they are able to certify that they made the corrections, the rent resumes at the contract rate. If the tenant fails to pay the reduced rent, and also the contracted rate after the situation has been rectified, the judgment is changed to one in favor of the landlord, and the tenant can be evicted.

Generally, the landlord is obligated to keep the conditions of a property in compliance with the applicable building and housing codes, which "materially affect health and safety." The defendant alleging the premises are uninhabitable, checks off the applicable boxes on a form. The following is a list of things the landlord must provide:

1.   Effective waterproofing and weather protection of roofs, walls and doors.

2.   Plumbing and gas facilities conforming to applicable laws and maintained in good order.

3.   Water supply approved under applicable law capable of producing hot and cold running water.

4.   Heating facilities.

5.   Electrical lighting.

6.   Premises at time of commencement of rental agreement, free from debris, filth, rubbish and vermin.

7.   Adequate garbage and rubbish receptacles.

8.   Floors, stairways and railings maintained in good repair.

9.   Door locks and window locks, if necessary.

In addition to defending the UD action, the tenant has an independent action for damages in civil court or small claims court, but that is a separate action. It is highly recommended that you, as a tenant, hire a lawyer to bring such an action. Remember, that you cannot use a lawyer in small claims court.

I have seen my share of slumlords appearing before me. Often when they are unable to evict the tenant for non-payment of rent because of a habitability defense, they will claim that the tenant caused the condition, but do not despair if you are a tenant. Here are some arguments you can make in response:

The dwelling substantially lacks any of the affirmative characteristics listed by statute (see above list), is deemed and declared substandard under the statute or contains lead hazards:

>   1.   A public official who is responsible for enforcing any housing law has notified the landlord or the landlord's agent in a written notice issued after inspecting the premises, of the landlord's obligation to abate the nuisance or repair the substandard or unsafe conditions. The conditions have existed and have not been abated for sixty days after the date the official's notice was issued, and the delay is without good cause; and,

>   2.   The conditions were not caused by the tenant's act or omission in violation of the statute.

If you, as a tenant, have facts that fit into one of the above items, you have a fighting chance to stay in the property at a reduced rent. If you, as a tenant, are aware that a a result of complaints to the government authorities about the property, there are findings of violations, you should request certified copies (certified documents are copies of important documents that need to be certified as true copies of the originals by a person authorized to do so. For certain documents, you must request a certified copy directly from the agency that issued or holds the original documents), or all correspondence and/or notices of violations from these agencies to present in court as evidence of the condition of the premises. You probably cannot use non-certified documents from the agencies to advance your case because they are considered hearsay and most likely not admissible.

The landlord typically responds to these uninhabitability claims by arguing that the tenant caused the condition at issue. Along with landlords, tenants also have obligations regarding the property. As the landlord, you can try to show that the tenant has not fulfilled the following requirements:

>   1.   Keeping the tenant-occupied part of the

premises clean and sanitary.

2. Disposing of all garbage and rubbish.

3. Properly using all fixtures and keeping fixtures clean and sanitary.

4. Not allowing anyone who is on the premises with the tenant's permission to destroy, or remove any part of the fixtures, equipment or structure.

5. Using the property as intended.

Items 1 and 2 do not apply if the landlord has expressly agreed in writing to perform these obligations. You will need to look at the lease.

I have had cases in which the tenant tried valiantly to show that the premises are uninhabitable. They have brought in pictures of the place to demonstrate its deplorable condition while the landlord brings in photographs of the place from before the tenant moved in, showing the pristine condition it was in. It becomes a battle of credibility. In one case, a tenant even brought in a live cockroach in a small plastic container. It certainly made an impression on me.

CONTRACT DISPUTES

7

What if you fell in love with a particular couch for sale by a private seller, you paid for it, and upon delivery discovered that what you received was not the couch you bought, or that the delivered couch was damaged, or what happens if you have a contract with someone and you disagree over the meaning of the terms of the contract? What can you do about it?

The very first thing you should do is take several deep breaths. In fact, if there is any way you can incorporate a meditation practice into your daily routine, it will provide you with a tremendous amount of clarity and calmness to help you deal with anything that comes your way, be it a lawsuit, or any other troublesome situation. Take a proactive approach to conflict. Instead of getting angry, pursuing revenge, or wanting to punish the other party – all reactive behaviors – try to engage the other party calmly with the goal of resolving the issue before resorting to a lawsuit, and see what happens. I promise you will feel better whether it is resolved or not.

If the other party is not willing to work with you in resolving the matter, you might be left with no alternative but to sue. In that case, the first question you need to ask yourself is if you have a case against the other party for breach of contract. You do if the following conditions are met:

> 1.   You and the other party entered into a

contract (a term defined below).

2.   You performed all, or a substantial portion of the significant things that the contract required you to do.

3.   The other party failed to do something required by the contract, and there was no contractual reason for the other party not to perform.

4.   The other party did something that the contract prohibited them from doing.

5.   You were harmed by the other party's failure to perform.

A. **What's A Contract**?

First of all, let us clarify what a contract is. It is an agreement between two or more persons or entities, including individuals, companies or organizations, which creates an enforceable obligation to do, or to refrain from, doing a particular thing. The elements required for a legal contract are:

- An offer.
- An acceptance.
- Competent parties who have the legal capacity in both mind and age to enter into a contract.
- Lawful subject matter.
- A mutual agreement.
- Consideration (something of value exchanged between the parties to a contract).
- Mutual obligations.

Disputes often arise over the "consideration" aspect of a contract. The term consideration is the label for the subject that is exchanged in a contract. The most common exchange is money for goods and services. If an agreement is made to pay for goods and services upon receiving them, then the contract becomes binding at the time of agreement, and not when the payment is made. Under these circumstances, the consideration is referred to as being executory. If the act has already been carried out (i.e., the goods have been exchanged for money), this is called an executed contract. However, the consideration in a contract does not always involve an exchange of money. For consideration to be enforceable, it must be legally sufficient. In other words, have enough value and be bargained for. A party cannot promise to do something where they already have a legal obligation to do so. For example, a police officer cannot collect a reward for the capture and arrest of a criminal. They are already obligated to capture and arrest criminals as a part of their job. For consideration to be of legally sufficient value, a party may refrain from exercising a right that the party is entitled to. An example of this is when you give up the right to sue someone in exchange for restitution (the act of making up for damages or harm). Let us say you hit the baseball out of the ballpark, but in the process, you broke the window of a house in the neighborhood. The homeowner agrees not to sue you for damages in exchange for your replacing their broken window.

Consideration must also be bargained for meaning, there is an exchange of promises and something of value where both parties gain a reward and, also, receive a detriment. In the sale of a couch, for instance, the seller receives money and owns one less couch, while the buyer gains a couch, but the detriment is that the buyer's bank account has been reduced by the cost of the couch.

I have covered quite a bit about landlord/tenant disputes over security deposits and UD cases in this book. It is worth mentioning here that lease agreements are contracts too and, therefore, subject to the requirements for a valid contract as enumerated above. The other aspects of contract law that are discussed in this chapter apply to leases as well.

B. **Ambiguous Language – But That's Not What I Meant**

199

There is an entire body of law devoted to contracts, which is too vast to cover in this book. However, I do want to address two areas of contract law here and then touch on the variety of remedies available for breach of contract.

The first area has to do with ambiguous language (an ambiguity is a vague or uncertain term) in contracts. There is a rule used by the courts to resolve disputes over ambiguous language in a contract. The *parol evidence* rule governs the admissibility of evidence that is outside the actual agreement when a dispute arises over a written contract. When parties put their agreements in writing, all prior oral and written agreements, and all oral agreements that were made at the same time as the current written agreement, are integrated into the writing. The written contract cannot be altered by oral (parol) evidence, provided that it has been legally executed by a person who intends for it to represent the final and complete expression of his or her understanding of the contract. However, when a writing is found to be ambiguous by a court, parol evidence (i.e., outside evidence) is admissible only to clarify, not to vary, the contract as written. Often courts rely on what is called *Rule of Construction*. This is a rule used for interpreting legal instruments, especially contracts and statutes. Most states treat the Rule of Construction as customs because they have not been codified and, therefore, do not have the force of law. In the case where one party knows, or has reason to be aware of the ambiguity, and the other does not, the court conveys the meaning given to the language by the party who does not know about the ambiguity – i.e., the party who is without fault. Also, the Rule of Construction calls for the court to interpret ambiguities against the party that drafted the contract. So, be careful when preparing documents. Unfortunately, despite the efforts of even the very best contract drafter, most every contract will contain some ambiguity.

C. **What About Those Contracts That Relieve One Party Of All Liability**?

The second issue touching on contract law that I want to mention has to do with exculpatory clauses in contracts. An exculpatory clause is a provision in a contract that relieves one party from liability. I am sure you have come across the following scenario, or one very much like it. You have just parked your car in a paid parking garage, and the attendant hands you a ticket with microscopic print on the back. In that teeny tiny print is a whole bunch of language relieving the parking garage operator of any liability in the event that your car gets damaged or stolen. Another example of an exculpatory clause in a contract is a dry cleaner's receipt that includes a disclaimer excusing the dry cleaner from any liability or damage to the item to be cleaned during the dry-cleaning process. In our everyday lives we are often handed receipts containing exculpatory clauses. These clauses are provisions in a contract that are intended to protect one party from being sued for their wrongdoing or negligence.

Other examples include a coat check at a restaurant, a clause in a trust agreement relieving the trustee from liability resulting from any act performed in good faith under the trust, and a lease that excludes the landlord from responsibility for damage, injury, or loss that occurs on the property. With this latter example, the exculpatory clause shielding the landlord could be found unenforceable if there is a lack of consideration for the limiting clause. In other words, when the landlord offers to charge lower rent or provide additional services to the tenant free of charge in exchange for the tenant's consent to the clause in the lease, the courts may view this as consideration for the clause, thus making the contract enforceable, but if the landlord offers nothing in exchange for the tenant agreeing to the exculpatory clause in the lease agreement, then the exculpatory clause probably cannot be enforced.

In the parking garage scenario, what happens when the parking attendant brings your car around for you, and you discover that it has an ugly dent in it that was not there before? The general rule is that exculpatory clauses are enforceable if they are reasonable, but you might be able to recover damages from the parking garage operator despite the exculpatory language on the ticket you were handed. Courts can overrule an exculpatory clause if they find it to be unconscionable, or unreasonable. Additionally, they cannot excuse liability for harm that is caused intentionally or recklessly. Courts will also consider a number of factors in determining whether or not to enforce an exculpatory clause, including:

- The clause should be conspicuous, meaning it should appear in bold print, in all capitals, or in a different color.
- The wording should be clear and understandable so that an ordinary person knows what they are agreeing to.
- The clause should be specific and state specific theories of liability, such as "negligence."
- The bargaining power of each party and public policy.
- The intent of the parties, particularly the intent of the non-drafter of the agreement to relieve a party from liability must be clear and unequivocal.

The laws vary from state to state. In California, there is a statute that declares that contracts exempting anyone from responsibility for injury to a person or property of another are against the policy of the law. In other words, if you find yourself in a situation in which you have been harmed by a company that has exculpatory language in its contract with you, you might be able to fight it and recover damages despite the presence of the language relieving the company of liabil ty.

D. **What Are The Remedies For A Breach Of Contrac** ?

You feel that the other party has not lived up to the te ms of your contract, so you bring a complaint for breach of coi tract. What can you hope to obtain if you win? When there a e two parties in a contract, and one breaches it, there are ger rally two types of remedies that are available to the non-b each- ing party - equitable remedies and legal remedies. Lega rem- edies most often are in the form of monetary damage that are awarded to help make the innocent party whole. There are several equitable remedies for breach of contract, i clud- ing specific performance, rescission and restitution. In ourts of limited jurisdiction, the primary remedy is for mo etary damages. Monetary damages for breach of contract u ually take the form of compensatory damages, which incluc : gen- eral damages and consequential or special damages. The other type of monetary damages that can be awarded are pu itive damages (defined earlier in this book), but these usua ly do not come into play in contract cases. The various ty es of remedies for breach of contract are described below:

E.   **Legal Remedies**

a.   **Compensatory Damages**, also call d ac- tual damages, cover the general damages and the loss di ectly, and necessarily incurred by the breach of contract. The se are the most common type of damages awarded for breac es of contracts. In our earlier couch example in which the rong couch was delivered, the buyer of the couch could insi that the seller take back the couch and deliver the right one If the seller refused and said that it could not supply the right ouch because it was no longer in stock, then the buyer coulc most likely bring a successful breach of contract suit agair t the seller. The general damages for this breach could incluc a re- fund of any amount the buyer had paid for the couch, pl s any expense incurred by the buyer in returning the couch back to the seller, and reimbursement for any additional cost the buyer incurred when purchasing the correct couch, or its closest equivalent, from another seller.

        b.   **Special Damages**, also known as consequential damages, cover any loss incurred by the breach of contract because of special circumstances or conditions that are not ordinarily predictable. These damages reimburse the innocent party for indirect costs. For instance, an innocent party may ask to be reimbursed for the loss of business profits that derived from not having access to the required materials to produce a product for a third party. To obtain damages for this type of loss, the non-breaching party must prove that this loss was reasonably foreseeable to both parties when they formed the contract or that the breaching party knew of the special circumstances or requirements at the time the contract was made.

With the couch scenario, if the seller knew that the buyer needed the new couch by a specific date because the buyer's old couch was going to be carted away before that date, and the buyer was scheduled to host an event at their home on the specified date, the damages for breach of contract could include all the aforementioned general damages plus payment for the buyer's expense of renting a couch until the correct one was delivered.

If you are the one who has been harmed by the breach of contract, do you have to do anything to minimize the amount that you are harmed? Yes, you have an obligation to mitigate the amount of damages to the extent reasonable. You would not be able to recover damages for losses that could have been reasonably avoided after the breach occurred. If you fail to use reasonable diligence in mitigating the damages, any damage award to you can be reduced by the amount that could have been reasonably avoided. With the couch example, if the seller cannot supply you with the couch as quickly as possible

Herbert L. Dodell

in order to minimize the period you will need to rent a couch.

How are compensatory damages calculated? This depends upon the type of contract that was breached and what sort of loss resulted. There is such a thing as a standard measure of damages, which is an amount that would allow the non-breaching party to buy a substitute for the benefit that would have been received had the contract been performed. Where the cost of the substitute is speculative, the non-breaching party may recover damages for the amount it cost them to perform its obligations under the contract.

Generally, contracts that involve the exchange of money or the promise of performance have a liquidated damages stipulation. The purpose of this stipulation is to establish a predetermined sum that must be paid if a party fails to perform as promised. The damages figure is agreed upon when the parties are negotiating the contract. The liquidated damages are usually found in contracts where it would be difficult to determine the actual amount that a party was damaged due to a breach. These clauses act as insurance for both parties. The person who breaks the contract knows ahead of time how much they would owe the other party. Similarly, the other party can negotiate an amount that would adequately cover their loss without having to go to court. Liquidated damages clauses are commonly used in real estate contracts. For buyers, liquidated damage clauses limit their loss if they default on the purchase. For sellers, they are compensated a preset amount, usually the buyer's deposit money in a timely manner if the buyer defaults. Here is an example – John agrees to buy Mary's house for $50,000. As part of the agreement, he must put down a deposit of $5,000. Both parties agree that if either of them does not follow the terms of the contract, the other person gets the $5,000 deposit. So, if John fails to follow through with the purchase, Mary gets to keep the $5,000. If Mary decides not to sell her home to John, she must return the $5,000.

Even if the jurisdiction in which the contract is drawn up

allows for liquidated damages clauses, the parties need to ensure that the clause follows the various requirements under contract laws. As with any contract clause or agreement, liquidated damages clauses should be drafted and reviewed by a competent contracts lawyer.

        c.   **Punitive Damages**, also called exemplary damages, are awarded to punish or make an example of a wrongdoer who has acted willfully, maliciously, or fraudulently. Whereas compensatory damages are meant to compensate the non-breaching party, punitive damages are intended to punish the wrongdoer for egregious behavior, and to deter others from acting in a similar manner. Punitive damages are based on the theory that the interests of society and the individual harmed can be met by imposing additional damages on the defendant. These damages have been characterized as "quasi-criminal" because they fit somewhere between criminal law and civil law. They are awarded to a plaintiff in a private civil lawsuit, but yet they are not meant to compensate the plaintiff for losses suffered at the hands of the defendant and, therefore, more like a criminal fine. Punitive damages are awarded along with compensatory damages. They are, however, not typically awarded in breach of contract cases. Why not? For one thing, punitive damages usually require a stronger intent than is necessary in standard breach of contract cases. For example, a plaintiff seeking punitive damages may have to prove that the breaching party acted intentionally in a malicious or fraudulent manner. Some states specifically prohibit plaintiffs from recovering punitive damages on breach of contract claims. Punitive damages are granted more often in tort (from the French for "wrong," a civil wrong or wrongful act, whether intentional or accidental, which causes injury to another) cases to punish intentional or reckless misconduct that results in personal harm. They are also often awarded to injured plaintiffs suing companies that have made allegedly unsafe or defective products as a way of sending a message to the manufacturer. You will find much more on the subject of torts in Chapter 8.

F. **Equitable Remedies**

Equitable remedies are those that are imposed when monetary damages would not adequately compensate the non-breaching party. The following types of equitable remedies may be available to you.

        a.   **Restitution** is a remedy designed to restore the injured party to the position they occupied before the contract was formed. Parties seeking restitution may not request compensation for lost profits caused by the breach. Instead, the goal of restitution is to return to the plaintiff any money or property given to the defendant under the contract. In the couch example, restitution would entail the seller returning the buyer's money and taking the delivered couch back. Plaintiffs typically seek restitution when the contract they have entered into is voided by the courts due to the defendant's incompetence or incapacity. The law allows incompetent and incapacitated parties to not fulfill their contractual duties so long as the plaintiff is not made worse off by the non-fulfillment.

        b.   **Rescission** is a remedy that ends the contractual duties of both parties. This remedy is used when one or both of the parties is induced to enter into a contract by mistake, fraud, undue influence, or duress, and seeks to have the contract set aside. Rescission is also available if both parties prefer to cancel the contract and return any money that had been advanced as part of the contract.

In my discussion of judicial discretion in Small Claims Court, I offered an example of when I rescinded a contract between the parties before me. The case involved a new leased car that turned out to be a lemon. I rescinded the lease agreement and required the car dealer to take back the faulty car.

c.   **Reformation** requires the contract be valid, and it allows the parties to modify the contract, so it more accurately reflects what the parties intend. This remedy also gives the court the ability to change the substance of a contract to correct inequities that were suffered. However, the courts are reluctant to rewrite contracts to reflect the parties' actual agreement, especially when the contract as it was written contains a mistake that could have been rectified through a more careful and thorough review of the terms before the contract was signed.

d.   **Specific Performance** is an equitable remedy that forces one party to perform, as nearly as practicable, his or her duties specified by the contract. This remedy is available only when money damages are inadequate to compensate the plaintiff for the breach. This type of remedy is rare and is most often demanded when the subject matter of a contract is in dispute. Specific parcels of land, famous paintings, heirlooms and antiques are all unique or rare items for which specific performance is usually available as a remedy. Courts are hesitant to order specific performance because it requires ongoing monitoring of the contract by the court. Keep in mind, too, that specific performance can never be used to compel the performance of a personal service, since doing so, would be akin to slavery.

e.   **Attorney's Fee And Costs** - In a breach of contract claim, the prevailing party may be able to collect the attorney's fees and costs they incurred in pursuing legal action. Some states, however, only permit these damages if they are specifically provided for in the contract. If you anticipate that you will succeed in a breach of contract case, you should include a request for attorney's fees in your pleadings. Also, when your contract is initially drafted, it might be wise to include a clause allowing for the recovery of attorney's fees by the prevailing party in the event that a dispute arises over the

Herbert L. Dodell

contract.

WHAT IF SOMEONE HARMS MY PROPERTY OR ME PHYSICALLY – PERSONAL INJURY LAW

8

What happens if someone takes a slug at you? What if you get violently ill and need hospitalization as the result of a can of soup you bought and consumed from a grocery store? What if you get bitten by a dog, or you are the victim of a car accident caused by a drunk driver? These are all considered torts.

Tort law, also called personal injury law, is a major area of law that involves more civil litigation than any other type of law. While some torts are also crimes punishable with imprisonment, the primary aim of tort law is to provide relief for the damages suffered, and to deter others from committing the same harms. So, what is the difference between a tort and a crime? In a tort action, a private plaintiff as the injured party may sue for an injunction to prevent the continuation of the conduct that caused the tort (the tortious conduct) or for monetary damages. In contrast, a crime is a wrong against society or the state, and is punishable by incarceration or a fine. Some acts, however, can be both a tort and a crime. For example, if you use force to cause bodily injury to someone, you are committing a crime of battery, and you are also civilly liable to the victim for damages. One of the most notorious cases in which a defendant was brought to trial for a criminal act, and later sued for personal injury, revolved around the former football star, O.J. Simpson. After Simpson was tried for a double murder and acquitted, the families of the victims, Nicole Brown Simpson and Ronald Goldman, filed a civil lawsuit against Simpson for wrongful death. In that venue, the jury found him "responsible" for the two deaths, and the families were awarded compensatory and punitive damages totaling $33.5 million. In that case, winning the multi-million-dollar award was one thing, collecting it was another.

When bringing a tort action, it can sometimes be difficult to identify the proper defendants. The tortfeasor (a person or entity who commits a tort) who directly harmed the plaintiff whether it is a physician's assistant, a company, a store clerk, a delivery driver, or some other individual, may not have the financial resources to pay a large judgment if the suit is successful. This is one of the reasons why it would be helpful to be represented by a personal injury attorney. A competent attorney will be able to identify and bring suit against additional parties who are liable, based on their relationship to the tortfeasor, such as an employer or a landlord.

There is a legal doctrine – respondent superior (translated as "let the master answer"), which states that an employer may be held responsible for the actions of their employees performed within the scope of their employment. Under this doctrine, the employer could be found liable for the torts, including assault and battery of their employees committed within the scope of the employment. I touched on this notion in the section on Workplace Violence under Restraining Orders. For this doctrine to apply, there has to be a clear employer/employee relationship established. However, particularly with intentional acts, which may be criminal in nature, it is not always evident that the employer is liable. While the issue of whether the employee's acts were negligent, or intentional, is determined first, the courts commonly consider whether justice is served by holding the employer liable. Again, whether or not the employer can be held liable for an employee's intentional act depends on whether that act was within the scope and course of their employment, or at the direction of the employer.

Here is an example – Joe is employed as a security guard at a department store. His job is to walk around, thus creating a presence to deter shoplifting. A customer instigates an argument with Joe and is then ushered out of the store by another security guard. Joe, however, gets angry and follows the man out into the parking lot, throws a punch and then a full-blown fight ensues. Several days later the customer files a lawsuit against the store, seeking reimbursement for medical bills and payment for pain and suffering. Asking the customer to leave the store when he caused a problem is within the scope of Joe's employment, but losing his temper, chasing after the man and physically assaulting him outside, is not. Under these circumstances, *respondeat superior* probably would not apply, as justice would not be served by holding the employer responsible for Joe's illegal act.

In contrast to the Joe situation, here is an example in which *respondeat superior* is warranted. A woman is hired by a caregiver agency to provide in-home assistance to an elderly disabled man. The woman was hired despite having been fired from her three previous caregiving jobs for mistreating patients. The children of the elderly man complained that he had bruises and scratches all over and a bump on his head as a result of being mistreated by the caregiver. In their lawsuit against the agency, *respondeat superior* is applicable. Not only does the agency bear a responsibility for the misdeeds of their employee caregiver, but the employer may also be held liable for carelessly or negligently hiring an individual who has a history of abusing patients. Of course, the employer is not solely responsible. Both the employer and employee may be subject to civil liability, and the employee caregiver may also face criminal charges for her actions.

Can a parent be held liable for the torts of their minor children? A parent who fails to take reasonable steps to properly supervise a child – knowing their child has a particularly dangerous propensity – could be considered negligent if someone suffers foreseeable harm as a result of the child's action s. For example, if a child discharges a firearm kept in the hou e, and the parent did not exercise reasonable care in keeping i away from the minor, the parent could be held liable for any ir juries that occurred.

As in many states, California has passed parental res onsibility laws that place potential liability on parents (an legal guardians) when a minor causes harm to a person, o does damage to property. Parents are not always held liable or the torts of their children, but they do have a duty to ex rcise reasonable care so as to control their minor children t prevent them from intentionally harming others. There are three types of torts: intentional torts (e.g., intentionally hit ing a person); negligent torts (e.g., causing an accident by fai ng to obey traffic rules); and strict liability torts (e.g., liabil y for making and selling defective products).

A. **Intentional Torts**

Intentional torts are those wrongs which the defe idant knew or should have known would occur through th ir actions or inactions. Examples of intentional torts ii clude battery, assault, invasion of privacy, trespass and infl ction of emotional distress. Defamation is usually categori ed as an intentional tort, too, because the defendant delibe ately printed or spoke aloud the defamatory statement.

1. **Assault**

With as much television as most of us watch, you have probably heard the term "assault and battery" used cou itless times in law and police dramas, but what does this term nean, and are these two words – assault and battery – synony 10us? They are actually two separate offenses that fall unde tort law. Assault has more to do with apprehension and fear while battery is actual physical contact with another. As I 10ted previously, a person may be both criminally and civilly liable for assault and/or battery. The Penal Code (a body of laws establishing the criminal offenses for a particular jurisdiction) defines assault as an unlawful attempt, coupled with a present ability to commit a violent injury on another person. It defines battery as any willful and unlawful use of force or violence on another person.

In order to bring a civil suit against someone for assault, you would have to show that the other person intended to inflict harm on you, or to put you in fear that you were about to be hurt or, at least, touched in a harmful way by the offender. In most states, that apprehension or fear of imminent harm, as long as it is a reasonable response to the situation, is all that is necessary in order for an act to be considered an assault. Although the particular legal requirements vary by state, the following situations would most likely give rise to a personal injury lawsuit.

Somebody thrusts a fist in your face and threatens, "I'm going to punch your lights out."

Somebody points a toy gun at you in order to scare you. The fake weapon looks like the real thing and you believe that the person is actually going to shoot you.

You are walking across an intersection at a crosswalk. A driver accelerates the car at the intersection wanting you to believe you are about to get hit, and then they slam on their brakes at the last minutes, stopping the car just a few feet away from you.

Note that in the above examples, no actual contact or touching occurs. The threat alone is key. In fact, if contact does take place between the offender and victim, the intentional tort of "battery" often comes into play.

2. **Battery**

The definition of the intentional tort of battery varies from state to state but, typically, what is required is that one person (the offender) make purposeful and harmful or offensive contact with another person (the victim). The contact and the resulting harm to the victim can be direct and immediate (e.g., someone pushes you), indirect and immediate (e.g., someone hurls a rock that hits you), or indirect and remote (e.g., someone sets a trap that you fall into days later).

Keep in mind that the victim does not actually have to be physically harmed in order for a battery to occur under civil law. In most states, it is merely required that the contact be offensive or inappropriate to a reasonable person, and that the offender meant for the contact to take place.

The intentional torts of assault and battery often emerge from one event, but not in every case. Think of the example of someone raising their fist at you, coupled with the threat to punch you. This could be a case of assault without battery since no actual punch was thrown, and a battery can take place without an assault. For instance, if someone pushes you from behind it can lead to a tort action for battery, but if you never saw the person coming at you and did not feel any apprehension beforehand, you probably have no case for an intentional tort of assault.

3.   **Damages In Assault And Battery Tort Cases**

What can you hope to gain from an assault and battery tort case? Considering that no actual physical harm is required in most states, there is a wide range of potential damage awards in these cases. If you suffered no hard, or a negligible amount, filing a lawsuit may not be worth it in the long run, even though an assault or battery may have technically taken place. As with any lawsuit you are contemplating filing I urge you to first ask yourself some questions. Why are you filing the lawsuit? Is it strictly for ego-gratification reasons such as revenge, assuaging your anger, or as a means of punishment perhaps? If you have truly suffered harm, a lawsuit might be warranted and valuable to make you whole, or to prevent the offender from harming others in the future.

When an assault and battery incident leaves you in a hospital and requires extensive medical attention, a personal injury lawsuit may be the best way for you, as the victim, to get reimbursement for medical bills and compensation for consequences, such as pain and suffering.

4. Defenses In Assault And Battery Tort Cases

If you are the alleged offender, what defenses can you raise when you are accused of assault and/or battery? These are the most common defenses to a personal injury lawsuit in which assault and battery is alleged:

a. **Consent**: You could argue that the so-called victim agreed to the possibility of being hurt. A plaintiff could have a hard time winning a case if he or she was playing a contact sport. For example, by playing football, the player consented to certain physical contact, even if he was harmed by that contact.

b. **Privilege**: A police officer using force in the course of making an arrest might assert the defense of privilege. A lawsuit against a police officer for assault and battery probably would not be successful as long as the officer used a reasonable and appropriate amount of physical force while making the arrest. If you follow the news, you have probably seen many headlines lately about police brutality. Frequent accusations are made, but how often are successful lawsuits brought against officers?

c. **Self-Defense Or Defense Of Others**: If you can show that you responded appropriately to a threat of harm, then a lawsuit against you for assault and/or battery will probably not succeed. The crux of the matter is whether or not your response was a reasonable reaction to the situation. For example, if someone tried to throw a punch at you, but you stopped them by grabbing their arm to try to subdue them, you would probably not be liable for the intentional tort of battery. However, in that same situation, if you took out a gun and shot the person who threw the punch, you would not get away with claiming self-defense because your response would not be considered reasonable under the circumstances.

B. **Negligence Torts**

Most personal injury cases revolve around the doctrine of negligence. Negligence is the failure to exercise a degree of care that would be taken by a reasonable person under the same circumstances. The law surrounding negligence is based on the principle that every member of society must act responsibly and avoid putting others at risk. Negligence is measured by how careful a person was when the injury resulted, and how careful, according to the law, the person should have been.

To bring a successful negligence suit, you would have to show that a reasonably prudent person in the defendant's position would have acted differently under the circumstances. Some examples of torts of negligence are car accidents caused by drunk drivers, medical complications resulting from a doctor's carelessness and dog bites that occur when aggressive pets are permitted to roam free. The responsible party in each case ignored the risk posed to others and, consequently, the plaintiff was injured.

If you are able to prove negligence in a personal injury case, then the defendant must pay you (the plaintiff) for all injuries caused by the defendant's actions. Certain kinds of damages are easy to calculate, such as medical expenses and property damage. For other types, such as loss of earning capability and emotional distress, you might need to enlist testimony from experts. It may also be possible to recover punitive damages, which are meant to punish and deter particularly egregious conduct.

To defend against personal injury liability in negligence actions, you could argue that the plaintiff did not use due care, and thus is partially or wholly responsible for their own injury. As the defendant, you may also claim that the plaintiff "assumed the risk" by voluntarily participating in a dangerous sport or activity, or that it was implied that the plaintiff gave you permission to take action that ended up harming the plaintiff. Some of these defenses are similar to those listed above for intentional torts.

C. **Strict Liability**

There are situations in which defendants will be considered liable regardless of how careful they were in their conduct. A defendant is held strictly liable if someone is hurt while the defendant is engaging in a highly dangerous activity, even if the activity is legal and all precautions have been taken. Demolishing buildings, transporting hazardous materials and manufacturing explosives, all fall into this category.

Injuries caused by defective products are a common tort. Generally, strict liability is applied to defective product injuries. In these strict product liability cases, if you are the plaintiff, you need not show that the manufacturer knew, or should have known that the product was defective or dangerous. To establish a defective product case based on strict liability, you must show 1) the product was defective; and 2) the defect was the proximate cause of your injury and you suffered damages. Proximate cause is the primary cause of an injury. It is not necessarily the closest cause in time or space, nor is it always the very first thing that sets in motion a sequence of events leading to an injury. In most tort cases, proximate cause is a question of foreseeability. If the particular injury that resulted was a foreseeable consequence of the defendant's conduct, then proximate cause exists. The question courts ask is, "Was the injury foreseeable?"

If you are suing the manufacturer or seller of a product that caused you great injury, and it turns out that the product was, indeed, properly designed and properly manufactured what is left for you to claim? You can argue, perhaps, that the defendant did not adequately warn you of the danger associated with the use of the product. The manufacturer does have a duty to warn you about certain latent dangers that are foreseeable. These types of cases will often require the use of experts, whom your lawyer will bring in.

Why should strict liability be used for defective product cases? For one thing, manufacturers, which are often large corporations, are in a better position to incur the costs of the injuries caused by their products than individuals who are harmed. In addition, by requiring manufacturers to pay damages for injuries caused by their products, regardless of fault, the law encourages manufacturers to produce safe, dependable products. Nonetheless, liability can also be based on the theory that the manufacturer acted negligently by designing and selling an unsafe product. Under either theory, product liability cases have the potential to become large class action lawsuits, involving numerous plaintiffs and huge money judgments.

With any of these torts, the types of damages the injured party may recover include loss of earnings capacity, pain and suffering, and reasonable medical expenses. These damages encompass both present and future expected losses.

THAT'S NOT WHAT I THOUGHT I BOUGHT! FRAUD!

9

What happens if you bought what was advertised as a new car, but it has been giving you nothing but trouble since you drove it home, and you later discover that what you bought was actually a slightly used car? Do you have any rights?

This is just one example of consumer fraud, something that happens to people all the time. In California, businesses that sell goods, such as vehicles, must comply with the California Consumer Legal Remedies Act (CLRA). The law prohibits a wide range of deceptive, fraudulent and unfair business practices involving all types of consumer goods. Some of those prohibited practices include misrepresenting the source of the goods and services, representing reconditioned goods as new, advertising goods without having the expected demand in stock, claiming that a repair is needed when it is not, offering rebates that have hidden conditions, and misrepresenting the authority of a salesman to close a deal. The CRLA gives consumer fraud victims the right to recover both actual and punitive damages, as well as attorneys' fees from the offending business. Under this law, you might also be able to replace a defective vehicle and get reimbursed for related expenses, such as towing, repairs and rental car fees. California also has what is called a "lemon law." This law applies to motor vehicles that come with a manufacturer's warranty. Under the California Lemon Law, when a vehicle manufacturer is unable to repair a vehicle to conform to the manufacturer's express warranty after a reasonable number of repair attemp s, the manufacturer must replace, or buy back the vehicle. A so, in California, there is something called the California Car F iyer's Bill of Rights, which gives consumers who buy certifie l pre-owned vehicles certain rights.

We, as Americans, are constantly buying things. W shop in brick-and-mortar stores and online for everything fr m refrigerators to collectibles to scuba diving gear. We shop 24/7, so it should come as no surprise that sometimes there is ome-thing wrong with goods and services we buy, or in th : pur-chasing process itself.

There are federal consumer protection laws as well ; laws in many states, such as the aforementioned California st itute, that exist to provide against a variety of forms of frau i and unfair business practices. Your state attorney general m iy enforce these laws, or your state may have a separate con umer protection agency. All states can protect you from frau ulent business practices through their common law (judge made law). Usually to prove common law fraud, you must show that:

- The person doing business with you n ade a false statement of material fact (a fact ir port-ant to your decision to go through wi h the transaction);
- The person making the statement knew >r believed the statement was false; and
- You relied on the false statement an you suffered damages.

An example that meets all these elements of fraud an be found in the case of an antique dealer who informs yo l that a statue is a valuable Ancient Roman artifact. In real ty, as the dealer knows, the statue is a forgery. The dealer ha com-mitted fraud if you buy the statue based on the dealer's state-ment.

Certain types of fraud are categorized as criminal offenses. For a listing of frauds that are federal crimes, see the Criminal Law section.

Fraud is another area of law in which having good representation can be invaluable. A consumer law lawyer can give you advice about the best legal solution to your problem. Often the consumer protection laws give you enforcement power by allowing you to file a private lawsuit, and it may be possible to recover attorney fees if you win your case. Some of the laws permit a judge to award triple the amount you actually lost, encouraging the exercise of your consumer rights, even when your actual loss might be minimal.

In this consumer-oriented world we live in, being a smart shopper means more than simply looking for the best prices and quality for goods and services, it also entails knowing your rights and what action you can take if something goes awry.

When you feel as if you have been swindled, before rushing to sue somebody, it is a good idea to consider the various options. First of all, is this fraudulent act or unfair business practice worth your time, potential financial commitment and aggravation that a lawsuit will entail? Can you take a deep breath and walk away instead of reacting? Remember, that even if you do not pursue an action against the perpetrator of the fraud, eventually they will have to pay back their ill-gotten gains one way or another. There will be a negative consequence from their action (or cause and effect in universal principles), even if it occurs many years down the road.

I am not suggesting that you should not pursue justice if you have been wronged, only that you should think carefully about your true motivation for bringing a lawsuit. Is it driven by your ego? Are you itching to sue as a way to retaliate, or "get back" at the swindler? Perhaps you want to be made whole, or you want to protect others from being victimized by the party who committed the fraud, or if you are the person who committed the fraud, wouldn't it be better for you in the long run to make amends for harming the victim? Cou d you return the victim's money and take back the faulty or m srepresented goods? Both parties lose (and the lawyers win) fyou have to battle it out in court.

If you, as the defrauded party, still want to file a clai , you should ask yourself, as a result of the fraud, if your tota damages amount to less than $10,000? If so, you can file in Small Claims Court against the party who committed fraud a ainst you.

If the damages you seek to recover are greater than $10,000, then you would most likely benefit from the dvice of a lawyer. If you do seek the assistance of any attorne , you might consider asking him or her these questions:

1.   Could my consumer complaint l e the basis for a class action lawsuit?

2.   Can I file a lawsuit and a Federal Trade Commission complaint regarding my consumer issue?

3.   Can I choose whether to seek relief under federal or state law?

Under most circumstances involving fraud or unfai business practices, your best bet would be to settle with t e opposing party. If the defendant is a company or corpoi tion, depending upon their size, it will probably be less cos ly for the defendant to offer you something in a settlement t an to go to trial with all the accompanying costs.

TO SETTLE, OR NOT TO SETTLE, THAT IS THE QUESTION

10

When do most cases settle? There is merit to the saying, "The case settled on the courthouse steps." Once the defense counsel has done all the work leading up to a trial, thus maximizing their hourly billings, all that remains is the trial. Defense counsel runs the risk of losing this client for future matters because if the case is lost in court, the client will question why their attorneys let it get that far. I have known some defense firms that took cases all the way to trial, and then lost their client when an adverse result occurred. With insurance defense firms who rely on getting continuous business from insurance companies, they run the risk of losing this source of business if they take these cases to trial and lose. What happens is that the insurance companies start to question their attorney's billable hours. I tell the insurance companies that the time they will suffer the least financially is always at the start of a case. A former defense lawyer, whose firm relied greatly on the continued business of one of the large insurance companies, confided in me that if they lost that particular client, the firm would have to fold up its tent. You can use the insurance company's desire to cut back on their attorney fees as leverage to get them to settle a case with you.

I have handled a number of cases that did, indeed, settle on the courthouse steps. A case I tried for some wonderful clients, involved an insurance agent who had failed to offer adequate coverage for a home. This agent had been featured in advertisements for the insurance company, but turned out to be a horrible witness. He was smug, overconfident, and not very thorough. His deficiencies were obvious to the judge, who suggested once the jury left the courtroom to begin deliberations, that we settle the case. The judge surmised that, with his demeanor, the agent was not going to win any fans among the jurors.

You can also ask yourself whether you can afford to continue paying hourly fees to your lawyer. How do you feel about the risk of possibly losing your case? Can you handle the costs of a loss, including the potential liability you might face? The strongest case to be made for a settlement is that it is immediate and certain, and there is no opportunity for an appeal.

Because there is the potential for tax consequences in settlement agreements, in my practice, I regularly consulted with a tax specialist before reaching settlement deals for my clients. As a plaintiff in a personal injury matter, you will want to know whether or not the money you get from the defendant is considered taxable income. Particularly with complex contract cases in which there is a possibility of tax consequences as a result of a settlement, it is advisable to consult with a tax attorney who can, perhaps, help you to structure the settlement award so that you will not be taxed on it.

When there are multiple parties to a lawsuit that settles, there will be a "global settlement," which means that the case ends for all the parties involved. They can be difficult agreements to reach because everyone has to agree despite the fact that everyone has their own agenda. Working out a global settlement is certainly best left to an experienced lawyer.

Here is a case I was involved in that demonstrates the value of leveraging a settlement. My client was a chef at Hugh Hefner's Playboy Mansion. One day after work, as my client was leaving the mansion, the guard dogs on the property attacked him and bit his lip, which required plastic surgery to repair.

He sued the Playboy Mansion and Hugh Heffner. The defense argued that the chef's injury was covered under the Worker's Compensation insurance and, therefore, the plaintiff could not sue the Mansion or Heffner. We found a statutory exclusion, however, for employees who work for less than a certain number of hours. These employees are not covered under the Worker's Compensation law and, therefore, are permitted to sue.

Heffner did not show up for the deposition we had scheduled. I asked the court for an order to compel his appearance at the deposition, and for sanctions against him. A sanction is a financial penalty or punishment imposed by a judge on a party or attorney for violation of a court rule, or as a fine for contempt of court. If it is a fine, the sanction may be paid to the court or to the opposing party to compensate the other side for inconvenience or added legal work due to the rule violation. The judge granted both, requiring Heffner to show up at the time and place that I designated and to pay sanctions. Heffner's attorneys suggested we meet at the Playboy Mansion. I declined and instead told them to meet at my office on Sunset Boulevard (a very busy street) at 5:00 PM on a Friday, right in the heart of rush-hour traffic. My choice was designed to make it as inconvenient for them as possible to give us leverage over them.

At the deposition, I told Heffner who, by the way, was a very nice guy, that it was going to be a long, drawn out trial, and that he would have to sit in court for at least three weeks. He laughed, knowing exactly what I was doing – putting pressure on him to settle. Within weeks, Heffner's attorney called and said Heffner wanted to settle. He did not relish the thought of sitting in court day after day. A good lawyer knows which buttons to nudge an opponent towards a settlement.

In some instances, losing your case is more than just not winning the case. You can end up being saddled with huge expenses – the costs of litigation – that can be awarded to the winning party. When a client is on the losing end of a case, those expenses could put the client out of business. [ ]ttle-ment helps to eliminate that risk.

I had a very unusual case once, which exemplifies h(w ne-gotiating tactics can lead to a good settlement. The m; e cli-ent came into my office dressed as a woman. He was m rried and working as a clerk for the county. He had been sl ghtly injured in a car accident and had filed a claim against the party that hit him, seeking damages based on the trauma of th acci-dent. He was treated for soft tissue injuries, and somewl ere in that treatment process, had decided to transition to b(:ome a woman. He left his wife and underwent gender tran ition. The insurer refused to pay a sufficient amount, so the :lient hired me to represent him/her. We successfully ma(e the case that the trauma of the accident had triggered my c ient's latent desire to become a woman. We had a psychol)gical evaluation to support our claim. The insurance compa y set-tled with us, and paid my client the policy limit, whi(1 was far in excess of what they would have paid for the mi 1imal physical injury from the accident. In the negotiations I had advised the insurer that going to trial would be risky, hat a trial might result in an award much greater than the olicy limits if the jury believed that the accident precipitat(1 this life-altering event for my client. In the end, they we e not willing to take that risk.

How do you know how much to demand to reach a ettle-ment in a personal injury case if you are the plaintiff? How do you know how much to offer if you are the defer lant? How do you put a price on pain and suffering? For star ers, it depends upon whether you are the defendant or the pl; ntiff, of course. When I have represented defendants, I have c fered the bare minimum in the beginning. On the other ha1 d, if I am representing someone who has been injured and is seek-ing damages, I will ask for the whole shebang – as m ch as possible. Damage amounts in personal injury cases are t 1tally subjective. If you are the injured party – the plaintiff – d( )end-ing on the type of injury and how serious it was, you cou ld try to make a case that your injury resulted in a loss of income, in physical suffering, and/or emotional suffering. To come up with a dollar amount, you would first take a look at the life expectancy chart issued by the government. How long you are expected to live is based on your age, gender and race. This chart is attached to the jury instructions, and is usually referred to by the judge before sending the jury off to deliberate. If the judge mentions the life expectancy of the injured party, then when I am addressing the jury in closing, I will say something like, "Judge Smith just told you that the life expectancy of my client is seventy-five productive years." Then I will go ahead and present to the jury all the elements of the damages. I might bring in expert witnesses to testify to the weekly cost in pain and suffering that my client will have to endure.

To illustrate, let us say you were in an accident, and since then have suffered from debilitating headaches on a daily basis, we would put a dollar amount on how much you would be willing to pay each day to not have to suffer from those headaches, and then we would multiply that amount by your life expectancy. This formula is what is called a *per diem* argument. As another example, let us say you have lost a limb, or suffered some other injury that will reduce your quality of life. How do you put a price tag on that? Again, it is all very subjective. You (or your lawyer) could emphasize the activities that you used to engage in, but are no longer able to as a result of the injury. Were you an avid bowler? Did your job require you to do a lot of heavy lifting? Are you no longer able to drive because of the injury? You can make your pitch that your injury has cost you a great deal – your ability to work, to enjoy physical activity and to be free of pain.

An accountant serving as an expert witness can offer testimony as to damages from loss of income, wages and for medical expenses. As the plaintiff, the amount you will possibly be awarded will depend on whether or not the jury sympathizes with you, or likes you. Since the outcome of a trial is like horse races – always a guessing game – in most cases you should settle, but you can use all these expert opinions regarding things like loss of income, pain and suffering, and decreased quality of life, to bolster your settlement offer.

Personal injury lawyers are specialists. Obviously, some are better than others. It is a volume business often requiring the lawyers to turn over the cases quickly. The really good lawyers, however, know how to maximize the damages and are not in a rush. You want someone who can analyze and put forth a position showing who and how the accident occurred, using bio-mechanics. You also want someone who can present the best evidence of the damages, physical emotional and economic. One of the best lawyers in Los Angeles is Michael Kahn. He is well-versed in bio-mechanics and the diagnosis and treatment of injuries. I have learned a lot from him.

If you are the defendant, even if you do not believe you are liable for the plaintiff's damages, you should consider settling for an amount that will satisfy the plaintiff. You need to consider the costs of your defense, which will include bringing in your own experts to refute the plaintiff's experts and, of course, attorney's fees. It might go better for you to pay the plaintiff something than to possibly waste that same money on legal expenses and risk losing the case, leading to much greater financial liability. Of course, the dynamic is different if your insurance company does not pay the limits when liability is clear, it subjects itself to bad faith damages.

It is a whole different ballgame figuring out what amount to offer in a contract dispute as opposed to in a personal injury case. Damages resulting from a breach of contract are generally quantitative. Accountants as experts can play a big role in coming up with damage amounts.

If I could rewrite the laws, I would make a provision for awarding attorney's fees when cases do not settle. There is a procedure for seeking settlement. A party files a particular form, which is a statutory offer to settle for a certain amount of money. The party sends this form to their opponent, who has 30-days in total, or 10-days before trial, to accept or reject the offer – (a statutory offer is subject to a set of rules governing the procedure for offers and setting forth which expenses are recoverable). Let's say it is the plaintiff who offers to settle with the opposing party for $100,000, but the defendant does not respond to the offer. The case goes to trial. The plaintiff ends up with a judgment of $105,000. Since this figure exceeds the amount they had previously offered as a settlement with the defendant, they are entitled to recover from the defendant certain costs that are ordinarily non-recoverable, such as expert witness fees and the interest that has accrued on their damages from the time of the breach or other loss, but there is no provision for the recovery of attorney fees. I would like to see us adopt the British system in which the loser in court pays the prevailing party's attorney' fees. In general, the prevailing party is considered the party that comes out ahead. I think the prevailing party in a lawsuit should always be awarded attorney's fees, whether there is a contract providing for them or not.

If the defendant makes an offer to settle with you, as the plaintiffs, you must carefully consider whether or not to take the offer. If you accept the offer, know that that is all you are going to get. If you go to trial and are awarded a judgment for less money than the defendant's offer, you are saddled with all your costs, at least up to the time the offer was rejected, and will likely not collect attorney's fees, nor should you even if you prevailed. Attorney's fees are only awarded to the plaintiff if a component of the claim involves bad faith on the part of the insurance company, or as provided by statute, or if there is a specific provision in the contract that provides for the prevailing party to be awarded attorney's fees. I believe that in all cases, awarding attorney's fees and the amount to be awarded, should be at the discretion of the court.

In a recent case decided by the Supreme Court of Arizona, which may reflect a trend to compel the parties to settle or face a serious risk, it held that if a party does not accept a "statutory offer" made by the opposition (either the plaintiff or the defendant) to settle the case for a designated sum and receives less than the offer after a trial, then the non-accepting party does not get fees or costs after the date of the offer. This is so, even if that party won the case (either as the plaintiff by receiving damages, or the defendant who successfully defends the case). If there is a provision in the contract known as a "prevailing party" clause, the non-accepting party could become responsible for the offering party's attorney fees and costs, even though the offering party lost the case. I believe they decided the case that way because they wanted to encourage the parties to settle. By setting up a quasi-penalty, it increases the risk dramatically. That is the primary reason to settle. So, think carefully if you want to put the pressure on the other side. The number you choose should be high enough to satisfy you, and which you believe is reasonably obtainable, and low enough for the other side to take it seriously. It is about risk and exposure.

A second technique is called "high/low." No, we are not talking about a poker game, although there is bluffing. Here is how it works. One party, the plaintiff, picks a number they believe represents a reasonable verdict or judgment as the "high." It means that no matter what happens in a trial, the plaintiff will only get that number, no more. On the other hand, the parties agree to a "low" meaning that no matter what the verdict or judgment turns out to be, even if the plaintiff loses, they get the low. That reduces the risk of a shutout. The "high" is the reason the defendant will agree to a "low." This is all about negotiating the numbers. You just need to be prepared to give up what could be a runaway verdict or judgment in your favor in exchange for certainty that you will get something. There is also a possibility of "jury nullification," which means they ignore things they do not want to hear, including the law, and decide based on how they feel about the parties. This is unpredictable, so why take the chance if you do not think you are popular with the jury? When you are in the middle of a trial and contemplating whether or not to settle your case, you can ask yourself a number of questions. How did you or how will you come across to that jury or have come across? Are you likeable? What kind of impression is the other side making on the jury? What will it cost you to see your case through to the end, keeping in mind that in addition to the trial, there might be an appeal? What does your lawyer think about the strength of your case and how it is proceeding? Usually astute lawyers want to settle their cases to ensure that they get paid. This is primarily the situation for contingency fee lawyers. If your case loses, they get nothing. At least if you settle, they will walk away with some compensation. On the other hand, hourly fee lawyers view things differently. The longer the case drags on, the more money they earn.

Be realistic, the other side may take a tough stance, and your ego could get in the way. Do not let that happen. You could be very sorry later.

Every time you go to trial with a dispute, no matter how strong you believe your case to be, you run the risk of losing. Isn't it better to walk away with something from a settlement agreement than to walk away empty-handed?

You can also ask yourself whether you can afford to continue paying hourly fees to your lawyer, and how do you feel about the risk of possibly losing your case? Can you handle the costs of a loss, including the potential liability you might face? The strongest case to be made for a settlement is that it is immediate and certain, and there is no opportunity for an appeal.

These two techniques could end your misery, so take it seriously.

PLAYING PERRY MASON

11

For trial lawyers (not all lawyers step into a ourt-room), the actual trial is the fun part of the case. A c pable trial lawyer is able to play three roles. The trial is a pe form-ance and, therefore, you want your lawyer to play his r her part well – i.e., be a good actor. A trial lawyer should a so be a good salesman. Adept in selling your story to a judge c jury. Lastly, your lawyer should be a quasi-psychologist, sor eone who is able to read other people, figure out their stre gths, weaknesses and what makes them tick. You are just bout ready to step into the courtroom after many months, or ome-times years of preparation and waiting.

A.   But First – Pre-Trial Motions

Often before the trial begins, however, the att rneys make *motions in limine* which are requests to the court o ex-clude certain issues, testimony or evidence from beir ; pre-sented to the jury. These motions are filed with the court and a determination is generally made by the judge at a tatus conference. The latter is a pre-trial meeting of the att rneys before the judge to discuss matters concerning movi g the case towards trial. Once a party makes one of these mc :ions, the opposing side will file an opposition. The moving party gets no reply. The court decides these motions before th trial begins.

These rulings can have a profound effect on a trial. A federal case in which my client was accused of getting kickbacks serves to illustrate this point. The person who was paying the kickbacks kept a ledger with notations in it revealing that my client, the president of a women's casual clothing company, was taking kickbacks from the clothing manufacturer in Vietnam. He would purchase the clothing from the Vietnamese manufacturer, but would take a percentage of the money back in cash, under the table without telling his company. The guy getting the kickbacks had a bookkeeper. The bookkeeper had access to the ledger, which reflected the kickbacks. When my client had a falling out with the bookkeeper, the bookkeeper got even with him by providing the ledger to the company. I made a *motion in limine* that this ledger was not admissible because there was no way to authenticate the handwriting in the ledger. The judge agreed and excluded the ledger from trial.

Aside from serving as an example of a productive use of a *motion in limine*, this case also demonstrates how often jurors decide matters based on their fondness or antipathy for the various players in a trial. This includes their feelings not only about the parties to the case, but also about the lawyers and witnesses who appear.

A little more background about this case will illustrate what I mean. Our client sold the company to a company that was listed on the New York Stock Exchange. He then became the president of a division of the NYSE-listed company. He had been involved in numerous lawsuits in the past, and in an effort to insulate himself from liability, especially with respect to the collection of judgments against him, my client put all his assets in his mother's name. He put the company in her name as well as a trademark agreement. Once the NYSE-listed company discovered that my client was stealing from them, as described earlier, they fired him. They still owed my client's mother the balance of the purchase price for the sold company and royalties. His mother sued for the money owed to her, and he sued them for wrongful termination, and I represented the mother and her son. The mother had a very strong case and should have been awarded millions of dollars. However, the jury could not stand the son and considered him a crook. They awarded the mother only $450,000 (there was a potential for awarding her millions) and ruled against her son on the wrongful termination claim, and awarded the company $1.5 million in damages against the son, which included punitive damages. After the conclusion of the case, I asked the jurors why they had reached the verdict they did. One juror said, "We didn't want the son to get the money. We knew that if we had awarded the mother the full amount, the son would have taken the money from her because he had put everything in her name for his benefit."

To avoid having to pay the punitive damages, the son made a deal behind my back with the other side, foregoing the $450,000 for the mother, in exchange for the release of the $1.5 million judgment against him.

B.   **The Dreaded Non-Suit**

What if you are the defendant in a lawsuit, and it is abundantly clear that the plaintiff really has no case against you? Is there anything you can do to put a stop to this trial before you have to spend any more time and money defending yourself? There is something called a *motion for non-suit* or dismissal or for judgment in a non-jury trial that a defendant in a lawsuit, or in a criminal prosecution can make, asking the judge to rule that the plaintiff or the prosecution (in a criminal matter) has not and cannot prove its case. In other words, you are claiming there is just no substantial evidence to support a jury verdict for the plaintiff, or prosecution. As the defendant, if you move for a judgment of non-suit, you do not waive your right to offer evidence in the event that the motion is denied. One of the most embarrassing things that can happen to plaintiff's counsel during trial is when a defendant makes a successful motion for non-suit immediately after the plaintiff's opening statement. (For a more thorough discussion of the basic elements of a trial, including opening and closing statements, see chapter 12). Attorneys most often make this motion after the plaintiff or prosecutor has presented all the evidence they have. Sometimes it is made after plaintiff's opening statement. They can move for a non-suit, however, upon evidence being presented that proves to the judge that the defendant cannot lose. It is often made as an oral motion with the arguments taking place in judge's chambers outside of the jury's presence.

As the plaintiff, you should know that if the motion for a non-suit is made at the end of your opening statement, by law you should have an opportunity to "cure" the defect in the statement. To do this, make sure that the defendant has clearly specified the elements that they claim are missing from your opening statement, and then request judicial leave to reopen your statement to add in the missing elements needed to prove your case. Unless as a matter of law your case is unwinnable, the court should grant your request.

A judge could also dismiss a case, or order a non-suit when the plaintiff does not proceed to trial at the appointed time, fails to show they have a good cause of action, or fails to offer any evidence. A non-suit terminates the trial at the time it is granted and results in a dismissal of the plaintiff's case with judgment for the defendant.

A plaintiff or cross-complainant can dismiss the complaint or cross-complaint at any time with or without prejudice. Without prejudice means the complaint can be refiled subject, of course, to statutes of limitations. You should talk to your lawyer if you are considering dismissing your complaint, and instead bringing it to mediation.

What happens if you dismiss your complaint without prejudice, take it to mediation, and you and the opposing party fail to reach an agreement there? Can you still refile your case? You need to be aware that time has passed while your case was in mediation. It might be that too much time has passed and that you can no longer refile your case because the statute of limitations has run. If your case is dismissed with prejudice, that is its death knell. You cannot refile it. Often, the opposition will waive its rights to recover its litigation costs if you are willing to dismiss with prejudice.

C. **Presenting Evidence: A Good Performance and Demonstrative Evidence**

Assuming your case has not been dismissed, and it is going forward to trial, it is time to consider the evidence you will be presenting. This applies to both the plaintiff and the defendant. Particularly in personal injury cases, it is helpful to show the jury some physical evidence to aid them in understanding the injury. I use aids such as models, photographic blow-ups and even artists' depictions to show the human anatomy and the location of the injury.

If your case has the potential for substantial damages, you may wish to engage a company that will analyze your case with a view towards what will be most persuasive for the jury. You can use focus groups to determine what will most likely appeal to a jury and what approaches will not work.

Pre-trial research is aimed at developing jury selection and case-specific presentation strategies, generally requiring the investigation into the psychological and sociological characteristics of potential jurors. By utilizing social science analytical tools, the process determines how each characteristic is likely to influence the juror's perception of the case.

Psychological characteristics are behavioral traits that jurors display as individuals, whereas sociological characteristics consist of behavioral traits jurors display as members of a group. How the verdict in a jury trial is reached represents a unique form of human decision-making. It combines the psychological with the sociological. Pre-trial research is a guidance tool for preparing for trial and often may serve as a

FROM THE TRENCH TO THE BENCH

predictor of the outcome.

Pre-trial research is case specific because every case is unique. The particular jurors chosen to serve on a case and the actual courtroom events, which include the judge's rulings, the participants in the trial, the venue, and issues revolving around the jurors, all constitute a one-time-only occurrence. Therefore, it is never wise for counsel to rely on the research results for jury selection/case presentation recommended for one case to be used again for an entirely different case. Any carry-over research that could reasonably be transferred from one trial to another must be presented in a reliable, scientific manner. To blindly accept that certain strategies are going to work again without further exploration can be a dangerous course for your attorney to pursue.

When engaging a lawyer on a contingency fee basis, you might ask if they are willing to use this resource and pay for it. If you have a large case, and your lawyer will not pay for this type of company, you might consider finding a different law firm. These costs may be prohibitive for a sole practitioner or a small firm, so you might be better off with a larger firm.

If you are the plaintiff seeking damages for an injury, you need to be aware of any pictures the defense might intro- duce that will contradict your claims. For example, I had a client who complained of back problems, and the defense showed a video of my client running on the beach. I chal- lenged the investigator who had taken the video by asking him whether he had also taken pictures the very next day of my client, who was in so much pain that she could not get out of bed. That was the best I could do to get around the dam- aging video. Under similar circumstances, you could testify that despite your injury, you tried to exercise, and not to sim- ply lie around doing nothing.

An attorney friend of mine in San Francisco once asked me to try a case for him in Northern California. He had a conflict, so he could not take the case to trial. I had four days to prepare for trial. I represented the plaintiff who claimed

she had suffered back problems as a result of a recent ca accident in which her car had been rear ended. She was sui g the
owners of the car that hit her. The defendant's insuranc company claimed she was not injured, or that her injurie were
pre-existing because it had been such a minor impac . The
problem was that she had been involved in five prior acc dents
and two more recent ones. This case was a rear end acc dent,
but the car that hit her had only been traveling five mi s per
hour. It appeared unreasonable that she would be sui g for
damages from this minor accident, but I pointed out in court
that the night before the accident she had hosted a inner
party during which she had lifted a heavy cauldron o soup
and, that despite this action, she had no back problem that
evening. She maintained that her back problems only egan
the next day, after her car was rear ended.

I came up with a creative bit of demonstrativ evidence to make our case. I went over to Pier One Im orts,
a nearby store, and asked if they had any cracked dr king
glasses in storage that I could, perhaps, purchase. They f und a
cracked one for me and I also bought an identical intact glass.
My intent was to make the point to the jury that my c ient's
prior injuries made her more susceptible to an injury om a
minor accident (i.e., this most recent traffic accident). n the
courtroom, I brought in the two glasses. For dramatic ffect,
I covered the two glasses with a towel. When I remov d the
towel, the jury could see that one glass was cracked a d one
was not. I tapped the cracked glass with a hammer nd it
broke easily. Then, I tapped the second glass with equa force
and nothing happened to it. The jury found my little d mon-
stration convincing and came out in favor of my client, gree-
ing with my argument that the recent slight accide t had
caused her back injury. This case is illustrative of the cc cept
of the "thin-skulled plaintiff," meaning if the plaintiff i more
susceptible to an injury because of a pre-existing conc ition,
as the defendant you are stuck with whatever conditi n the
plaintiff is in when the accident occurs. In other word , you

must take the plaintiff as they are.

Another case that exemplifies a good use of demonstrative evidence was a medical malpractice case I tried. My client, the plaintiff, claimed that the doctor had committed malpractice in a tummy tuck procedure. We were arguing that the doctor botched the operation because, as a result of the surgery, my client's belly button was no longer centered, but rather on the side of her stomach. To illustrate my point, I had my client stand, lifting her blouse in front of the jury to show them where her belly button ended up. It was quite a sight and clearly effective because the verdict went our way.

D. **The Experts**

There is an array of performers in any courtroom drama. The legal system has spawned a cottage industry of experts, who are brought in to offer expert opinions on matters in dispute. Experts are the key to most cases. How do you find them? Your lawyer will take care of securing the experts, but you should know that they are generally very expensive. Try to get an estimate of the cost and get your lawyer to limit the expert's fees as part of the engagement agreement. In federal court, at least, there is a rule that requires you to disclose any experts you intend to use, their qualifications, and the basis for their opinions, well in advance of the trial.

Experts come from all walks of life. The most commonly employed experts are accountants, engineers, psychologists, members of law enforcement, forensic scientists and doctors, but nearly anyone can offer an expert opinion on any issue before the court, as long as expertise is needed to decide who is right or wrong, and the extent of damages involved, whether they are physical, emotional, or financial. In the section about hiring a lawyer on a contingency basis, I talked about one of the more unusual experts I used in a case – a cattle feeder who could testify that fat cows were more valuable than thin cows. As I previously pointed out, there are hired-gun chiropractors who are engaged by personal injury lawyers specifically to file medical reports attesting to injuries their clients have supposedly suffered.

In my years of law practice, I have encountered many doctors, regularly hired by insurance companies, who tend to find nothing wrong with plaintiffs who limp into their office. When I have been on the other side of these cases, representing the injured plaintiff, and knowing that the doctor will find absolutely nothing wrong with my client, I will accompany my client to the so-called independent medical evaluation, otherwise known as an IME. I will bring a court reporter along with me to record exactly what happens during these medical evaluations. We even record precisely what time the doctor enters the room. These doctors want to make this examination as brief as possible because they receive a flat fee for doing them. The reporter takes note of everything the doctor asks my client, the claimant to do, and I ask the doctor to state for the record everything that transpires. If the doctor refuses, which most often happens, I state for the record what is happening. Later, when we receive the report, which inevitably indicates no physical injury, we have a record. This record is useful for cross-examining the doctor at the deposition or at trial if it reaches that point.

I had a case in which I was able to challenge an expert witness doctor's assessment of my client's injury based on my own research. I was representing a woman who had been in a car accident, and the defendant's insurance company claimed she suffered no injury as a result. The insurance company used a doctor to confirm that she was not injured. He testified about a particular nerve in the body. During the trial, I went home during the lunch break and looked up information in my copy of *Gray's Anatomy* about that nerve (this was long before Google). When we resumed the trial after lunch, the doctor was still on the stand. I showed him my *Gray's Anatomy* book, and he confirmed that it was the authoritative work on the subject of the trigeminal nerve, which then allowed me to read from it without it being considered as hearsay. What I read completely contradicted what he had earlier testified to. I had successfully impeached his testimony by citing *Gray's Anatomy* as the authority. We also painted a picture of the doctor as a paid professional witness for the defense, who would provide whatever testimony the defense needed.

Often in personal injury cases involving automobile accidents, both sides make use of mechanical experts. This leads to a battle of the experts. Generally, I have found that the best way to attack an expert is not based on the opinion they offer, but rather pointing out the expert's bias. You can expose their bias by discovering their income derived from serving as an expert. I will ask the expert at their deposition how much they are being paid to provide an opinion, and then I will use this information against them at trial by multiplying that number times the number of cases that go to trial, or where they are settled. I have had cases in which the experts have made millions of dollars, often working repeatedly for the same defense law firms.

Plaintiffs' experts are no better. Yes, experts should be compensated a reasonable amount for their time and expertise. After all, cases are quite often won based on how convincing the experts are but, sometimes, they perform all sorts of unnecessary tests simply to drive up their bill.

Often expert testimony, when the expert is convincing can be invaluable for a case. I represented a client who slipped and fell getting on to a ferry. I hired an engineer to offer testimony. He timed the current and the tides that had been in effect at the time of the accident in order to show how the boat was rocking up and down while my client was boarding. In addition, there was not adequate handrail for her to hold. We won the case in no small part due to the effectiveness of the expert. This case also serves as a reminder that you should not underestimate the likeability factor of the parties. What do I mean? My client was a sweet elderly woman with whom the jury clearly sympathized.

E.   Protecting A Business Or Property During A Lawsuit

While you are stuck dealing with a lawsuit, what is going to happen to your business or property that is the subject of the dispute? The court can appoint what is called a receiver, whose job is to preserve your property while the litigation is ongoing, particularly between the parties who appear to have an equal right to use the property, but who are unwilling to acknowledge each other's interest. Receivers are bonded and generally receive a generous fee for performing their job. They are very capable of running up their bill. I had a case to which two partners in a bakery were having a business dispute. One of the partners (not the one I represented) applied to the court for a receiver to be appointed in order to preserve the status quo of the business. There was a hearing on the request, at which we argued against the need for a receiver. The court sided with my client's partner and appointed a receiver. In this case, the parties ended up settling, but not before the receiver earned a nice bit of change.

F.   Jury Instructions

For a full run-down of the various elements of a jury trial, including jury selection, opening statements and closing arguments, presenting evidence and more on jury instructions, see chapter 15, the section devoted to criminal law.

Either at the Final Status Conference (the last pre-trial meeting of the attorneys for both sides to inform the court as to how the case is proceeding), or shortly before the trial begins, the parties submit jury instructions. Your lawyer should devote plenty of attention to preparing these instructions because they can help you win at trial. Your jury instructions are supposed to give the jury guidelines as to how to properly apply the applicable law to the particular issues and facts in your case. Depending upon particular instructions given, they have the potential to cause prejudicial harm to your case and, therefore, you want them to be written in such a way as to encourage the jury to view the evidence as supporting your theory of the case. If there are issues you want to raise that might lead to a change in the law, you can ask for the most favorable instruction warranted by a good faith argument for a change in the law.

You will have to provide opposing counsel and the judge with your requested instructions. There is a meeting between the judge and the parties' lawyers after the parties have closed their case, and before the jury is instructed, to determine the content of the instructions to the jury, and to note any objections the lawyers may have, to the instructions prepared by the opposition, or proposed by the judge. You will want to review the other side's jury instructions before the conference. You should file your requested instructions, your objections, and the final version of instructions with the court. If the court insists upon holding the final conference before the trial, you should ask to have an opportunity for another conference after all the evidence has been introduced because the evidence may give rise to the need for different or additional instructions. Insist on the presence of a court reporter so that all your requests for instructions, your objections, and the court's rulings will be on the record.

When it is time for the jury to deliberate, listen carefully to the court's oral instructions, comparing them to the instructions the court agreed to give, and make sure they are the same as any written instructions that will be submitted to the jury. If they are different, the focus will be on the oral instructions in the event of an appeal. If there is a mistake in the judge's oral instruction, ask the judge to correct their instruction and advise the jury that the instruction was given by mistake. If the error was serious enough, you could move for a mistrial. In any event, be sure to keep a copy of all your requested instructions, the other side's requested instructions and the instructions actually given. Make sure they are all filed with the court.

Some judges give the jury instructions before the closing arguments and others given them afterwards. If it i done before, you can refer to the instructions in your closing argument by saying something like, "You just heard the judge instruct you on the law you must apply to the facts of th case. This is what he said..." If the instructions are to be given after your closing argument, you can still refer to them by saying something like, "The judge will tell you about the law you must apply to the facts of this case. He will tell you ...." I have found that holding the instructions in my hand, or using a blow-up of them, can have an impact on the jury.

During your opponent's closing argument, you should be on the look-out for misstatements of the law, or of the court's instructions. Make sure that opposing counsel's visual aids reflecting the instructions are correct. If an error or misstatement occurs, consider whether it rises to the level of cause for a mistrial. At a minimum, ask the court to instruct the jury correctly on the point. Many judges give a copy of the instructions to the jury.

WILL THIS CASE EVER END? JUDGMENTS AND APPEALS

12

What happens if you are not happy with the outcome of your trial? Are you stuck with the verdict no matter what? Most of what follows applies to both civil and criminal matters.

A. **Prejudgment Remedies**

You might have some options before the judgment is handed down. Whether you are a plaintiff or a defendant, you may be able to file for a writ with the Court of Appeals for relief pending the outcome of your lower court case. There are different forms of remedies. Three types of writs are efforts to have the appellate court order something to be done, not done, or produced. These are rarely granted because the appellate court usually tells the submitting party to wait for a judgment and then appeal. In my opinion, filing a writ at this point is not worth the expense. Writs of execution or possession are entirely different than an attempt at appellate court relief before the end of the trial. Those writs are sought in the trial court and are designed for collection, temporary relief, or possession of property.

   1.   **A Writ Of Prohibition**: With this writ, you are asking the appellate court to prohibit certain action by the trial court.

   2.   **A Writ Of Mandate**: Filing this writ, you are ask-

ing the appellate court to order the lower court to do ome-thing.

3. **A Writ Of Habeas Corpus**: This type of writ is only for criminal cases and, in Latin literally means "you have the body." It is used to order a prison official to bring an inmate to court so it can be determined whether r not that person is being lawfully held, or should be released from custody. If the prisoner argues successfully that the incarceration violates a constitutional right, the court may order the prisoner's release. Habeas corpus relief may also be sought to obtain custody of a child, or to gain the release of a detained person who is insane, is a drug addict, or has an infectious disease. Most often though, it is used to get someone released from jail or prison.

Writs of prohibition and mandate are rarely granted. Here is a misdemeanor case I handled, in which we filed for a writ of mandate, with a request for a stay of the lower court judgment. At the trial court, my client was charged with building a patio extension without a permit and some other building violations. It was also alleged that he built part of the patio on his neighbor's property. My client believed that it was solely on his own property that he had built the patio. We made a deal with the prosecutor that so long as my client fixed the violations on his property within one year, my client could withdraw his plea of no contest (in a plea of no contest in a criminal case, the defendant receives a conviction and some sort of punishment, but the defendant isn't actually admitting guilt. The primary advantage of a no contest plea is that it cannot be used as an admission of liability in a related civil case).

In compliance with the deal, my client remedied the building violations on his property, but he did not fix the part of the patio on his neighbor's property. The judge wanted to make the neighbor, whom he described as the victim, whole.

After refusing to allow my client to withdraw his pleas of no contest, which was the deal as a condition of my client's probation, the judge required him to bring up to code the part of the patio that was on his neighbor's property. He ordered this despite the fact that my client had already upheld his end of the deal with the prosecutor by fixing the violations on his own property. This meant that my client would have to bring the neighbor's property up to code, something he had no legal right to do, in order to avoid jail time. My client filed a writ to prevent imposition of the sentence. The appellate court denied the writ. He then appealed the judge's decision. Ultimately, the appellate court affirmed the judge's decision. In my opinion, it was a terrible miscarriage of justice. Why did the judge require my client, the defendant, to pay an exorbitant damage award, or be in violation of probation? The simple answer is because he could. He wanted to punish my client for building an addition on his property without a building permit, and for encroaching on the neighbor's property. The judge seemed carried away by his own sense of power.

4. **A Writ Of Attachment**: There is another type of writ called a writ of attachment, which can prevent a defendant from disposing of his or her property to avoid paying a judgment. As the plaintiff, you can apply to stop the defendant from transferring their assets. If a party transfers their property specifically to avoid paying a judgment, this transfer can be set aside as a fraudulent conveyance. When you apply for a writ of attachment, you must post a bond with the court in case the trial does not go in your favor. When you need an attachment, you have to show that it is likely you will win your underlying case, and that you will be harmed if the attachment is not granted.

B. **After The Judgment – Now What**?

Often after a verdict is rendered, the losing party will

claim that the judge or jury reached the wrong conclusion and, therefore, they want to file an appeal of the verdict. Before anyone can file an appeal, however, the parties must wait for the judgment. This is a formal document signed by the judge containing the verdict as well as anything else that should be included, such as whether or not accrued interest is recoverable, and attorney's fees, too. On the subject of interest, if the interest is recoverable in a civil case, the amount (as dictated by state statute) will be added to the verdict amount. The same goes for attorney's fees. If there is some sort of contract between the parties that provides for attorney's fees to the prevailing party, the amount can be added to the judgment at the application of the party who won the case. It bears repeating that in insurance cases in California, the attorney's fees are recoverable when the insured, or its assignee, is seeking benefits under their policy, and there is a finding of bad faith on the part of the insurance company. What are considered reasonable attorney's fees is a recurrent issue.

If you are not happy with the contents of the judgment, you can object. It is not uncommon for a losing party to seek to reduce the judgment, or contest the attorney's fees. The judge plays a significant role here. We can decide what we think is reasonable with regard to the judgment amount and the attorney's fees. Because this is a discretionary call on the part of the judge, the chance of a reversal on appeal is slight. The appealing party would have to show abuse of discretion on the judge's part. In any event, appeals are expensive and involve a protracted process.

C.   **The Perils Of An Appeal – A True Cautionary Tale**

A recent case I was involved in as an attorney, illustrates the unpredictability of appeals, even when one has great confidence in the outcome. This particular appeal is also an example of an appeal based on jury and judicial misconduct.

This is a case that I referred to both in the sections on Cross-Complaints and Jury Selection. Here are the details of that case. My client (APP) was a manufacturer of motorized scooters. The company had a major customer (CSK), a chain of automobile parts stores that purchased the scooters to be sold in the thousands of retail stores it had across the country. These scooters were a hot item for a while, but when the market cooled, CSK found itself stuck with an excess of inventory that was not selling as well as before. CSK wanted to maintain good relations with its customers, so it informed them that they could return the scooters for a full refund, even though there was nothing wrong with them. CSK, in turn, sent the scooters back to APP, the manufacturer. They returned so many that my client ultimately went out of business. As part of CSK's contract with my client, if CSK paid within 30-days for the inventory of scooters they were keeping, they would receive a prompt payment discount from my client. In order to get this prompt payment discount, they dated the checks much earlier than they were actually sent, put them in a drawer, and then sent them to my client using the date on the checks to support the discount. In this way, they were taking discounts they were not entitled to. CSK was not paying on time, and a CSK employee even admitted that the checks were not being sent on time.

The trial was held in Arizona because CSK was based there, and the contract provided that in the event of a lawsuit, the case must be filed in Arizona. We presented all this evidence to the jury, which made for a very strong case. Two of the chief executives of CSK were eventually indicted for fraud for "cooking the books." I called these executives as witnesses, and they both pleaded the Fifth Amendment before the jury. After a three-week trial that involved thousands of pages of written exhibits, and a great deal of undisputed testimony, the jury deliberated for less than two hours. They awarded my client only $10,000 because that was all th t CSK admitted it owed my client. CSK had filed a counter laim. They jury found against them. This was one of those c ses in which the jury was not willing to award much of anyth ng to either side.

I was so surprised by the outcome of this cas that I hired a private investigator to learn how the jury re iched this insupportable verdict. The investigator interview d the two dissenting jurors, which can be done after a judgme it has been rendered, and discovered something disturbing. 1 uring the deliberations, one of the other jurors had asked the ailiff how long it generally took for deliberations. The bail f had responded, "An hour or two would be plenty." This cer ainly established a particular mindset. Also, one of the diss nters told our investigator that one of the majority jurors ha 1 said in the jury room, "Let's get out of here; who cares abo t this case?" It just so happens that we wanted this juror, a t ttoo-covered woman, on our jury panel because we assume l that she would not have any sympathy for a big corpora e de-fendant. Aside from showing how unpredictable appe s can be, this case also demonstrates how selecting a jury c 1 be a gamble (you saw more related to this observation in tl e jury section).

The result in this case possibly could have be n far different if we had rejected the tattooed juror in favor c f hav-ing the proper alternate juror sit in the deliberatior but, from a spiritual perspective, we ended up with a jury w were supposed to get. Was my client paying off a debt from ome, long ago action? There is no sure thing in jury trials. As ve all know, nothing is certain except death and taxes.

After learning about the bailiff's comment to the juror, we moved for a new trial, based on jury and judicial m scon-duct. The trial court judge refused to grant a hearing n the motion for a new trial. We appealed the denial of the h aring to the Arizona Court of Appeals. The appellate court over-turned the trial court's ruling, saying that the lower court should have granted a hearing on the motion. CSK took the case to the Arizona Supreme Court. The state Supreme Court overturned the Court of Appeals, and ruled that the trial court was correct in denying the motion for a new trial. We were flabbergasted by the decision, certain that the Arizona Supreme Court would affirm the Court of Appeals. The state Supreme Court concluded that the bailiff's comment was not prejudicial, which it certainly was, and that the comment was a "throwaway," not necessitating a hearing on a new trial. The defense had argued that allowing for a new trial would open the floodgates for every disgruntled litigant to seek a new trial. I am guessing that this notion was behind the higher court's decision. They don't want to see parties, criminal defendants especially, coming back and complaining that they did not get a fair trial. Obviously, the scheduling of a hearing, reassembling the jurors, and starting over would clog the system. Unfortunately, my client was denied due process all for the sake of expediency.

On a personal note, I noticed that my reaction to this outcome was quite a bit different than it would have been in the old days. Upon reading the Arizona Supreme Court decision, the old me would have ranted and raved, and engaged in every kind of reactive behavior. Instead, because over the years I have learned to change my consciousness, I recognized that there was a message contained in the unfavorable results of this lawsuit. So, I looked for the message. Could it be that this case ended this way to give me new, rich material to use as examples in this book? This one case alone touches on the subjects of judicial misconduct, jury selection, appeals and the benefits of settlement.

D. <u>Other Appeal Matters: What Are Your Chances</u>?

In my experience with cases appealed on the grounds of judicial misconduct, Courts of Appeal tend to rubber stamp the trial court judge's ruling. As an example, I handled a case for a client, who had suffered serious damage to his ome. The insurance company would not agree on the extent of the damages. The matter went to an insurance appraisal he aring, as provided for in the Insurance Code. The code require s that each party select an appraiser, and the two appraiser then select a third person called the umpire. If they cannot agree on an umpire, the court will appoint one. Each of the th ee appraisers is required to be unbiased and impartial in the con- siderations. The cost for the appraisers is split betwe n the parties.

In this case, the insurance company chose an app aiser they regularly used (who was dependent on the insura ce in- dustry for employment). The two appraisers selected a re- tired judge to serve as the umpire. He was reputed to be plaintiff oriented and, thus, our side was satisfied wit this choice. During the appraisal hearing we adjourned for lunch. Much to our surprise, when we went across the street to grab a bite, there was the insurance company appraiser having lunch with the defense lawyer and one of the witnesses. Wh n we returned after lunch, I raised with the umpire the impro riety of this supposedly impartial appraiser dining with a w ness. The umpire was not concerned and simply sloughed it c f.

After the hearing concluded, the panel voted -1 to support the insurance company position. We petition d the Superior Court for review, based on the misconduct. V e had also learned that the retired judge/umpire had done some work for the insurance defense firm in the past, but h d not disclosed this potential conflict of interest prior to the hear- ing. We then appealed to the Court of Appeal, whic also affirmed the appraisal panel's finding. It was a surprisir out- come given the obvious misconduct, but it reaffirm d the reality that appeals courts are reticent to overturn the deci- sions of the lower courts.

In many instances, a winning party who is aw rded costs (attorneys' fees and other trial expenses) will orego those costs in exchange for the losing party waiving their right to appeal. Often the losing party cannot afford to spend money on an appeal, and cannot afford to post a bond to prevent collection of the judgment while the appeal is pending. In California, it takes the better part of a year or more for an appeal to be decided at the Court of Appeal level. In about 2% of cases, the highest court in the state, the California Supreme Court, will grant review, which adds another six months or longer to the appeal process. While the court of appeal must hear an appeal as long as the parties follow the procedural rules for filing and meet all deadlines, the Supreme Court's decision to grant review is purely discretionary.

The Supreme Court exercises its discretion to hear cases when there is a split in decisions on the same matter of law among the lower courts, thus requiring the court to clarify just what the law of the state is on that issue. I tried a case against a prominent insurance company resulting in a trial court verdict against my client, and a subsequent loss in the appeals court. The California Supreme Court granted review, meaning that they were interested in the legal issues raised in the case. Insurance law at the time was undergoing changes. That the highest court in the state decided not to allow the California Court of Appeal decision to stand, and was willing to hear an appeal, was an indication that, perhaps, we were going to prevail in this matter. The insurance company was concerned and settled the case because they did not want to risk the possibility that the California Supreme Court would establish new law that could be used against them in future cases. In considering whether to appeal a judgment, you, or your attorney, needs to weigh the risks and the possibility for success.

E.   How Far Can You Go? Paying The Judgment And The Appellate Process?

The appellate process begins with the filing of a Notice

of Appeal. You must comply with the jurisdictional requirements, meaning you must file the appeal in the proper court, and abide by the time period requirements. If you are interested in appealing a decision, you need to find out when the judgment has been entered (a competent attorney will know this), and the date of the notice of entry of judgment that appears in the court records.

What happens if you cannot or do not want to pay the trial court judgment against you? If you want to stay the judgment (in other words, not have to pay the money owed to the plaintiff as per the judgment) from the trial court pending your appeal, you must post a bond, usually within a few weeks of the judgment. This bond is called a *supersedea bond*, or more commonly known as an appeal bond. The bond is a third-party guarantee to pay the judgment to the plaintiff if you lose the appeal. Federal and all state courts require losing defendants to post a bond, or some other form of security to stay the plaintiff's execution of the judgment.

Let's say you own a company, and the judgment is for a huge amount of money, maybe even millions of dollars. Posting a bond could be devastating for the company and its employees, particularly in cases where the defendant is required to post the bond within a few weeks of the adverse judgment. A conversation about what it might cost you to appeal an adverse judgment is a critical one to have with your attorney very early on when you are meeting to evaluate your case or discuss strategy. The cost of posting an appeal bond can weigh heavily in your decision about settling the case.

If you have lost your case, you are not required to post a bond in order to appeal the decision, but you must post a bond or some other form of security in order to stay collection of the trial court judgment. If you choose to appeal without posting a bond, the plaintiff is free to execute on the judgment they won at the trial level while the appeal is pending. If you, as a defendant succeed on appeal, you would then have to file a separate action to recover from the plaintiff the judgment money you already paid, and you would need to collect on any judgment you obtained as a result of the appeal. Once you hand over thousands, or even millions of dollars to the plaintiff for what is potentially a meritless case, there is no guarantee that you will even be able to get your money back after the appeals process. There are great expenses attached to trying to recover your money in this way. You would have to file a lawsuit, win it, and then seek to collect on the judgment. The appeal bond allows you, as a defendant, to avoid these problems.

From the plaintiff's perspective, the appeal bond ensures that if the appellate court eventually affirms the lower court's judgment, there will be money to pay the plaintiff that judgment. It might be years in the future, but at least it enables the plaintiff to collect from the defendant eventually. Without a bond, the plaintiff could worry that by the time the case winds its way through the appellate process, the defendant might go bankrupt, or otherwise be in a position that would make collection difficult or impossible.

The appeal bond requirements vary from state to state in terms of the amount of the bond that must be paid. The appeal bond is usually in the amount of one and a half times the original judgment, however, some states have enacted a cap on the dollar amount that a defendant must post. Your lawyer needs to know what the particular requirements are for the state in which your case is being heard.

How do you obtain a bond? There are many surety companies that write appeal bonds. A surety is an individual or company that agrees to honor another's obligations in the event of that other's default. As the defendant against whom the judgment was rendered, you are the principal who needs the bond. The surety company sells you the bond. The terms on which sureties offer bonds vary, so it is a good idea to consult with a bond broker to find the best options and prices. Generally, you will need to provide collateral, such as your house if you own it. Since surety companies tend to be risk adverse, some may require full collateral to cover 100% of the bond, and you will have to pay a premium on the bond. Premiums are typically measured by the amount of the bond, usually some percentage of the total bond. Once you obtain the bond, you file it with the trial court. In some jurisdictions, the act of filing a bond in the proper amount creates a stay of enforcement of the judgment. In other words, you won't be forced to pay the money that you owe the plaintiff as per the judgment in the case. In other jurisdictions, particularly the federal courts, a trial judge must approve the bond before any stay of enforcement takes effect. What happens if you lose the appeal? Then, the surety will have to make payment to the plaintiff on your behalf, and you will be required to reimburse the surety, or they will take the collateral.

Will a court accept any other form of security to stay a judgment? An appeal bond is not the only form of security that will enable you to obtain a stay of enforcement of the judgment. In some jurisdictions, you can deposit cash with the court, or provide fewer liquid forms of security, such as treasury notes, stock shares, and letters of credit. There are cases in which a defendant can seek a stay without providing any security. This happens when a defendant cannot obtain a bond or deposit funds sufficient to secure the judgment, because the judgment exceeds the defendant's assets. On occasion a court will allow an unsecured stay of the judgment. You need to ask for it and show justification.

As a defendant, you can appeal merely because you lost in the trial court, but it is risky unless there is a reasonable chance of success on appeal. You must have good grounds for filing an appeal, and there are serious consequences for lawyers who file meritless appeals and, of course, you should keep in mind that appeals are time consuming and expensive. After filing a Notice of Appeal, you must designate the record on appeal within ten days of filing. In other words, you must tell the trial court which documents and testimony you want included in the record of appeal. There are two parts to the record for your appeal: A record of the documents filed in the trial court, and a record of the oral proceedings that took place during the trial. You must order the record from the court reporter. Depending on the length of the trial and the amount of testimony, the cost of copying the record can be prohibitive, but you must pay for it before the appeal can proceed.

In California, it takes about five to six months before you need to file the appellate brief. Then, of course, the respondent has an opportunity to file their brief, and inevitably, they will request an extension. The appellant (the party appealing the lower court ruling) gets to file a reply brief to the respondent's brief. About 60 to 90 days after the submission of the reply brief, the parties are notified of a date for oral argument. The oral argument usually takes place a couple of months after the notice of oral argument.

I am not convinced that oral argument makes much difference in the outcome of an appeal, but it does serve a purpose. The justices (at the appellate court level they are called justices, rather than judges), who sit on the panel of three justices to hear a particular case, read the briefs, circulate a draft opinion before the oral argument, and have a chance to ask questions at the oral argument. If the members of the panel disagree about the case, they often ask questions to solicit a response that will support their position. Oral argument is generally offered as a recap of the case, and the lawyers invite questions from the judicial panel. The questions asked will give you a good indication of the direction the court is leaning. For example, in a case against an insurance company for loss of inventory, I represented a plaintiff company that bought old widgets, and stored them in a warehouse. The case eventually wound up before the Ninth Circuit Court of Appeals. This was the case I referred to earlier in which the lower court judge had granted summary judgment, because she claimed she could not read a report. One of the justices kept asking me "softball questions," questions that wei easy to answer. Clearly, that particular justice was sympath tic to our case, and wanted the other members of the circuit t hear my answers. We won the appeal. He wrote the opinion.

At the conclusion of the oral arguments, the app ellate court will state that the matter is submitted. The de ision will be rendered anywhere from within a week to s veral months, according to the court's schedule, requiring a 1 iajority of the justices to make a ruling. In a Court of App al, it requires two out of three to agree. In the state Supreme ourt, four out of seven. Once the decision is announced th ough a written opinion, the case is either over, a particular ower court ruling is reversed while the other rulings are uph ld, or the case is sent back to the lower court for proceeding con-sistent with the ruling.

There is still one more opportunity for review, ar 1 that is with the United States Supreme Court, the highest court in the land. The Supreme Court can hear just about an kind of court case, as long as it involves federal law, includi g the Constitution. A petition for review must be filed with t 1e Supreme Court, and most often, that petition is denied. C nce it is denied, there is nowhere else to go – the case is finally ver.

WHAT HAPPENS IF I'M NOT HAPPY WITH MY LAWYER?

13

Most often, clients are pleased with their attorneys if they win their case. However, sometimes, even after a case is won, a client might claim that he or she could have gotten a greater award given the strength of their case, but their lawyer was simply not as thorough as they should have been. It should come as no surprise that when clients lose their cases, they often place blame on their attorneys. Under either condition, when it comes time to pay the lawyers' fees, clients sometimes refuse to make payments, or they dispute the charges. To avoid such conflicts, it is important to have an executed retainer agreement between the client and the lawyer.

Unfortunately, what began as a cooperative mutually beneficial relationship between the attorney and client, can become contentious if the outcome of the lawsuit is not what the client had expected or hoped for, or if the client is unwilling, or unable to pay the lawyer's fees. In California, the client has the right to demand non-binding arbitration of any fee dispute. If the client does not avail himself or herself of this right, the lawyer is left no choice but to bring a lawsuit seeking recovery of the fees the client owes. Often, this lawsuit brings a cross-complaint from the client against the attorney for legal malpractice. It is a good idea for lawyers to wait for one year after the cessation of the attorney/client relationship to bring a lawsuit against the client. After a year, the former client can no longer sue the lawyer for malpractice, because the statute of limitations has run.

If you sue your attorney for legal malpractice, you are waiving the attorney/client privilege from your original case. This means that the attorney you are suing can bring up every communication that took place between you and the attorney when they represented you. In order to prevail in a legal malpractice case, you must first retry the original case in which the attorney represented you, and demonstrate that you would have won that case if not for your incompetent attorney. This is called a case within a case.

Here's an illustration of how these legal malpractice cases work. A lawyer neglects to file certain legal documents within the statute of limitations. His client sues him for legal malpractice. In his defense, the lawyer argues that the plaintiff, his former client, would not have won the case anyway. The plaintiff, who is suing his former lawyer, will have to put on the original case in order to prove that he would have won. Meanwhile, the lawyer has to defend the legal malpractice suit by proving, which can include calling witnesses and offering evidence, that the lawyer's actions could not have affected the outcome of the case, that it was not a strong case in the first place. Of course, his former client will argue the opposite – that it really was a winning case.

As a client, before getting embroiled in a serious dispute over fees with your attorney, consider the expense and time required for defending the attorney's collection suit against you, or for bringing your own legal malpractice suit (in which you will have to retry the case), not to mention the anxiety it will cause you. What is the end result you are hoping to achieve? If the attorney represented you in a competent manner, don't they deserve to be compensated for their work? Is it really the attorney's fault if the case did not go your way? You should stop and think about what the upside is for you in refusing to pay the fees owed, and encouraging a lawsuit to be brought against you. Demonstrating anger against your attorney and the desire to blame someone for the unsatisfactory outcome of your case are reactive behaviors. By doing what is right which, under these circumstances, is probably to pay the fees, or at least work out an arrangement with your attorney to pay them over time, you will be taking a proactive approach. Sometime down the road, you will be rewarded for taking this proactive stance now. Although you might not experience an instant gain from doing the right thing, you will be rewarded eventually. As I have said previously, time separates cause and effect. It might be months, years, or even decades before you will reap the benefit of your actions, but you eventually will. Conversely, if you insist upon taking out your disappointment on your attorneys, there will be consequences sometime in the future resulting from the choice you have made to react. You might not see the connection because so much time has passed in between events, but there will be an effect caused by your choices.

If you are not satisfied with the results of your case, perhaps you can discuss the possibility with your attorney filing an appeal. Or, alternatively, you can choose to accept the loss and say to yourself, "I needed to cleanse something I did in the past." It might be comforting to tell yourself that the results could have been a whole lot worse, and that you needed the lesson gained from this experience. You will be unlikely to repeat the behavior because you absorbed the lesson. By accepting the outcome of the case, you can reduce your anxiety level. Even the worst trial or situation contains sparks of holiness, and it is our responsibility to release these sparks into the world.

A.   **Can I Fire My Lawyer Along The Way?**

You have the right to change lawyers at any time. What happens if your lawyer no longer wants to represent you? Do you have to pay them for the work they have already done, or a percentage as provided in the retainer agreement? Generally, if the lawyer wants out, he or she will forfeit the contingency fee, but can recover what is called *quantum meruit* (reasonable value of services). When you get a new lawyer, often the former and current lawyers will work out the financial concerns between themselves. In a worst-case scenario, there will be a fee dispute between them that can be decided in arbitration.

What happens to the work that the attorney has already done? You have the right to most documents held by your attorney, other than "work product" that relate to the case. You just need to ask for them. In some states, however, the lawyer might have some rights to retain a file until the client pays a reasonable amount for the work done on the case.

What if I feel that my lawyer has acted unethically? A lawyer's conduct is governed by the rules of professional responsibility in the state or states in which they are licensed to practice. The rules are commonly administered by a disciplinary board attached to the state's highest court. The rules include detailed codes of conduct for specific situations. If a lawyer's conduct falls below the standards set out in the rules, they can be disciplined by being censored, reprimanded, suspended from the practice of law, or most serious of all, disbarred (having their law license taken away).

B. <u>What Happens To Lawyers Who Don't Follow The Rules</u>?

Lawyers can be sanctioned for litigation misconduct. For example, a lawyer may not file a frivolous claim (a claim that has no merit). Most often, lawyers are sanctioned during the pre-trial activities. The sanctions can result from violations of the rules of discovery, from missing appearances, filing frivolous motions, or other conduct that antagonizes the judge. A sanction is always punitive. Monetary fines are the most common sanctions, but a judge can impose other types of sanctions as well. The sanction can be tailored to the particular case. For instance, if a party refuses to obey a discovery order, or an order to produce requested evidence, a judge can order that the evidence sought be construed in favor of the requesting party, refuse to allow the disobedient party to make claims or defenses related to the evidence, stay or postpone the case until the discovery order is obeyed, dismiss the action, render judgment for the requesting party, declare the disobedient party in contempt of court, or issue any other order that is just under the circumstances.

In a recent case, I sanctioned a lawyer who did not show up for the second half of a trial after he was ordered back to court. It took us the better part of the afternoon to sort things out, including telephonic conferences with the lawyer. It was a waste of opposing counsel's time since he had to spend the afternoon sitting in court, waiting for the no-show lawyer to appear. You can see the sanctions I imposed if you take a look at the minute order in the appendices. If the court awards sanctions against a lawyer in excess of $1,000, the lawyer must notify the State Bar. Also, lawyers can be sanctioned by the Bar Association for matters such as overbilling and refusing to hand back a client's files.

The American Bar Association has set forth model rules for professional conduct of lawyers. The following preamble to these rules will give you a good idea of the standard of conduct you should expect from your lawyer:

"As a representative of clients, a lawyer performs various functions. As advisor, a lawyer provides a client with an informed understanding of the client's legal rights and obligations and explains their practical implications. As advocate, a lawyer zealously asserts the client's position under the rules of the adversary system. As negotiator, a lawyer seeks a result advantageous to the client but consistent with requirements of honest dealings with others. As an evaluator, a lawyer acts by examining a client's legal affairs and reporting about them to the client or to others.

In all professional functions a lawyer should be competent, prompt and diligent. A lawyer should maintain communication with a client concerning the representati)n. A lawyer should keep in confidence information relating) representation of a client except so far as disclosure is requ ed or permitted by the Rules of Professional Conduct or othe law."

As a judge, I sanctioned a plaintiff for refusing o answer interrogatories, which had caused the defendant t have to make a motion to compel the plaintiff to answer. I that case, I awarded the defendant $1,000. I have also sanct oned a party for frivolous discovery and for refusing to parti ipate in discovery. I mention this to show you the risk if) ou or you attorney chooses to play games. The Hugh Heffner case I discussed earlier is an example of when, as an attorney, have asked for sanctions against the opposing party. After F ffner did not show up for the deposition, I asked the court fo sanctions against him. The judge awarded us monetary sanc ions, and ordered Heffner to show up for the deposition at th time and place I designated. Further, the court said that if e did not comply, the court would strike the answer (elimin te all or a portion of the defendant's answer in their pleading , thus allowing the case to result in a default judgment against him.

If you think you have a valid complaint abou how your lawyer has handled your case, you should file a complaint with the disciplinary board of the highest court i your state. If the complaint concerns the amount of attorney s fees, you might be referred to a state or local bar associatio 's fee arbitration service. Try to work it out with your lawy r directly before filing a complaint. Accusing your lawyer f unethical conduct is a very serious matter. Registering th s sort of complaint might punish the lawyer for misconduct, ut it will probably not help you recover any money. You s ould consider very carefully the future effect of the wheels yc 1 will be setting in motion. Filing a complaint against your lav yer is reactive behavior. Is it the right thing to do, or are you l shing out at your attorney to assuage your anger, or to retalia e because you were displeased with the results of the case? Think about your motivation before you act.

CLASS ACTION SUITS: TO JOIN OR NOT TO JOIN, THAT IS THE QUESTION

14

When a group of people suffer damages as a result of misconduct, negligence, or other causes, but the individual damages are small, it would be impractical and unduly expensive for any one person to sue the party or parties causing the damages. The cost of the attorney's fees alone would exceed what any one member of the group could recover. Class actions (a type of lawsuit in which one or several persons sue on behalf of a larger group of persons, referred to as "the class") allow attorneys to vindicate the rights of a large number of people under circumstances in which no individual party has sufficient economic incentive to bring suit on their own. In this way, some class action suits have benefitted society.

In a class action suit, a person, or persons, may seek damages against an offending party on behalf of a vast number of people. In that case, the class will consist of plaintiffs. A class can also be comprised of defendants when those who have caused the damage are too numerous to sue individually. One or more members of a class may sue or be sued as representative parties on behalf of all only if:

1.   The class is so numerous that joining all the members together is impracticable;

2.   There are questions of law or fact common to

the class;

3.   The claims or defenses of the representative parties are typical of the claims or defenses of the class; and,

4.   The representatives will fairly and adequately protect the interests of the class.

The court must certify the class before a class action lawsuit can proceed.

A lawyer, or lawyers more like it, will represent the class and either settle the case, or take it to trial. The class will be responsible for paying the lawyers' fees. Most of these cases will be handled on a contingency fee basis, meaning that the attorneys will take 40% off the top. For example, if a case settles for $1 million, the attorneys take the first $400,000, plus reimbursement of costs, with the remaining amount being divided among the class members, which probably constitute a very large number of people. In the end, the class members will most likely end up with an insignificant sum of money. Since the costs of the lawsuit are recouped first in these cases, often the lawyers are the only ones who make any money.

If you receive notice of the action and are informed that you might get a recovery, it does not cost you anything to participate, so why not agree to join the class? On the other hand, you are given the right to "opt out" of the suit, thus enabling you to pursue the case yourself, and not be bound by the fees to be paid to attorneys for the class. The problem is that you need to have significant damages of your own to convince an attorney to take your case on a contingency. The benefit of opting out is that you can take advantage of the discovery conducted by the attorneys for the class. Usually there is a committee that does the work because it would be unwieldy for hundreds of lawyers to participate in the case. The courts have developed ways to limit the expense and chaos when hundreds of lawyers are involved. The documents must be kept in a depository, available for use by any litigant

A fairly, well-known, example of a colossal class-action suit involved the Dalkon Shield, an intrauterine contraceptive device found to cause severe injury to a disproportionately large percentage of its users. As many as 20,000 women made claims against A.H. Robins, the manufacturer, mostly related to the device having caused pelvic inflammatory disease and loss of fertility. The massive number of claims in the Dalkon Shield case makes it one of the largest class-action lawsuits in United States history. It sparked a grass roots coalition of women who fought for justice against a company that was apparently aware of the possible harm resulting from the use of its product. A.H. Robins filed for bankruptcy protection because of the rising number of lawsuits filed against it. Eventually, a $2.4 billion trust fund was set aside to compensate for injuries caused by the birth control device, and nearly 100,000 women were notified of their options for collecting from the fund. Some Dalkon users were offered as little as $125 because they could not locate their medical record twenty years after the fact. Others were offered only $150,000 to compensate for miscarriages and infections that required removal of their reproductive organs. Meanwhile, the attorneys representing the class earned millions of dollars from handling all the lawsuits connected with the case.

In class-action cases, the court controls all notification, and requires the class-action attorneys to pay for the printing and mailing of the notices. If you receive a notice, read it carefully, as it contains the time limits for opting out of the class and for approving or not approving of a settlement, as well as other requirements. A typical case is one in which credit card holders are overcharged for their credit card usage. Since the amount of damages is negligible for each individual, they become a member of a class. For the most part, you should accept the offer to join a class unless your individual damages are much greater than what you would recover from participating in the class-action suit.

269

HELP! I'VE BEEN CHARGED WITH A CRIME

15

Up to this point, I have been primarily discussing civil cases, as opposed to cases falling under the criminal law system. A civil case involves a dispute between two people or more, or parties, on a particular issue in which one party sues the other(s). The judge or jury will determine liability, and the amount of damages. The court may require the party at fault to compensate the injured party, or to fulfill an obligation, such as abiding by the terms of a contract.

In contrast, under criminal law, the offense, or crime, is viewed as an act against society rather than an individual. Consequently, it is not the victim's responsibility to bring a criminal case against the perpetrator. Instead, a government prosecutor (representing the "People") will bring legal action against someone for the commission of a crime. If the defendant is found guilty, they might have to pay a fine, serve time in jail or prison, or be put on probation. Jail time, or incarceration, which entails the loss of one's personal freedom, is a more severe penalty than the monetary fines that result from civil cases. Since the stakes are so much higher in a criminal case than between the parties in a civil matter, there are a number of judicial safeguards in place to protect the rights of a defendant. These safeguards include the presumption of innocence, the right to an attorney, the right to be free from self incrimination, the right to compel witnesses to testify in their defense, and the right to cross-examine witnesses who testify against them. The burden of proof is much higher in criminal cases – the prosecution must prove the defendant's guilt beyond a reasonable doubt.

I have a lot of experience in criminal matters stemming from my work in the District Attorney's Office, and from my representation of defendants in criminal cases. I have handled all kinds of criminal cases, including murder, arson, insurance fraud, DUIs, rape, drug and white-collar cases. I even represented street-walkers on Sunset Boulevard. Those were fun.

As a criminal defense lawyer, my main goal was to create doubt about the guilt of the defendant in the minds of the jurors. The most important thing we can do for our clients in these matters is to plant the seeds of doubt that our clients committed the crime for which they are being prosecuted.

You might ask how I could possibly defend people accused of committing violent crimes like rape and murder. The only way our legal system can work is if every defendant, even those accused of the most heinous crimes, is given a fair trial. I looked at my role as that of ensuring that the prosecutors in these cases prove their burden that the defendant is guilty beyond a reasonable doubt. That being said, I must admit that years ago I gave up representing defendants who allegedly committed violent crimes. The turning point for me was the rape case *People v. Hughes*. The defendant had been accused of raping 20 women in the San Fernando Valley (of Los Angeles). I was retained for the preliminary hearing (held when a defendant pleads not guilty at the initial appearance). Since there was no jury present at this stage, the defendant, who was in custody, was handcuffed and shackled to a chair. As each victim took the stand to testify about what he had done to her, he would rattle the shackles and whisper in my ear, "She loved it," and even gave me a detailed description of the event. Obviously, he was held to answer in this case.

I went home that night and, despite my firm belief in the presumption of innocence, and the requirement that the prosecution prove its case, I was so upset by the experience with this despicable defendant that I decided I would stop defending those accused of violent crimes. Of course, I still believe every defendant deserves the best possible defense, but now my attitude is – let someone else do it. The lawyer who represents them does not have to be me.

A.   **I've Been Arrested – What Do I Do**?

A police officer approaches you in your car, or knocks on the door of your home and says, "You're under arrest." What should you do? First, be aware that you are only under arrest once a police officer takes you into custody, and you are not free to walk away from the arresting officer. If you are in custody, you have certain rights that must be explained to you before you can be questioned by law enforcement officials. If you have ever watched any television police dramas, you are probably already familiar with these rights, known as *Miranda Rights*. They are designed to protect a suspect's rights under the Fifth Amendment to the United States Constitution to be free from self-incrimination. You most likely have also heard on television courtroom dramas when someone in the witness box "pleads the Fifth," and refuses to answer a question.

The following Miranda rights must be read to you only if you are in police custody and under interrogation:

- You have the right to remain silent and to refuse to answer questions;
- Anything you say may be used against you in a court of law;
- You have the right to consult an attorney before speaking to the police and to have an attorney present during questioning now or in the future;
- If you cannot afford an attorney, one will be appointed for you before any questioning if you wish; and,

- If you decide to answer questions now without an attorney present, you will still have the right to stop answering at any time until you speak to an attorney.

Even if you are innocent of the crime for which you have been arrested, this predicament might just be your lot because of some wrongful conduct in your past. Remember, as I have noted previously, you might not see the connection between what is happening to you now and some earlier action for which you are now paying the price, because of the time that has passed between the events. These are the sort of uncomfortable and even painful situations in life that are often necessary to effect change. There is truth in the adage, *No pain, No gain*. You now have the opportunity to be proactive to do what you can to make amends between the period of your arrest and trial. If you send out the right signals, good energy will bounce back, if not necessarily immediately, it will eventually.

The police do not always need a warrant to stop someone and pat them down. A police officer may stop and detain you based on reasonable suspicion. If the police reasonably suspect that you are armed and dangerous, they may also frisk you for weapons and search your immediate surroundings to make sure you have no weapons, contraband, stolen goods, or evidence of a crime. The police can also search your car if they take possession of it.

B.   **Book 'Em**

After you have been arrested, you will be taken to the nearest police station and booked. Because the court consider booking to be an administrative process, your Miranda rights do not have to be read to you, and the police do not have to allow you to contact a lawyer until after the booking process is complete. Keep in mind though, that whatever you say about your case to the booking officer, can be used against you in court. The booking process can be prolonged and humiliating, and consequently, leaves suspects vulnerable to the power police officers wield over them, and might cause the suspect to start talking freely to the officers. As a suspect, you are well advised to only answer the booking officer's questions and to say nothing about your case. If you have information that you think will help your case, you should wait and tell it to your lawyer.

During booking, a police officer typically does the following:

- Takes the suspect's personal information, including name, date of birth and physical characteristics;
- Records information about the alleged crime;
- Performs a record search of the suspect's criminal background;
- Takes fingerprints and photographs and searches the suspect;
- Confiscates any personal property carried by the suspect, such as keys and wallets, to be returned upon the suspect's release; and,
- Places the suspect in a holding cell or local jail.

Also, sometimes the suspect will be required to provide a handwriting or DNA sample, and participate in a lineup. After your personal items are collected, an officer will ask you to sign an inventory of those items, which will be placed in safe-keeping until your release.

In many states (including California), as a suspect, you are permitted to make one or more free local phone calls as soon as booking is completed. This is your opportunity to call an attorney, a bail bondsman, and friends or relatives, so you can post bail, or at least hear a friendly voice. Be cautious about what you say over the phone, however, as police officers and others might overhear your conversations, or be monitoring the phones.

If you are being held, but not booked within a reasonable period of time, usually several hours or overnight, your attorney can seek a *writ of habeas corpus* from a judge. The writ is an order by the court instructing the police to bring you before the court in order for a judge to decide if you are being lawfully held.

C.   **I'm Stuck In Custody – When Will I Be Charged With A Crime**?

Arrests for crimes and prosecution are intentionally bifurcated to protect citizens against abuses of police power. Police officers make arrests based on probable cause that a crime has been committed. On the other hand, prosecutors file charges only if they are convinced that they can prove a suspect is guilty beyond a reasonable doubt.

Some crimes are obviously much more serious than others. Criminal activity runs the gamut from citations for traffic violations such as speeding, which usually result in a relatively small fine, all the way to murder and rape. Shoplifting, resisting arrest, simple battery, or public drunkenness, are all misdemeanors, and may carry a jail sentence of one year or less. The city attorney for the city in which the crime took place handles misdemeanors.

The most serious crimes are felonies, and they include robbery, kidnapping, rape and murder, and carry a maximum sentence of more than one year. The District Attorney's Office will prosecute felony cases. If the crime is a matter of federal law (i.e., laws created by Congress), the United States Attorney's Office will prosecute on behalf of the United States. Examples of federal crimes include the sale and distribution of narcotics, bank robberies, fraudulent dealings that impact interstate commerce, wire fraud, mail fraud, tax fraud, or any crime in which the United States is defrauded, gun law violations, environmental crimes and civil rights violations. These cases are heard in federal courthouses throughout the country. For cases arising under state law (i.e., laws created by state legislatures), state and local prosecutors will bring suit. States prosecute a far greater number of cases than does the federal government.

Charging you with a crime is at the discretion of the prosecutor, who can base their decision on the totality of the circumstances, including your past criminal records. (Remember my reference in the introduction to the *Groundhog Day* effect? Are you engaging in the same negative behavior repeatedly)? However, prosecutors charging decisions are primarily centered on the police, or arrest report given or sent to them by the arresting police officers. The prosecutor will review the arrest report, which generally contains a summary of the occurrences leading up to the arrest, details such as the weather conditions, dates, specific times, locations and witnesses' names and addresses. Based on the arrest report, prosecutors can decide to file charges on all the crimes for which the officers arrested a suspect, they can file charges more or less severe than what the police leveled, or they can opt not to file any charges. The arrest reports also often play a critical role in how much bail is imposed, the outcome of preliminary hearings, and whether or not the prosecutor will be amenable to plea-bargaining. Keep in mind, however, that police reports are one-sided, and because they are considered to be hearsay, they are usually not admissible at trial.

If you have been arrested for a serious felony, a prosecutor might seek the assistance of a grand jury to review all the information, and determine whether to bring criminal charges, or an indictment (a formal accusation initiating a criminal case, presented by a grand jury and often required for felonies and other serious crimes) against you. The grand jury sometimes replaces the preliminary hearing as a method by which criminal charges can be filed. A grand jury is comprised of a panel of private citizens, chosen in a similar manner to juries. Their job is to consider the evidence presented by the prosecutor and decide whether there is probable cause to believe a crime was committed, and if the defendant committed it. The grand jury can even issue subpoenas to compel witnesses to testify or to produce documents and other evidence.

When you are in custody, you have the right to a speedy trial, meaning that the prosecutor must typically decide within 72-hours what to charge you with. In California, the decision must be made within 48-hours after you are taken into custody. The prosecutor is not bound by the initial charges, however, and once additional evidence is available, can change the crimes with which you are charged.

Given that most head prosecutors are elected officials who might have their sights set on higher office, often their decisions on what charges to file are influenced by public opinion, and what they think will help advance their careers. For example, a district attorney might choose to prosecute every shoplifting case, no matter how weak, in order to appeal to the abundance of shopkeepers in his or her district. I tell you this to impress upon you the importance of securing a lawyer to represent you in these criminal proceedings. Defense lawyers with experience will know what motivates prosecutors who must sometimes be seen by the public as taking a hard stance on certain cases, even though a prosecutor might be willing to negotiate later on in the process. Only experienced defense attorneys will understand how to navigate this landscape.

D. **Finding An Attorney**

Defendants in criminal cases, who face the possibility of going to jail if convicted, have a constitutional right to counsel. As I emphasized with regard to civil suits, it is in your best interests to find a good attorney, or if you cannot afford one, to allow the court to appoint one for you. Government appointed attorneys – public defenders – are charged with zealously defending a criminal defendant's rights. If you have the financial wherewithal, however, you should engage an experienced criminal defense attorney. Where do you find one? First, you should seek a referral from a relative or friend. If they do not know of any criminal defense lawyers, you might ask the bail bondsman for a recommendation. Also, you should be aware that there are usually lawyers waiting around the jailhouse seeking clients to represent.

If you are a suspect and have been arrested, charged with a crime, and taken to jail, you will be given a form to complete regarding your income. If you have the means to pay a lawyer, you will not be given a court appointed attorney.

E.   I've Been Arrested For Drinking And Driving – What Do I Do?

Since so many cases involve DUIs (Driving Under the Influence), DWIs (Driving While Intoxicated) and OUIs (Operating Under the Influence), I thought it would be helpful to have a separate section devoted to this subject. These terms cannot always be used interchangeably. They refer to different offenses depending on the state. For example, in some states, a DUI only refers to driving under the influence of certain drugs, while DWI refers to driving under the influence of alcohol. In California, you can be charged with DUI when you have a concentration of .08 percent, or more alcohol in your blood system. This is the standard measurement used in every state to determine whether you are considered an "impaired" driver.

By the way, you can get a DWI when driving vehicles other than cars and trucks, including ATVs, golf carts, and even bicycles. Obviously, combining drinking, taking drugs, or certain medications, with driving is never a good idea, but what happens when you get pulled over because an officer suspects you of driving under the influence? How should you respond if drinking was not necessarily the cause of your erratic driving? If a police officer suspects you of driving under the influence, they will require you to pull over to the side of the road, will ask you to step out of the car, and will likely administer three standardized field sobriety tests to you. One test is the horizontal gaze test. You have seen this one in movies and public service announcements. The officer will have you watch a pen or flashlight as he or she moves it slowly back and forth. The officer will be watching for jerkiness in the way your eyes track the object. This involuntary shaking is called nystagmus and usually only happens at the extremes of someone's periphery vision. However, for an intoxicated person, this shaking can occur within 45 degrees of the center. If you failed this test, you probably have a blood alcohol content (BAC) of .08 or greater, which is the legal limit, but there are so many other causes of nystagmus, most of which have nothing to do with drinking. Some people's eyes simply behave that way, and that is unfortunate for you if you get stopped for DUI.

Then there is the walk and turn, or "divided attention" test. With this test, the officer gives you multiple instructions, telling you to walk a straight line while looking down and counting out loud, and then pivoting, and going back the other way. It is hard to keep your balance and follow multiple instructions if your brain is impaired by alcohol.

Finally, there is the one leg stand test. This is another divided attention test to make sure you do not fall flat on your face. You will be told to stand on one foot with the other about six inches above the ground, while counting out loud. The officer will be looking for swaying and other balance problems. You might find yourself subjected to some other field test. These may include bringing your index finger to your nose, touching the tip of each finger with your thumb while counting after each tap, hand clapping and counting backwards.

Evaluation of these tests is purely subjective. If the officer thinks you are drunk, it will be his or her word against yours. You can refuse to take these tests, but that might result in your being arrested. At the very least, the officer can testify in court about your refusal.

What about the chemical tests – blood, breath and urine? Do you have to take these? There are implied consent laws in every state that contend that simply by driving on the roads, you are agreeing to take a chemical test to determine your BAC. These tests are given at the police station or at a clinic. The police will usually give you the option of which test to take – breath, urine or blood. You must take a chemical test, although the specifics of which test you must take and when it must be given, vary from state to state. In some states, a chemical test must be given within a certain period of time, usually within a few hours of when you were driving. However, even if you took the test outside of the specified time frame, and cannot be charged with having a BAC over .08, you might still be found guilty of a DUI, based on the officer's observations of your impairment and driving. By refusing to take the test, you run the risk of severe penalties, possibly worse than if you were found guilty as a result of the test. The penalties vary from state to state, and can include a combination of jail time, a fine, and suspension of your license and, as with the sobriety field tests, when your case goes to court, the prosecution can use your refusal against you to prove that you refused to take the test because you knew you were intoxicated and would fail to pass. Generally, it is not beneficial to you to refuse to take a chemical test. You should know that you can be charged with a DUI, even if you are pulled over for some other reason than erratic driving if your BAC is .08 or higher. Some states assume that any amount of alcohol or certain drugs in the bloodstream constitutes impairment. If you have been drinking, it could benefit you to allow some time to pass before taking the test.

In California, you must take a breath, urine or blood

test if you are lawfully arrested by an officer, who has probable cause to believe that you have been driving under the influence of alcohol or drugs, legal or illegal. The test must be given at the time of your arrest, and you should be given the choice of a blood, urine or breath test. In the field, you will be asked to take a preliminary breath test, even if you have not been arrested. The breath test requires you to blow into a small machine called a Breathalyzer. The officer can use the results of this test to show probable cause that you were driving under the influence. You do not have to take the preliminary test, but if you refuse, and the officer has some other reason for suspecting you of drinking and driving, he or she could still arrest you. It does not trigger an automatic suspension of your license as does a refusal to take a breath, urine or blood test after an arrest. If you are arrested, the officer should tell you that if you refuse to take a chemical test, you will be fined, will lose your license, and you could be sent to jail if you are later convicted of a DUI. In California, the penalty for refusing to take the blood, breath or urine test begins with a one-year suspension of your license.

What if you have been stopped for impaired driving, and you have not been drinking, but rather you have been smoking marijuana, or perhaps have some other drug in your system? Is there a test for detecting substances other than alcohol in your system? As of this writing, state officials have proposed using new technology to catch the increasing number of motorists who are driving while high on drugs. The newly introduced legislation in California would allow law enforcement officers to use oral swab tests to strengthen a case when there is probable cause that a driver is impaired, and the driver has failed sobriety field tests. The new technology is a hand-held device to test the oral swab for the presence of marijuana, cocaine, amphetamines and pain medications, including opiates. There are currently test programs around the country in which oral swabs are used to detect drugs in place of the more complicated blood and urine test.

The first time you get a DUI, it will probably be charged as a misdemeanor and not a felony. However, even first time DUIs can become felonies if you kill or severely injure someone while driving under the influence. It can also become a felony if you have a particularly high BAC, or if your license was restricted, suspended, or revoked before you drove while intoxicated. Also, in some states, your third or fourth DUI can turn into a felony charge even if no one was harmed.

If you are charged with a DUI, in all likelihood, your driver's license will be suspended. How will you get home, you might wonder? The officer will probably take you in a police car to the station and you will have to leave your car where it was when you were stopped. Your driver's license will be confiscated at the station, and there you will be given the choice of which chemical test to take. It is generally best to choose the breath test, because you will get the results immediately, unlike with the blood and urine tests in which there could be a delay analyzing them at the lab. The longer the delay, the more likely it is that you will have to spend time in jail. It is also advisable to choose the breathalyzer given that there is a defense that can be raised against the results – gum or candy can affect the BAC reading.

At your arraignment, you can request a temporary driver's license from the judge, or a restricted license to allow you to drive to and from work or school. Generally, the requests are granted in the form of a recommendation to the Department of Motor Vehicles, which the DMV routinely follows. The DMV will send you a written notice that your license has been suspended or revoked. You can request a hearing before the DMV. If you successfully plead your case at the hearing, they might return your license to you, but the chances of them doing so are about the same as you winning the lottery. Of course, if you fail to make a convincing case, your license will probably be suspended for a period of time. The length of time depends on factors such as your BAC, and if you have any prior DUIs on your record. Remember, if you refuse to give a blood, breath or urine sample at the time of your arrest, your driver's license will be automatically suspended, and this is the case even if you are not convicted of a DUI.

How can you get your driver's license back? The most common way is by completing an educational or therapeutic treatment program. Many states have passed "habitual offender" laws, which means that if you have been convicted of multiple DUIs, you could lose your license for years, or maybe permanently. If this is not your first DUI offense, you might be penalized by having to install an Ignition Interlock device in your car. This device prevents drivers from starting their cars if their BAC is to high. You might also be penalized with a fine, jail time, and probation. Once your DUI conviction is official, it will remain on your record, and thus show up on any background checks that potential employers might run. If you are convicted of a second and third DUI, prior convictions will likely affect your sentencing, even if they occurred many years before.

Another possible way to regain your license from the DMV is to file with the Superior Court a petition for a writ of mandate to compel the DMV to restore your license, or you can file a writ of prohibition to prevent the DMV from suspending or revoking your license. These measures are rarely successful. You would need to show an abuse of discretion on the part of the DMV, a very difficult burden to meet.

After you are arrested for a DUI (or DWI or OUI), the next step is to go to court for an arraignment. That is where you will be formally charged with a crime and you must respond with a guilty or not guilty plea. You can obtain a form from the court called, "DUI Advisement of Rights, Waiver and Plea Form," also known as a "Tahl Waiver," a copy of which is in the Appendices. The form contains standard terms, conditions and an indicated sentence for DUIs. In other words, an account of what you can expect to happen. Of course, there may be variables, which could change some of the terms. Especially if this is your first offense, in some counties, a plea bargain could reduce your charge to reckless driving (often defined as a mental state in which the driver displays a wanton disregard for the rules of the road. It is a major moving traffic violation), depending on the test results. Not all counties will allow this kind of plea.

Although reckless driving is a serious offense, it carries a much less severe penalty than a DUI conviction. Both reckless driving and DUI charges can result in jail time, but the time that must be served is much less for reckless driving. It can be anywhere from no jail time to a few days in jail, as opposed to a DUI, which can land you in jail for up to a year. In addition, drivers arrested for a DUI typically must spend at least a few hours in jail after an arrest, while drivers charged with reckless driving, may simply be ticketed and allowed to drive home. Also, the license is usually not restricted or revoked in reckless driving case, as it is in DUIs. Reckless driving with a BAC lower than .08 is called a "wet reckless." The penalty is the same as reckless driving.

At this point, you should ask yourself if you need a lawyer. The answer is maybe yes, maybe no. Ask yourself, "Can a lawyer do something for me under these circumstances that I can't do for myself?"

Do not pay heed to attorneys who advertise, "Friends don't let friends plead guilty." This is nonsense. It is very difficult to win cases in which either the breathalyzer or blood and urine tests indicate a blood alcohol level of over .08. The form for indicated sentences applies whether you have an attorney or not. While the form looks complicated, it really isn't. Most of the provisions deal with waivers of constitutional rights or subjects not germane to your case. In most cases, there will be probationary conditions. Usually, you would be on probation for 36 months (with no requirement that you report to a probation officer). If you violate any of the probationary terms, or are caught driving on a suspended license, it is essential that you hire an experienced criminal lawyer. It is possible to have probation revoked and then reinstated with additional terms, such as community service. A good lawyer might be able to accomplish this for you. Before you engage one of those lawyers who advertise, and imply that they can do better than you can, I suggest you ask the following questions:

1. What is the basis for the fee? Many of these firms who advertise will make a "motion to suppress evidence," or seek a dismissal based on the nature of the police stop, before any testing was administered. Most of the time, these motions go nowhere. The motions are "boilerplate," meaning the identically worded motion is used repeatedly with only the names, times and dates changed to fit the particular case. Only if your facts fit neatly into the boilerplate motion does it made sense to file one, but for the most part, you will spend thousands of dollars on what will most likely turn out to be worthless motions. Ask the lawyer what they are going to do for you (besides filing useless motions) for the fee they charge. Does it include a trial, if necessary, with a competent and experienced trial lawyer? Who is that lawyer? Take a look at their resume. Many of the firms who advertise farm out the cases to local firms who pay them a referral fee. The advertising lawyer does not do the legal work. You need to know who is going to appear at the arraignment, and speak to the city attorney or district attorney on your behalf. What kind of reputation does the attorney have?

2. Ask what defenses the attorney will raise to the DUI and driving with a BAC of .08 charges. In order to prevail, you will need to create a reasonable doubt in the mind of at least one juror. You will need an expert to attack the accuracy of the equipment used in the testing and question the numerical results. The prosecutor will have their experts. Be prepared to spend a lot of money on your experts, thousands a day, probably.

3.   Ask the attorney to analyze the significance of the test you took. If your BAC is more than .08, it is not going to make much of a difference unless you go to trial and convince at least one juror that the reading of the chemical test was wrong. The indicated sentence is on the form included in the Appendices. If the attorneys say your results will make no difference as to whether or not you are convicted, you should ask him or her what they are going to do about this damaging test reading.

4.   Ask the lawyer about their success rate with the DMV. In most cases, the penalty for DUI is statutory, and there is no way around it. Suspension of your driver's license might be determined by statute, and a lawyer will not be able to do anything about that.

5.   Ask the lawyer what they expect will happen with the DMV. If they tell you that there is a good chance they can get your license suspension reversed, ask what they base this belief on. Often, they will tell you whatever they think will get you to hire them. What do they intend to do for you? You are not asking for a guarantee, just what the possible, or likely outcomes are, if the attorney gets involved.

Listen to the lawyer's promises, and then follow your gut. Do you believe what they are telling you? If not, you should look elsewhere for a lawyer. The prosecutor will talk to you, and you might be able to work out something on your own with him or her, that is acceptable to you. The prosecutor pretty much follows the standard form that has the penalties spelled out.

If you choose to fight the charges, you will go to trial. At a trial, you or your attorney will have to argue that the breathalyzer is not an accurate barometer of your BAC, or that the machine was not calibrated properly. Your lawyer might even bring in an expert on this subject. Today, there is a cottage industry of doctors and other experts who will testify about the factors that make the reading of these Breathalyzers inaccurate. As well, your attorney can argue that your driving was fine, and that you only had one drink. It is best i your attorney can bring in witnesses to attest to this fact. As an example, I defended a DUI in which my client contende l that she only had one glass of wine to drink, and had been d iving perfectly fine. She had been out with two friends, wh each had one glass of wine. We brought in her passengers whc testified that they each had one glass of wine, and that my c ient's driving was fine. We also introduced a receipt from t e bar showing the sale of three glasses of wine.

In another case, my client was charged with a D JI because he failed the field sobriety test of walking in a st aight line. My client had custom made shoes to help him w :h his balancing problems. In a dramatic gesture, I set his shoe n top of the jury rail for the jurors to see that the shoes wei ? specially made. I then pointed out that my client could no walk a straight line under any circumstances. It was enough o create doubt in the minds of the jurors and we won the case

If you get caught driving intoxicated, consider hat it was meant to happen. Could it be that by getting st pped, your life was spared, or perhaps, you were saved froi des- troying an innocent life? Before you decide to fight th DUI, or after you have fought the charges and lost, conside why this has happened to you. Is this your opportunity to c eanse yourself so that in the future your life will not be p gued by chaos? Although you may have lost the case, in the grand scheme of things, you have actually won. You have mo d to- wards the light, and away from negativity and the dema ids of the ego.

F.   How Can I Get Out Of This Jail? – Posting I ail

If you are arrested for a minor offense, you night merely be given a written citation, and released after s gning the citation and promising to appear in court at a late date. If you are arrested for a serious crime, in all likelihoo , you will only be released from custody by providing some ort of assurance that you will show up in court for all hearings and for the trial. To this end, the district attorney will either recommend that bail be set to make sure you will appear, or that you be kept in custody with no opportunity to post bail. Bail is security in the form of a sum of money that is exchanged for the release of an arrested person as a guarantee of that person's appearance for trial. If you can demonstrate that you are not a flight risk, and you have substantial contacts (i.e., a job, family, etc.) in the community that will keep you in the area, the court may release you on your own recognizance. You will try to make your case for being released on your own recognizance, or having a bail amount set, to the duty judge (the judge on duty when you are arrested). The judge sets your bail amount and, in many jurisdictions, there is a preset schedule listing the bail amounts for particular crimes. Other times, bail is determined on a case-by-case basis. The Eighth Amendment to the United States Constitution states that excessive bail shall not be required.

Defendants who are not released on their own recognizance, but want to get out of jail, will have to post bail. Once you post the requisite amount of bail in cash with the court, you will be released from custody. If you fail to appear in court on the mandated date and time, however, you forfeit the money to the court, and the court can issue a warrant for your arrest. If you do not have sufficient cash to post the entire bail, the court will accept something called a bail bond. A bail bond is a promise by an insurance company that the company will pay the full amount of the bail if the defendant fails to show up for court proceedings.

The insurance company, through a bail bond agency, will charge a premium for posting the bond. For example, if the court sets your bail at $10,000, the insurance company could charge $1,000, a 10% premium, to post the bond on your behalf. The insurance company will require a guarantor to sign for the bond. The guarantor will agree to pay the insurance company the $10,000 if you, as the accused, do not show up. If you appear at trial, the court will return the insurance company's bond (called "exoneration"), and the company will keep the $1,000 premium for posting the bond. If you flee, however, the insurance company forfeits the $10,000 it posted with the court, and will require the guarantor to reimburse the insurer for that amount. The company might also engage bounty hunters to locate the defendant, and bring him or her to court. If you are familiar with the former reality TV show, *Dog, The Bounty Hunter*, you will have a picture of what bounty hunters do. Duane, "Dog," the bounty hunter, along with his wife, pursued all kinds of fugitives, which often entailed sitting in his car, waiting for the hunted person to come out of some sleazy motel or bar. If the bounty hunters are successful in locating and bringing in the defendant, the company's bond will be returned. You will want to find a bail bondsman who is local and close to the jailhouse.

With particularly heinous crimes, or where the defendant will most likely flee the jurisdiction, or possibly harm members of the public, bail may be denied altogether, and the defendant will be kept in jail as a pre-trial detainee. You might also be labeled a pre-trial detainee if you are unable to post bail for your release.

Recently, California passed legislation (effective October 1, 2019) that eliminates the posting of bail with a judge determining the outcome for release without bail. If you are arrested before October 1, you can still pitch the judge to apply the new law.

G. Now What? The Arraignment

The first stage of the courtroom proceedings is called the arraignment. In some states, arraignments are only required in felony cases. During a typical arraignment, a person who is charged with a crime is called before a criminal court judge. At the arraignment, the judge does the following

- Reads the criminal charges against the

defendant;

- Asks the defendant if they have legal counsel, or need the assistance of a court appointed attorney;
- Asks the defendant how he or she answers, or pleads to, the charges – does the defendant plead "guilty," "not guilty," or "no contest?"
- Decides whether to change the amount of bail, or to release the defendant on their own recognizance; and,
- Announces the dates of upcoming proceedings in the case, such as the preliminary hearing, (felonies), pre-trial motions, and the actual trial.

A plea of no contest (*nolo contendere*) means that you do not contest the charges made against you. This type of plea is often part of a plea bargain with the prosecutor. It results in a criminal conviction just like a guilty plea, and will appear on a criminal record. However, if the victim of the crime later sues the defendant in civil court, the no contest plea cannot be offered into evidence against the defendant as an admission of guilt. On the other hand, a plea of guilty can be used in civil cases as evidence of the defendant's guilt. A judge only accepts a *nolo contendere* plea if they feel that it is made voluntarily and intelligently. Even at this stage, it is still possible for the defense to reach an agreement with the prosecutor.

H.   **Plea Bargaining**

The settlement of the case can occur at any time, from the very first court appearance at the initial arraignment up to, and even, during the trial. Guilty pleas are frequently the result of negotiations between the defense attorney and the prosecutor. The process of negotiating is called *plea bargaining*, and the agreement itself is called a *plea agreement* or *plea bargain*. In the plea bargain, the defendant, through their attorney, agrees to plead guilty to some, or all of the charges against them. In exchange for certain assurances from the prosecutor. Sometimes the prosecutor agrees to dismiss one or more of the charges, or consents to make a recommendation to the judge about the sentence to be imposed, or agrees not to object to a sentence proposed by the defense attorney. This agreement is binding on the government (as represented by the prosecutor).

A common strategy used by prosecutors is to "overcharge" a defendant in order to ultimately get the conviction they are hoping for. Why do prosecutors overcharge those accused of a crime? Overcharging gives them leverage. They have to regularly move a large volume of cases through the court system, and can accomplish this through plea-bargaining, as described above. Prosecutors will often file a felony charge, when a misdemeanor charge is more appropriate. This happens especially with what is known as "wobblers," those crimes that could be charged as either a misdemeanor or a felony. A felony has far more serious consequences, and can land a defendant in state prison, as opposed to county jail (for a misdemeanor). Defendants are often motivated to plead out these cases as quickly as possible for fear of being incarcerated in state prison. An example is when a prosecutor is convinced that there is a reasonable likelihood of obtaining a conviction for petty theft, a misdemeanor, so he or she chooses to charge the defendant with burglary, a felony. The prosecutor does so, knowing that the defendant will be willing to plead guilty to the lesser offense of petty theft, which should have been charged in the first place! Also, the prosecutor might threaten the defendant with a trial, in which case the defendant runs the risk of losing, and suffering a lengthier sentence than the prosecutor is offering in a plea bargain.

Another advantage for the prosecutor in overcharging defendants, has to do with bail. Generally, bail is established by a bail schedule, based on the seriousness of the offense.

When the bail is set artificially high, because the prosecutor has overcharged, it is more difficult for the families to bail out their incarcerated loved ones. If a defendant is stuck in jail while his or her case is pending, there is greater pressure on the defendant to plead guilty quickly if it means being released from custody, and possibly receiving a lesser sentence, or even probation.

I had a case in which my client was charged with murder for accidentally shooting his best friend. After some negotiations with the prosecutor, my client ended up pleading to an *involuntary manslaughter* charge (this charge usually refers to an unintentional killing resulting from recklessness or criminal negligence, or from an unlawful act that is a misdemeanor or low-level felony, such as DUI). My client got no jail time and was put on probation. The evidence is often overwhelming against a criminal defendant, so sometimes the best they can hope for is to negotiate the amount of time they will have to serve. Also, the defendant can put in a request for where they want to be incarcerated.

As a component of the plea agreement, the defendant may agree to testify about crimes about which they have knowledge. Thus, a prosecutor may use the plea bargain to secure the testimony of a minor player in a crime in order to convict a more significant criminal.

The guilty plea is made before a judge with a court reporter taking down everything that is said in the proceeding. If you are the defendant entering a guilty plea, be aware that the judge will question you about your plea. Before the judge accepts the guilty plea, they will ask you in open court if you are pleading guilty voluntarily, if you understand your right to plead "not guilty," and to demand a trial, if you understand the terms of the plea agreement and the consequences of the guilty plea. The judge will also question you to determine whether you have been coerced by the prosecutor into entering the plea, and whether there is a factual basis for the plea. If the judge is not satisfied by your responses to the questions, the judge will reject the guilty plea.

In certain felony cases involving non-violent drug offenses, a different type of settlement might be possible. Defendants charged with first-time drug offenses, and defendants who suffer from drug addiction, may be eligible to attend classes, or other rehabilitation programs. If they successfully complete all the required programs, they can have their case dismissed through something called "Deferred Entry of Judgment" (DEJ) or drug diversion. Some defendants who commit these types of non-violent drug possession offenses may be eligible for long-term drug treatment instead of incarceration.

I. <u>Next Stop – The Preliminary Hearing</u>

When a criminal complaint is filed, other than for misdemeanors, the defendant has the right to a preliminary hearing. Preliminary hearings are held only in cases in which the defendant pleads not guilty at the arraignment or initial appearance. However, if the prosecution obtains an indictment from a grand jury before the date of the preliminary hearing, the need for a preliminary hearing is moot. The primary purpose of the preliminary hearing is to weed out charges that are clearly groundless to save defendants the anxiety and expense of having to defend themselves at a trial against unwarranted accusations. The hearing typically takes place shortly after the charges are officially filed against the defendant. The judge, defendant, defendant's attorney, the prosecutor, and any witnesses and victims subpoenaed, will be at the hearing. It is sort of a mini trial in which testimony is taken under oath and the prosecution must satisfy a judge that there is probable cause to believe a crime has been committed, and that the defendant committed that crime. It is a slight burden to meet. Prosecutors usually present just enough evidence to convince the judge that there is probable cause to hold the defendant for trial. The prosecution can offer testimony from

FROM THE TRENCH TO THE BENCH

witnesses, and can even introduce case-related evidence, such as a weapon. The defense has the right, and most often will, cross-examine the prosecution witnesses to learn what they will be testifying to, and to gauge their demeanor. However, if the judge believes that defense counsel is simply trying to obtain discovery of the prosecutor's case (which is precisely what I would try to do as the defense attorney), through cross-examination of the government's witnesses, the judge can cut off the cross-examination. After the prosecution has completed its presentation, the defense has the right to put on its own case, but is not required to do so, and generally doesn't. The defendant can waive the preliminary hearing altogether and, if so, the case is usually scheduled for another arraignment and trial.

Why would a defendant waive their right to a preliminary hearing? They might wish to avoid the adverse publicity associated with a public airing of the evidence or, perhaps, they might be concerned that once the prosecution begins mounting the evidence to present at the hearing, the prosecution might realize that the initial charges filed against the defendant are too light. Also, defense counsel might advise the defendant to waive their right to the preliminary hearing to avoid having to reveal their evidence, or defense strategy before the trial.

I use the hearing as an opportunity to discover what the People's case is all about. Defense counsel receives a copy of the police report and any other documents relevant to the case, so we have advance notice of what will be presented at the trial. For example, in a DUI, or drug possession case, the prosecutor will supply the defense with lab reports or blood or chemical tests that were performed and may be used in the case. The prosecution often must reveal the identities of their key witnesses, and the nature of their testimony, information that can be of great value in preparing the defense. A possible outcome of the preliminary hearing for the defendant is that they might recognize for the first time the strength of the prosecution's case, and be propelled to seek a plea bargain.

One important difference between preliminary hearings and trials is that hearsay evidence is frequently admissible in preliminary hearings. In California, for instance, in preliminary hearings, the hearsay rule is not applied, so the police officers can testify as to what others have said to them. Since, as defense lawyers, we can discover the identity of the witnesses to the crime from the police report, we can subpoena the witnesses and elicit their testimony at the preliminary hearing. I have gotten valuable testimony in this way that I later used to impeach the witness's testimony at trial.

Once the preliminary hearing concludes, if probable cause is found, the defendant is "held to answer," meaning they are held for a trial before a jury. If the judge decides that probable cause has not been established, the court dismisses the case, and the defendant is released. In some cases, the prosecutor can later file another complaint against the defendant, based on the same crime. At any time, the prosecutor may decide to voluntarily dismiss the charges (this is called *nolle prosequi*, a Latin phrase meaning "be unwilling to pursue"). The vast majority of preliminary hearings conclude with the defendant being held to answer.

J.   **What Happens After The Preliminary Hearing?**

After the defendant is bound over for trial, the prosecution will probably file an information (a sworn written statement charging that an individual has engaged in a criminal act). The difference between an information and an indictment is that the latter is presented by a grand jury, while an information is presented by a duly authorized public official such as a public prosecutor.

Defendants out on bail typically remain free following the preliminary hearing, but must appear in court at the next scheduled hearing. Defendants, who are still in custody, stay in jail awaiting their next court appearance. They can, however, renew their request for bail, or reduced bail at the preliminary hearing. A judge at the preliminary hearing might grant bail if the actual facts presented at the hearing convince them that the defendant is less dangerous, or less of a flight risk, than the police report had indicated.

Depending upon the seriousness of the crime and the jurisdiction, the case will proceed in one of three ways:

- The defendant is arraigned a second time before a higher-tier court (at this juncture, lots of deals are made);
- The parties begin plea negotiations (which can be done at the initial arraignment), or they begin a trial in the court that conducted the preliminary hearing; or,
- The judge will set a date for either a pretrial conference, a trial, or both.

K.   **Pretrial Hearing And Motions**

The next phase of the criminal case involves the lawyers filing motions and probably engaging in a pretrial conference. If you are the defendant, your attorney may make various motions in order to get your case dismissed on legal grounds, such as a motion to have certain evidence thrown out of court because the police acted improperly when seizing this evidence. This is known as *the fruit of the poisonous tree.* Your attorney might also make a motion to compel the district attorney, or the police, to disclose other pieces of evidence, which could exonerate you.

The pretrial hearing or conference (pretrial conference and pretrial hearing are generally used interchangeably) is a meeting of the parties to an action, along with their attorneys, held before the court, prior to the beginning of the actual courtroom proceedings. It may be requested by a party to the case, or ordered by the court. The reasons for conducting a pretrial conference are as follows:

- To expedite disposition of the case;
- To help the court manage the case;
- To discourage time-wasting pretrial activities;
- To improve the quality of the trial through thorough preparation; and,
- To facilitate a settlement of the case.

Pretrial conferences do not delve into the guilt or innocence of the defendant, however, attempts to settle or plea-bargain often take place at these conferences.

The pretrial hearing is an excellent time to put into practice the spiritual principles that I have referred to throughout this book. Actually, any moment in time is the appropriate time to incorporate spirituality into your life. It is not too late to set aside your ego and think long and hard about why you are being prosecuted. If you were in the wrong, maybe it is time to acknowledge what you have done, accept your punishment, and try to do the right thing going forward. Even if you are innocent of the crime, by having to defend yourself, perhaps you are now paying the price for some past misconduct. This should encourage us to embrace rather than avoid problems and obstacles. In essence, they are opportunities for transforming our lives and growing in a positive direction. If our primary goal in life is to seek light and goodness (i.e., reach a higher spiritual plane), we need to understand that light will be found when we traverse the difficult challenges in our lives. It will be found in the situations that are out of our comfort zones. Being a defendant in a criminal case is certainly one of those situations.

Maybe, at this point, before going to trial, you need to carefully consider that a plea agreement might be your best option, that whatever happens is meant to happen. If you have done something wrong, and insist on a full-blown trial, you risk an unfavorable outcome. If you can negotiate a settlement, you probably should because whatever the terms of that settlement are, at least you know that your punishment could have been worse. Remember, everything happens for a reason.

Pretrial conferences in criminal cases are used to determine matters such as what evidence will be excluded from trial, which witnesses will be permitted to testify, what the specific issues in the case are, schedules for the submission of pretrial briefs and motions and rulings on motions submitted before the conference. Pretrial conferences save valuable time for the courts and jurors by narrowing the focus of the trial, and resolving preliminary matters. As well, they establish the court's ability to fairly and impartially administer justice by facilitating discovery and reducing the element of surprise at trial. Once the conference is concluded, the judge issues an order reflecting the results of the conference. This order will control the future course of the case.

L.   **A Jury Of Your Peers**

It is time for the trial to begin, but first a jury must be selected. To learn more about the process of jury selection, take a look at chapter 5. In both civil and criminal cases, the jury is chosen from a list called a *venire* or jury pool that has been compiled by the court. Different states have different methods of compiling names for the jury pool. In some states, including California, the list is derived from voter registrations or driver's license records. Most states require that a court official screens the list of names of potential jurors to eliminate those who are unqualified or ineligible under state law. Some factors that would result in disqualification for jury service are: The person is not a United States citizen; the person is under the age of 18; the person is not a resident of the jurisdiction in which the trial will take place; or, the person has been convicted of a felony.

An adult criminal defendant has the right to a trial by jury. The twelve jurors are called "the finders of fact." They must listen to all the evidence presented by both the prosecution and the defense, and determine if the prosecution has proven the defendant's guilt beyond a reasonable doubt. All twelve jurors must agree in order to either convict or acquit. If the jury cannot agree, a mistrial will be declared by the court, and the case may be tried again before a different jury, it may be dismissed, or the prosecutor and defendant can agree to a plea bargain to a lesser charge.

Aside from when the jurors cannot agree on a verdict, there are other reasons for a court to declare a mistrial. Anything improper or unfair that occurs during a trial that cannot be cured, is grounds for a mistrial. The only remedy is the opportunity to start over. Attorney misconduct can lead to a mistrial. For instance, an attorney offers a document into evidence, knowing full well that it is not admissible, but does it anyway in order to get the information before the jury, is grounds for a mistrial. Having been exposed to this document, it is impossible for the jurors to wipe it out of their minds. Once you ring the bell, it cannot be un-rung.

M.   **The Main Event – The Trial**

Although a trial is the most high-profile phase of the criminal justice process, most criminal cases are resolved long before trial – either through guilty or no contest pleas, plea bargains, or dismissal of the charges. If you, as the defendant, have not reached a plea agreement, and jury selection has been completed, it is time for the main event – the trial. Aside from jury selection, the trial consists of the following elements: Opening statements by the prosecution and the defense, witness testimony and cross-examination, closing arguments, jury instructions and, finally, jury deliberation, rending of a verdict, and sentencing if there was a conviction.

1.   Opening Statements

Will the opening statements make any difference in your trial? There was a study done by the University of Chicago concluding that 90% of juries decide the cases they hear after the opening statement. The prosecution will make the first opening statement, followed by the defense. The attorneys cannot introduce evidence during their opening statements. However, they are permitted to offer a preview of coming attractions. The statement usually contains the following phrase: "The evidence will show..." If at all possible, your attorney should avoid giving their opening statement just before or immediately after lunch, or at the end of the day. Before lunch, jurors will be hungry and watching the clock for their lunch break. After lunch, they will be ready to snooze. At the end of the day, they will likely be thinking, "When can we get out of here and go home?"

2.   Presenting Evidence

Next, the prosecution and the defense each have a turn to present evidence and call witnesses before a judge and the twelve members of the jury. The order of how the evidence is presented, and when the witnesses are called are tactical decisions on the part of your attorney, and should be discussed with you. The judge's task is to ensure that the prosecution and the defense adhere to all the rules of evidence when presenting their case to the jury. Just as in civil cases, witnesses will testify, some of whom might be called to the stand as experts on some aspect of the case, there will be cross-examination of them by the other side, and physical evidence, such as a weapon used in the commission of the crime, can be introduced.

If you are the defendant, should you testify in your criminal trial? Criminal defense attorneys will generally advise against defendants testifying on their own behalf. There are a number of reasons for this. For one thing, if you are too adamant in professing your innocence, you might not be believable to the jury. Maybe you are familiar with the line from *Hamlet*, "The lady doth protest too much, methinks!" The line basically suggests that when a speaker asserts something too frequently and fervently, they might make themselves appear defensive and insincere. Also, the jurors might think you are lying if you do not make eye contact with them, or you make too much eye contact, or you seem too nervous, or you look over at your lawyer too much. Even with pretrial preparation, the way a defendant comes across on the witness stand is unpredictable.

It is up to the government to prove their case against you. During the trial the jurors will be reminded by the judge, the prosecutors and your defense attorney, that as the accused, you have a right not to testify. Further, the jury is told that if you do not testify, that fact shall not be held against you, or even commented upon by the prosecutor.

Another reason to avoid taking the stand in your own defense is because prosecutors are adept at cross-examination. They can trip you up in your testimony, can reveal through questioning all kinds of skeletons in your closet that you would not want uncovered, and can ask questions to which there is no good answer.

When should you testify in your own defense? Only when your lawyer tells you to. Most often, a lawyer will advise their criminal client to testify when it appears to be the only way they can get a crucial piece of evidence before the jury, or they need the defendant to refute the testimony of a chief witness against them. I had just such a case. It was a drug deal matter. The star witness for the prosecution had made a deal with the prosecutor for immunity from prosecution in exchange for his testimony against my client, the defendant. My client had been arrested for possession of cocaine for sale. He was caught delivering a box of drinking glasses that had bags of cocaine hidden in a false bottom of the box, underneath the glasses. My client said he thought he was simply doing a friend a favor by delivering the box to someone for him, and that he had no idea there were illegal drugs hidden inside. The star witness for the prosecution claimed that my client knew just what he was doing, and that he was aware of the drugs in the box. I was compelled to have my client testify because he was the only one who could refute the prosecution's witness, by saying that he did not know about the drugs. He turned out to be a very poor witness, but in that particular case I had no choice. I needed his testimony. The jury did not believe my client and, in the end, he was convicted.

Something interesting happened after the trial, however, I received a call from the witness saying that he wanted to recant his testimony. At that time, he was imprisoned in Chino State Prison, a medium security prison. I went there to meet with him. I had to pass through one metal gate, and then wait in an enclosure between that gate and a second gate. While I was stuck in the space with both gates closed on either side of me, suddenly a deafening alarm sounded. I had to remain locked in that space until the prison guards were able to take care of the prison disturbance that had precipitated the setting off of the alarm. After they opened the second gate for me, I had to walk down a long concrete corridor that runs through two rows of prison cells, filled with prisoners glaring at me. Some were walking down the hallways. You can imagine my apprehension. When I came face to face with the former witness, he handed me a declaration indicating that he had lied at the trial, and that my client had not been aware of the drug transaction. The witness admitted to having only given that testimony because it allowed him to make a deal for himself. I have since learned that this happe s frequently, which explains why there are innocent people n jail. Of course, I made a motion for a new trial on the basis f this declaration, but the motion was denied. The judge exp ained that all too frequently witnesses recant their testimor and, therefore, he was not convinced that the witness's cha ge of heart should be believed.

The best cross-examination consists of leading questions that often begin with the words, "Isn't it true t at..." Here's a case I tried, which shows how important an ffective cross-examination can be. My client, the defendar , was accused of grand theft from a storage space of propert supposedly owned by the alleged victim. The defendant cl imed that he had power of attorney from his former mother- 1-law to control the property. The alleged victim also clain ed to have power of attorney over the property. In essence, th s was a credibility issue. The alleged victim described ever thing he claimed was in the storage room. As I cross-examine him, I elicited from him great details about the contents, inc ading the size and number of items. I then got him to comm nt on the size of the storage space, and was able to show that given the size and number of items he had enumerated, the was no way to squeeze all of it into the storage space. By sting so many things supposedly housed in the storage roo 1, the alleged victim was trying to bolster the amount of his laim, but it backfired, making him out to be not credible. My lient was found not guilty.

3. __Closing Arguments__

The next step in a trial, after all the witnesses ha e testified, and the evidence has been introduced, is for each de to make their closing argument. The prosecution goes firs then the defendant, and then the prosecution has an oppor unity to rebut the defense's closing argument. Neither side ca comment on evidence that was not introduced during the t al, or mis-state the law. The court sets the amount of time we have for closing arguments.

Does the closing argument affect the verdict? Personally, I think that by that time, the jury has already reached their conclusion but, then again, it could be beneficial because it enables your lawyer to recap the evidence in a way most favorable to you. I make it my practice to argue without notes and use blowups of key documents that I had earlier introduced into evidence. I have learned from juror feedback that this shows I have command of the situation, something that impresses them. One tactic you can use during the closing is to point out that in the other side's opening statement, they promised to prove something, and you can remind the jury that the promise was not kept. It goes to the credibility of the other side.

Many trial lawyers believe biblical quotes are effective. I usually close with this quote from the biblical book Micah: "It has been told thee O man what the Lord doth require, only to do justice, love mercy, and to walk humbly with your God." Does it work? I have no idea if quoting scripture is truly helpful, but it just might motivate the jury to give my client's case serious consideration.

4. **Jury Instructions And Deliberations In Criminal Court**

Once closing arguments are completed, the judge instructs the jury, unless the judge chose to give the jury instructions before the closing arguments. In this phase of the trial, the judge gives the jury the set of legal standards it will need to decide whether the defendant is guilty or not guilty. The judge determines what legal standards should apply to the defendant's case, based on the criminal charges and the evidence presented during the trial. The prosecution and defense can provide input and make arguments to the judge regarding the instructions. The judge will instruct the jury on the proper legal principles it needs to consider, including finding s the jury will need to make to arrive at certain conclusio: s. For example, if the defendant has been charged with volu ntary manslaughter, in the instructions, the judge may sta e the elements of voluntary manslaughter, advise the jury ,f the elements of related crimes such as involuntary mansla: ghter and second-degree murder, and tell the jury precisely what findings they would need to make in order to convict t le defendant of each of those crimes.

After receiving instructions from the judge, the __ :rors, as a group, must consider the case through a process :alled deliberation. Before sending the jurors out of the cour: :oom to the deliberation room, the judge will advise the ba iff to take charge of the jurors, and will admonish the jurors ot to communicate with anyone outside of the jury room abc it the case.

The jurors must try to reach an accord as to wl ether or not the defendant is guilty or not guilty of the cr me(s) charged. The deliberation, the first opportunity the ju y has had to discuss the case, is a process that can last any vhere from a few hours to several weeks. Before reviewing tl e evidence, the jurors must elect a foreperson, someone to :ct as the chairperson and spokesman for the jury. The juro s can convey questions and requests for "read-backs" of testi nony through the foreperson.

Most states require the jury in a criminal case to be unanimous in their findings of guilty or not guilty. I such states, if the jury fails to reach a unanimous verdict, an finds itself at a standstill (i.e., a hung jury), the judge may d :clare a mistrial, after which the case may be dismissed, or th trial may start over from the jury selection stage.

An example of a case which resulted in a mistri: , was one in which my client was accused of raping a 15-ye :r old girl. The jury verdict was 11-1 for acquittal. The lo: e dissenter had lied during *voir dire*, claiming that none f her friends or family members had been molested or rape . We later discovered that her niece had been raped, and the juror's desire to see my client convicted was motivated by her bias. A mistrial was declared, which meant that the case could have been refiled. I convinced the judge to dismiss the case in the interest of justice, and he agreed.

The facts of the case were as follows: The 15-year old girl was the niece of the defendant's girlfriend. The defendant was a married man, and when he refused to leave his wife, the allegation of rape was made against him. The girl alleged that he had climbed into the apartment through a window. That allegation made no sense since the man had a key to the apartment. Also, the girl described the man as having a full head of hair, which did not add up given that the defendant was balding. In her statement to the police, the girl indicated that the alleged rapist had unzipped his pants. I had the defendant bring the pants to court. When the girl was on the witness stand, I held up the pants with only the back of them facing her. I asked her if these were the pants he had unzipped. She said, "Yes, they were." Then I turned the pants around and showed them to the jury. There was no zipper in the pants, they only had buttons. On top of all these inconsistencies in her testimony, there was evidence that the girl had had sex with her boyfriend the day that the alleged rape had occurred. One can easily conclude that the girl's aunt contrived the rape story to get back at the defendant for refusing to leave his wife for her.

After a defendant is convicted, the defendant has the right to appeal the conviction. Conversely, the prosecution cannot appeal an acquittal (a finding of not guilty). This is because the Fifth Amendment to the United States Constitution prohibits the prosecution of a defendant twice for the same alleged offense. That would be considered double jeopardy, a term that comes from the language in the Fifth Amendment: "No person..(shall) be subject for the same offense to be twice put in jeopardy of life and limb." However, the Fifth Amendment does not prevent a defendant from being charged twice for the same type of crime. Let's say you were charged with simple assault against John Doe and found not guilty, and the case was dismissed. You can still be charged with assault again, against a different person in an unrelated matter.

If you are the defendant, and your case ends in a mistrial, are you now free to go home and carry on with your life? As I mentioned already, in criminal cases, in most states, the jurors must be unanimous in finding the defendant guilty. If the jurors are not in unanimous agreement, the result is a hung jury, and the judge declares a mistrial. The prosecutor may try the defendant again in a new trial with a whole new jury. It might seem as if this retrial violates the Fifth Amendment's protection against double jeopardy, but re-prosecuting a defendant after a mistrial is permissible under the Fifth Amendment because the original jury was unable to reach a verdict, and so the defendant was not in jeopardy – in danger of being convicted.

I once defended an arson case in which the jury made a grave mistake. They found the defendant, my client, not guilty only because they thought all twelve jurors had to agree on a verdict no matter what. The jury in that case did not know about such a thing as a hung jury. If they had, each juror could have decided the way they wanted to, and allowed for a hung jury if they could not all agree. In so doing, the case could have been refiled by the prosecutor. Instead, the end result was that my client was found not guilty and, therefore, could not be retried, all because the jury was not well informed enough to be aware of the concept of a hung jury.

What happens after the jury deliberates and reaches a verdict? The jury foreperson informs the judge, and the judge typically announces the verdict in open court. At some trials, the jury foreperson hands the signed verdict form to the court clerk or bailiff, who then gives it to the judge. The judge looks at it, hands it back to the clerk who, while everyone in the courtroom is holding their collective breath, reads the verdict out loud. If you are unhappy with the verdict, is the defendant, you can ask the judge to "poll the jury." At this point, the judge will ask the jurors one by one if this is, indeed, their verdict. This will allow you to see which, and how many, of the jurors were in favor of the verdict, and to ascertain whether the requisite number of jurors reached the verdict. Finally, the jury is dismissed and the jurors are free to talk about the case with anyone. You will be surprised to learn what aspects of the trial swayed the jurors, and what mattered most to them. As I have noted earlier, jurors are human and, sometimes, decide based on their emotions, gut feelings, likes and dislikes.

In the most serious criminal cases, the jurors might need to be sequestered. This means that the judge will direct the jurors to be held in accommodations, usually a hotel, and not exposed to any media and other sources of information that might influence their decision in the case until the trial has concluded, and they have reached a verdict. While it used to be implemented in high profile cases, such as the O.J. Simpson trial, sequestering happens very rarely any more. It is extremely costly, and the current thinking is that isolating a jury causes more problems than it solves.

5.   **Sentencing**

The judge will interpret the verdict for sentencing. Defense lawyers should be familiar with the proclivities of the sentencing judge. Some gain reputations for being either particularly tough, or particularly lenient in sentencing. Having this understanding of the judge can be useful in plea bargaining before the sentence is handed down. You can still negotiate with the prosecution after the verdict is rendered and before sentencing, although you have more leverage before the verdict. You, as the defendant, can seek to strike your prior convictions as part of your plea bargaining with the prosecution, because if the judge is allowed to consider them, you will most likely receive a tougher sentence.

I find it valuable to put together a sentencing memorandum for the judge in which we list all the positive attributes of the defendant. These can be based on probation reports if they show that the defendant adhered to the terms of his or her probation. Also, if the defendant had no prior convictions, we would note this in the memorandum, and we would indicate the defendant's willingness to undergo rehabilitation, and also include any family issues for the defendant that might tug at the judge's heartstrings. As an example, I once represented a young man who had committed multiple burglaries in order to feed his drug habit. These were serious offenses considering that he was stealing from people's homes when they were present. Nevertheless, I was able to convince the judge to put him in a drug rehabilitation facility, allowing him to rehabilitate himself, as opposed to sentencing him to prison. The judge, presumably moved by the young man's plight, decided to give him this second chance.

Once the sentence is imposed, it is rare for a sentencing judge to be reversed, or the sentence modified, unless it is a matter of law. At the time of sentencing, it can be beneficial for the defense to offer restitution before a judge proposes it. Restitution is the return to the property owner of their property, or payment to them of the monetary value of the loss. Sometimes restitution is made part of a judgment in negligence and contract cases. In criminal cases, which this section covers, one of the penalties that can be imposed is requiring the return of stolen goods to the victim, or payment to the victim for the harm caused. Restitution may be a condition of granting a defendant probation, or giving them a shorter sentence than normal. With restitution, at least the victim will gain something, as opposed to getting nothing from the defendant if he or she lands in prison.

The sentencing options are determined by law, and can range from no jail time and probation, to imprisonment in the state prison. In most serious cases, called capital felonies, or murder with special circumstances, the defendant faces a sentence of life imprisonment without the possibility of parole, or even the death penalty. Crimes which elevate murder to a capital felony, or constitute murder with special circumstances include: Murder of a peace officer, murder for hire, prior conviction of murder, murder of a kidnapped person, murder during a sexual assault and multiple murders. If the defendant has been convicted of one of these offenses, a separate proceeding called a penalty phase is held. At this proceeding in which both sides present evidence to either mitigate or aggravate the sentence, the jury decides what the penalty should be. If the jury decides in favor of execution, the judge has the power to overrule that determination, and to sentence the defendant to life imprisonment without the possibility of parole.

From a Kabbalistic perspective, your punishment is essentially a debt that you need to pay for something you have done. Even if you are innocent of the crime, the judgment has perhaps been imposed for some previous misdeed. You have actually been found guilty for the purpose of the lesson, and this might end up benefitting you in some way. It could be that during the course of this case, you have met someone who brings something positive into your life, an opportunity that would not have presented itself otherwise. Then there is also the possibility of an appeal. Who is to say that after you have lost your case, if you change your consciousness, begin to shed your selfish ways and start giving more, you won't win your appeal?

6.   **Appealing The Conviction**

If you have been convicted and want to appeal, the appeals process begins with your attorney filing a notice of appeal in the trial court. By appealing, you are asking a higher court to review certain aspects of the case for legal error, as to either the conviction, or the sentence imposed. In an appeal, as the defendant - you are now called the appellant -

you would argue that because of certain legal mistakes which affected the jury's decision and/or the sentence imposed, the case should be dismissed, or you should be retried or resentenced. The appellate court will review only the record of the proceedings in the lower court, and does not consider any new evidence. The records consist of the court reporter's transcripts of everything said in the court by the judge, the attorneys and the witnesses. Also, everything admitted into evidence such as documents or objects, becomes part of the record. The appellate court reaches its decision based on the record and the written legal briefs (documents stating the facts and points of law of a client's case) filed by both sides of the appeal. The appellate court may hear oral argument from each side before deciding the appeal.

Appeals are complicated matters, and attempting to appeal your conviction without the benefit of counsel, leaves you at risk for missing a deadline, or failing to follow the mandatory rules for filing appeals. You might lose your chance to raise a particular argument, or even benefit from some change in the law if you do not follow the rules. It is always best to seek representation for an appeal.

PARTING THOUGHTS

16

Why did you pick up this book? Do you have a goal in mind? Perhaps you can use the principles in this book to help you achieve that goal.

Do you believe that whatever happens in our lives is destined to occur, or is it random? Either way, it would seem that we have no control over our lives, but actually we do. Sometimes it seems like things happen suddenly, for no apparent reason, and with no prior warning. In reality though, nothing occurs out of the blue, and there are no completely random events. Everything that transpires in our lives can be traced back to a seed that was planted in our past. Both good and bad occurrences pop up in a seemingly unexpected way, only because time has separated the cause – what we have done – from the effect, or result. We often do not recognize the connection between some past conduct of ours and a current happening, because the element of time has intervened.

You have the opportunity to direct the course of your life by the choices you make now. According to a best-selling author and Grammy Award winner, "(t)he decisions we make in each moment allow us to experience either the worst or best versions of our lives." The choice is ours. You can be conscious of the way you interact with others, and with your environment to the point of shedding any reactive emotions, like hatred, anger, and a desire for revenge that you carry within. Instead, you can choose to live by the Golden Rule, the most common phrasing of which is: "Do unto others as you would have them do unto you." After all, some version of this ethical concept known as the Golden Rule is at the heart of every religion.

In the world of the law, as in life, as I have said before, everything happens for a reason. If you are stuck in the legal system, try asking yourself what brought you there. Is the lawsuit, or the event that precipitated the lawsuit, a message sent to let you know that, perhaps, you need to change your consciousness, your way of approaching the world? Can you forego the temporary gratification that might come from winning a lawsuit, or punishing someone whom you believe wronged you, in favor of long-term fulfillment? Going forward, can you let go of trying to satisfy your ego and, instead, try to be a more giving person? Remember that true spiritual growth only takes place during challenging times, when we are confronted with hardships and obstacles. As Sophocles said, "There is no success without hardship." So, even if it is uncomfortable, doing the right thing will always bring you closer to the light, and it bears repeating – we get what we need.

Although not involving the law at all, one of the best illustrations of the aforementioned concepts of getting what we need, and things happening for a reason, can be seen in the success story of the beloved children's author, Dr. Seuss. Theodore Geisel (aka Dr. Seuss), down in the dumps after the 27th rejection of his first book, was lugging the manuscript and drawings for *Mulberry Street* home to burn. As he was walking home, he bumped into an old acquaintance from college on Madison Avenue in New York City, who asked what Geisel was carrying. "That's a book no one will publish," Geisel answered. That very morning, his acquaintance had been made editor of children's books at a publishing house. The man invited Geisel up to his office. He and his publisher bought *Mulberry Street* that day. Geisel would later say in regard to the meeting with his old acquaintance, "If I's been going down the other side of Madison Avenue, I'd be in the dry-cleaning business today."

I wonder if I had been walking on a different street, or on another day of the week in Manhattan all those years ago when I met the woman selling Kabbalah books, would my life have taken an entirely different path. It is not too late for any of us to alter the course of our lives. We just need to recognize and be receptive to the messages we are sent.

Perhaps by picking up this book, you are like I was when I happened to pass by the woman selling the books. You were ready to receive this message and "the teacher appeared."

Hopefully, you have found the overview of the law and the spiritual principles in this book to be informative, and that this book will serve as a useful guide for both your journey through the legal world and your spiritual sojourn. You might want to open it and let the light in, and then, to quote Dr. Seuss, "Oh the places you'll go."

ACKNOWLEDGMENTS

Write Wisdom: I would like to thank Loren Stephens, president and founder, for her overall comments and input, which made this book professional and interesting. Most especially, I want to thank Betsy Rosenthal, who took mountains f material and stories I gave to her, and made this book a easy read.

Contract Lawyers: Perry and Jane Fredgant, who ma le me look pretty smart, even though much of the work wa done by them. They are the unsung heroes. To Burton Mark Se ikfor, the finest lawyer I have ever known. We have been w rking together for more than 30 years. He was the most pessi iistic person on every case. He was always finding something rrong with it. His genius was the ability to find a way arou nd it. There is no one better.

S. Marcus Aurelius: The Grammy Award winning pro lucer, song writer and hit maker with whom I spent many lours talking about the book. He helped me with creative dec sions, including the cover. I am very appreciative to my good iend.

Elliot Norman Johnson: I met Elliott when h was homeless and sat at the entrance to the courthouse ith a cup for donations. One day I stopped and we talked. Tl it developed into a real friendship. We often had long and f iitful conversations. Elliot is very spiritual and kept remindi ig me to "stay focused." The good news is that he is no longer n the street.

Rav and Karen Berg: The spiritual principles the have taught me, and which I am sharing in this book is wh it life is all about. It motivated me to write this book. It could not have been done without them. Thank you

Essex Ins. Co. v. Five Star Dye House, Inc. (2006) 38 Cal.4th 1252
– Cal.Rptr.3d -; - P.3d – [No. S131992. July 6, 2006]

ESSEX INSURANCE COMPANY, Plaintiff, Cross-Defenda t and
Appellant, v. **FIVE STAR DYE HOUSE, INC.**, Defendant, ross-
Complainant and Respondent.

(Superior Court of Los Angeles County, No. BC 156517 Ken-
neth R. Freeman, Judge).

(The Court of Appeal, Second Distr. Div. Five, No. B1(7295,
125 Cal.App.4th 1569).

(Opinion by Kennard, J., expressing unanimous view f the
court).

COUNSEL:

Carroll, Burdick & McDonough, David M. Rice, Laurie J. F elper,
Troy M. Yoshino, Don Willenburg, John D. Boyle, Do na P.
Arlow; Murchison & Cumming, Jean M. Lawler; Edmund ì. Far-
rell and Bryan M. Weiss for Plaintiff, Cross-Defendant a d Appellant.

Wiley, Rein & Fielding, Laura A. Fogan, Gary P. Seligma ; Sinnott, Dito, Moura & Puebla, Randolph P. Sinnott and hn J.
Moura for Complex Insurance Claims Litigation Assoc ation
as *Amicus Curiae* on behalf of Plaintiff, Cross-Defenda t and
Appellant.

The Dodell Law Corporation, Herbert Dodell and Ge ald J.
Miller for Defendant, Cross-Complainant and Responde t.

Gianelli & Morris, Robert S. Gianelli, Sherril Nell Ba cock;
Ernst & Mattison, Don A. Ernst and Raymond E. Mattis n for
Consumer Attorneys of California as *Amicus Curias* on ehalf
of Defendant, Cross-Complainant and Respondent. [38 al.4th
1255]

OPINION

KENNARD, J.

In *Brandt v. Superior Court* (1985) 27 Cal.3d 813 (*Brandt*), this court held that in a tort action against an insurance company for breach of the duty of good faith and fair dealing, an insured may recover as damages those attorney fees that are incurred in the same action and are attributable to the attorney's efforts to recover policy benefits that the insurer has wrongfully withheld. We reasoned that when an insurer's tortious conduct consists of depriving its insured of policy benefits, the attorney fees that the insured reasonably and necessarily incurs to obtain those policy benefits constitute an economic loss proximately caused by the insurer's tort, and thus those attorney fees (now commonly referred to as *Brandt* fees) are recoverable as tort damages. (Id. at pp. 817-819).

The issue here is this: When an insured assigns a claim for bad faith against the insurer, and the assignee brings a tort action against the insurer that includes a claim for wrongfully withheld policy benefits, may the assignee recover *Brandt* fees? Our answer is "yes." [38 Cal.4th 1256].

I.   FACTS AND PROCEDURAL BACKGROUND:

Luis Sanchez, doing business as L.A. Machinery Moving (hereinafter Sanchez), was in the trucking business, specifically, transporting commercial machinery. In June 1994, Sanchez contracted to deliver two commercial dryers to Five Star Dye House, Inc. (Five Star), a designer jeans manufacturer that uses dryers in the manufacturing process. During transportation of the dryers, one fell while on Sanchez's truck and was damaged. Five Star refused to accept delivery of the damaged dryer.

Five Star sued Sanchez for negligence (the underlying action), seeking as damages the profits it lost while the damaged dryer was being repaired. Sanchez tendered defense of the action to his liability insurance carrier, Essex Insurance Company (Essex). Essex denied coverage, however, and refused to defend Sanchez in the action. Sanchez undertook a defense using his own funds; the trial resulted in a judgment against him for $1.35 million, plus costs.

Sanchez then assigned to Five Star all of his claims and causes of action against Essex. In exchange, Five Star agreed to delay execution on the judgment in the underlying action until the claims against Essex for the judgment amount were exhausted. Notwithstanding the assignment, Sanchez remained liable for the full judgment amount, plus interest.

Essex then filed this action in superior court for declaratory relief against both Five Star and Sanchez. Essex sought a declaration that it did not have a duty to defend Sanchez in the underlying action. Under the assignment from Sanchez, Five Star cross-complained against Essex for, among other claims, breach of contract and tortious breach of the covenant of good faith and fair dealing. During the course of the litigation, Sanchez was dismissed as a defendant in the declaratory judgment action, based on his assignment of all claims to Five Star. [38 Cal.4th 1257].

The trial court found the existence of an insurance contract between Sanchez and Essex, potential coverage under that policy for Five Star's claim against Sanchez, and bad faith by Essex in not defending Sanchez in the underlying action. The court awarded Five Star $1.6 million in damages against Essex, but it denied Five Star's request for Brandt fees.

The Court of Appeal affirmed the trial court's judgment against Essex, but it reversed as to the denial of attorney's fees. The Court of Appeal held that when an insured assigns a bad faith cause of action against an insurer, the assignee receives the right to recover the policy benefits in full, including Brandt fees. The court expressly disagreed with another Court of Appeal decision, *Xebec Development Partners, Ltd. v. National Union Fire Ins. Co.* (1993) (*Xebec*), which held to the contrary.

We granted Essex's petition for review to determine

whether assignment of a tort action against an insurer for wrongfully withholding policy benefits includes the right to recover *Brandt* fees.

II.   LEGAL BACKGROUND:

A.   The American Rule and Brandt

[1]   Embodied in the Code of Civil Procedure section 1021, the "American rule" states that except as provided by statute or agreement, the parties to litigation must pay their own attorney fees. In addition to its various statutory exceptions (see, e.g., Civ. Code, §   1717), the American rule is subject to common law exceptions that this court has created. (*Trope v. Katz* (1995) 11 Cal.4th 274, 279). *Brandt*, **supra**, 37 Cal.3d 813, is the source of one such exception.

[2]   In Brandt, an insured sued the insurer for breach of the implied covenant of good faith and fair dealing, seeking damages that included attorney fees. (*Brandt*, **supra**, 27 Cal.3d at p. 816). Citing the American rule and Code of Civil Procedure section 1021, the trial court struck the portion of the complaint seeking attorney fees. (*Brandt*, **supra**, 37

Cal.3d at p. 816). We held that when an insurer denies coverage in bad faith, the insured can recover attorney fees in an action to recover the policy benefits. (Id. At p. 817). [38 Cal.4th 1259].

After observing that an insurer's breach of the covenant of good faith and fair dealing is a tortious act, we reasoned in *Brandt*, "When such a breach occurs, the insurer is 'liable for any damages which are the proximate result of that breach.' [Citation.]"

When an insurer's tortious conduct reasonably compels the insured to retain an attorney to obtain the benefits due under a policy, it follows that the insurer should be liable in a tort action for that expense. The attorney's fees are an economic loss – damages – proximately caused by the tort. [Citation.] These fees must be distinguished from recovery of attorney's fees qua attorney's fees, such as those attributable to the bringing of the bad faith action itself. What we consider here is attorney's fees that are recoverable as damages resulting from a tort in the same way that medical fees would be part of the damages in a personal injury action. (*Brandt*, **supra**, 37 Cal.3d at p.817).

In a tort action for wrongful denial of policy benefits, *Brandt* allows the insured to recover as tort damages only the attorney fees incurred to obtain the policy benefits wrongfully denied. (*Brandt*, **supra**, 37 Cal.3d at p. 819), but attorney fees expended to obtain damages exceeding the policy limit or to recover other types of damages are not recoverable as *Brandt* fees. See *Cassim v. Allstate Ins. Co.* (2004) 33 Cal.4 780, 811-812 [attorney fees to obtain emotional distress damages and punitive damages not recoverable under *Brandt*]. This follows from the rationale of *Brandt*. The tort of bad faith against the insured entitles the insured to recover the policy benefits in full, undiminished by attorney fees, but not to recover attorney fees in general. Allowing recovery of attorney fees incurred to obtain damages beyond the policy limit or to obtain punitive damages would allow the insured to recover attorney fees as attorney fees, violating the American rule, embodied in *Code of Civil Procedure* section 1021, that parties generally must pay their own attorney fees. "Rather, *Brandt* merely entitles the insured to all of the benefits due under the policy, undiminished by the expenses incurred in retaining an attorney to recover under the policy." (*Cassim v. Allstate Ins Co.*, **supra**, at p. 815 [conc. opn. of Baxter, J.]).

This court has in various decisions affirmed *Brandt's* rule awarding attorney fees to an insured who is injured by the bad faith conduct of the insurer. (*Cassim v. Allstate Ins. Co.*, **supra**, 33 Cal.4th at p. 806, fn 10; *White v. Western Title Ins. Co.*

(1985) 40 Cal.3d 870, 890; see also *Track Mortgage Group, Inc. v. Crusader Ins. Co.*(2002) 98 Cal.App.4th 857, 867; *Campbell v. Cal-Gard Surety Services, Inc.* 38 Cal.4th 1259 (1998) 62 Cal.App.4th 563, 571-572. The *Brandt* rule is now a well-settled but narrow exception to the general rule that each party to litigation must pay its own attorney fees.

B. The General Rule of Assignability

[3] California, as set forth both in case law and by statute, maintains a policy encouraging the free transferability of all types of property. (See *Civ. Code* §§ 954, 1044, 1458; *Farmland Irrigation Co. v. Dopplmaier* (11957) 48 Cal.2d 808, 222; *Robert H. Jacobs, Inc. v. Westoaks Realtors, Inc.* (1984) 159 Cal.App.3d 637, 645) fn. 3 "[I]t is a fundamental principle of law that one of the chief incidents of ownership in property is the right to transfer it." (*Bias v. Ohio Farmers Indemnity Co.* (1938) 28 Cal.App.2d 14, 16).

This "chief incident of ownership" applies equally to tangible and intangible forms of property, including causes of action. Originally codified in 1872, section 954 states: "A thing in action arising out of the violation of a right of property, or out of an obligation, may be transferred by the owner." An assignment is a commonly used method of transferring a cause of action.

Although the assignability of causes of action is derived from the common law, section 954 had the effect of liberalizing restrictions on the types of action that may be assigned to a third party (*Wikstrom v. Yolo Fliers Club* [1929] 206 Cal. 461, 464). We summarized the resulting state of the law as to assignability of claims in *Reichert v. General Ins. Co.* (1968) 68 Cal.2d 822 (*Reichert*). In *Reichert*, the plaintiff purchased a 325-unit motel and received assignments of multiple fire insurance policies for the premises. (Id. at pp. 825-826). Later, a fire caused significant damage to the motel. (Id. at p. 826). After the insurance companies failed to indemnify the plaintiff for the damages, the plaintiff lost possession of the motel in bankruptcy. (Id. at pp. 826-827). When the plaintiff sued the insurance companies for the resulting loss they demurred to the complaint on the ground that the plaintiff's causes of action had passed to the trustee in bankruptcy (Id. at pp/828-829). Under bankruptcy law, the trustee in bankruptcy received all causes of action that the bankrupt could have assigned. (Id. at p. 829, citing 11 U.S.C. § 110). Thus, whether the plaintiff's causes of action against the insurance companies were assignable was the central question in Reichert, (Reichert, **supra**, at pp. 829-830). [38 Cal.4th 120].

The court in *Reichert* defined when a cause of action is assignable: "As a general proposition it can be said that only causes or rights of action which are not transferable or assignable in any sense are those which are founded upon wrongs of a purely personal nature, such as slander, assault and battery, negligent personal injuries, criminal conversations, seduction, breach of marriage promise, malicious prosecution, and others of like nature. All other demands, claims and rights of action whatever are generally held to be transferable." (*Reichert*, **supra**, 68 Cal.2d at p. 834, quoting *Wikstrom v. Yolo Fliers Club*, **supra**, 206 Cal. At p. 463). We conclude that the plaintiff's causes of action against the insurance companies for breach of their duties under the insurance policies were assignable, and thus they passed to the trustee in bankruptcy. (*Reichert*, supra, at pp. 830, 835-837).

Actions for bad faith against insurance companies can introduce problematic elements into this seemingly bright-line rule defining assignability of causes of actions, as shown by this court's decision in *Murphy v. Allstate Ins. Co.* (1976) 17 Cal.3d 937 (*Murphy*). There, the plaintiff sought a judgment obtained in an earlier tort action by bringing a direct action against the tortfeasor's insurance company, alleging breach of the insurer's duty to the insured (the tortfeasor) by refusing to settle within policy limits. (*Murphy*, **supra**, at pp.939-940). The trial court granted judgment on the pleadings for the defendant insurance company, and the plaintiff appealed. (Id. at p. 939).

The plaintiff argued that the action was authorized by Insurance Code section 11580, subdivision (b)(2) or, alternatively, by former *Code of Civil Procedure* section 720 (*Murphy*, **supra**, 17 Cal.3d at p. 940). This court found that the plaintiff could not pursue the claim under Insurance Code section 11580, subdivision (b)(2). That provision merely made the judgment creditor a third-party beneficiary of the insurance contract, allowing the judgment creditor to enforce only those contract provisions that were designed to benefit injured claimants. The duty to settle and the covenant of good faith and fair dealing, however, were designed to benefit the insured, not injured third party claimants. (Id. at pp. 942-944).

This court in *Murphy* next considered former *Code of Civil Procedure* section 720, which then provided: "If it appears that a person or corporation alleged to have property of the judgment debtor, or to be indebted to him, claims an interest in the property adverse to him, or denies the debt, the judgment creditor may maintain an action against such person or corporation for the recovery of such interest or debt...." (*Murphy*, **supra**, 17 Cal.3d at p. 945, fn omitted. See now *Code of Civil Procedure* § 708.210 ["If a third person (38 Cal.4ᵗʰ 1261) has possession or control of property in which the judgment debtor has an interest or is indebted to the judgment debtor, the judgment creditor may bring an action against the third person to have the interest or debt applied to the satisfaction of the money judgment."]). Under this provision, the judgment creditor may assert only those causes of action belonging to the judgment debtor that are assignable. (*Murphy*, **supra**, 17 Cal.3d at pp. 945-946). Thus, this court in *Murphy* addressed the question whether the insured's causes of action against the insurer for breach of the duty to settle and breach of the covenant of good faith and fair dealing were assignable. (Id. at pp. 945-946).   Under the particular facts at issue, we concluded that although the cause of action itself was assignable, it potentially included damages that were not assignable and therefore not recoverable in an action under former section 720 of the *Code of Civil Procedure*. (*Murphy*, **supra**, 17 Cal.3d at p.946). "The insured may assign his cause of action for breach of the duty to settle without consent of the insurance carrier, even when the policy provisions provide the contrary. [Citation]. However, part of the damage arises from the personal tort aspect of the bad faith cause of action. [Citation]. And because a purely personal tort cause of action is not assignable in California, it must be concluded that damage for emotional distress is not assignable. [Citations]. The same is true of a claim for punitive damages." (*Murphy*, **supra**, 17 Cal.3d at p. 942).

This court in *Murphy*, described the bad faith action against the insurer as a "hybrid cause of action," one comprised of both assignable and non-assignable components (*Murphy*, **supra**, 17 Cal.3d at p. 946). Because the cause of action could not be split, allowing the injured claimant to proceed under former section 720 of the *Code of Civil Procedure* would deprive the insured of any opportunity to recover the non-assignable damages (emotional distress damages and punitive damages), and thereby "defeat the very purpose of the cause of action." (*Murphy*, **supra**, at p. 946). Although we concluded in *Murphy* that the action was barred, we suggested how an assignment might be used in this situation to protect the interests of both the insured and the claimant: "Requiring assignment before the claimant may proceed would, of course, insure notice to the insured that the claimant wished to proceed against the insurer. At that point the insured would have the choice of partially assigning and then joining in the action, or of bargaining for a release from liability in excess of coverage. The release would permit the insured to protect himself from continued exposure to personal liability. Further, because the judgment creditor would then both own and control the [38 Cal.4th 1262] cause of action against the insurer, he could attempt to satisfy his judgment thereby. Finally, the insured could protect his right to non-assignable claims for punitive, emotional and personal injury damages." (Id. at pp. 946-947).

C.   Conflicting Court of Appeal Decisions

In *Xebec*, **supra**, 12 Cal.App.4th 501, Xebec Corporation entered into an agreement with Xebec Development Partners (XDP), whereby XDP would provide nearly $14 million to Xebec Corporation for research and development, and Xebec Corporation in exchange would assign to XDP the rights to new technology (Id. at p. 517). Later, XDP sued Xebec Corporation and two of its officers for misappropriating the funds earmarked for research and development. (Ibid.) National Union Fire Insurance Company (National Union) claimed it had not received timely notice of the lawsuit and, on this basis, declined to defend the Xebec corporation officers in the suit, which resulted in a stipulated arbitration award against Xebec Corporation and the two officers, on which judgment was then entered, in excess of $9 million. (Id. at pp. 521-523). The arbitration settlement agreement included provisions under which Xebec Corporation assigned to XDP its rights against National Union (Id. at p. 523). Under this assignment, XDP sued National Union for refusing in bad faith to defend the officers of Xebec Corporation in the original lawsuit. (Id. at p. 524).

The action was tried to a jury, which returned a general verdict against National Union for more than $7 million, and the trial court awarded XDP attorney fees under *Brandt*, **supra**, 37 Cal.3d 813. (*Xebec*, **supra**, 12 Cal.App.4th at pp. 526, 571). In a lengthy opinion dealing with a variety of issues arising from the complicated underlying factual situation, the Xebec Court of Appeal reversed the trial court's ruling as to the award of *Brandt* fees to XDP, devoting just over one p ge to that issue. (Id. at pp. 571-572).

The Court of Appeal in *Xebec* observed that XD ꞌ was "a third-party claimant" and a "stranger to the policy." *Xebec*, **supra**, 12 Cal.App.4ᵗʰ at p. 572). As an assignee of the in ured, XDP "could assert only those rights the insureds had ha l, and it could assert the rights only in the stead of the in ured-s." (Ibid). Because none of the insureds had incurred att rney fees to compel payment of policy benefits, the Court of A ppeal concluded that XDP could not assert their rights under I andt, nor could it assert a right to *Brandt* fees on its own beh lf because "the fees it thus incurred cannot be construed ¿ ; tort damages to XDP, because National Union had no duty t ꞌ XDP to pay policy benefits to anyone." (Ibid. italics in origina). (38 Cal.4ᵗʰ 1263).

In this case, the Court of Appeal expressly dis greed with that analysis. It focused on this court's language i Murphy, **supra**, 17 Cal.3d at page 942, and in *Reichert*, **sup a**, 68 Cal.2d at page 834, articulating the principle that a tort claims are assignable under section 954 except thos of a purely personal nature. The Court of Appeal here rea oned that *Brandt* fees constitute an economic loss and are nc t personal in nature, and therefore under section 954 the ri ght to recover *Brandt* fees is assignable. It rejected Essex's arg ment that because *Brandt* fees are tort damages, only fees in urred by the insured are recoverable. It observed that the ri ht assigned by Sanchez was the right to recover the policy bene-fits in full, "undiminished by the attorney fees incur ed in bringing the actions to recover those benefits," and tha "[t]he identity of the party incurring attorney fees to vindica e the insured's rights under the insure policy is irrelevant.....'

III. ANALYSIS

[4]   We start from the proposition that assig iabil-ity is the rule. (§954). From that general rule we accept chose

tort causes of action, "founded upon wrongs of a purely personal nature." (*Reichert* **supra**, 68 Cal.2d at p. 834). Actions for bad faith against an insurer have generally been held to be assignable (*Communale v. Traders & General Ins. Co.* [1958] 50 Cal.2d 654, 661-662), including claims for breach of the duty to defend (*Hamilton v. Maryland Casualty Co.* [2002] 27 Cal.4th 718, 728). Although some damages potentially recoverable in a bad faith action, including damages for emotional distress and punitive damages, are not assignable (*Murphy*, **supra**, 17 Cal. 3d at p. 942), the cause of action itself remains freely assignable as to all other damages (Id. at p. 946).

Here, the claim that Sanchez assigned to Five Star is based on Essex's tortious breach of its contract obligation under the policy to defend its insured, Sanchez, in the lawsuit brought against him by Five Star. In suing on this assigned claim, Five Star has not sought damages for emotional distress or punitive damages, or damages for injury to reputation or other personal interests. What Five Star has sought to recover as tort damages is the monetary value of the policy benefits wrongfully withheld by Essex.

As this court has explained, "[w]hen an insurer's tortious conduct reasonably compels the insured to retain an attorney to obtain the benefits due under a policy, the fees incurred for those attorney services are an economic loss-damages-proximately caused by the tort." (38 Cal.4th 1264) (*Brandt* **supra**, 37 Cal.3d at p. 817). Those attorney fees do not possess any of the personal aspects that preclude assignment of other tort damages, such as damages for emotional distress. They are not damages arising "from the personal tort aspect of the bad faith cause of action." (*Murphy* **supra**, 17 Cal.3d at p. 942).

We reject Essex's argument that because *Brandt* fees are tort damages, they are recoverable only if incurred by the insured personally, rather than by the assignee. "As a general rule, the assignee of a chose in action stands in the shoes of his assignor, taking his rights and remedies......" (*Salaman v.*

328

Herbert L. Dodell

Bolt (1977) 74 Cal.App.3d 907, 919). Had Sanchez broug it the bad faith action against Essex, his right to recover *Bran* t fees would be unquestioned. As the assignee of Sanchez's claim against Essex, Five Star stands in his shoes, and so m y assert his right to recover any *Brandt* fees incurred in pro ecuting the assigned claim. We agree with the Court of Appeal here that the right that Sanchez assigned to Five Star w is the "right to recover the policy benefits in full, undiminisl ed by the attorney fees incurred in bringing the action to re cover those benefits." Were we to accept Essex's argument, Sanchez would no longer be assigning the right to recover the policy benefits in full. Essex also argues that allowing Fiv Star, an assignee, to recover *Brandt* fees from it would not serve to make the insured whole, which is the essential purp se of *Brandt* fees, because, under the terms of the assignmen from Sanchez to Five Star, the amount that Five Stars recov ers as *Brandt* fees will not reduce Sanchez's liability on the jud ment in the underlying action. We disagree. In exchange f r the assignment, Five Star agreed to defer collection of the judgment against Sanchez until "all efforts to collect the jud ment against Essex......have been exhausted." (See fn. 2 ante.) Thus, all sums recovered from Essex, including *Brandt* fees, v ill be credited against the judgment in the underlying actio , directly reducing Sanchez's liability to Five Star.

Disallowing recovery of *Brandt* fees in cases such s this would result in a windfall for the insurer, whose liabil ty for tortious conduct would be significantly reduced beca se of the fortuitous circumstance of the assignment of the ba faith claim. As we have recognized, recoverable *Brandt* fee may exceed the contract benefits wrongfully withheld. (*Ca im v. Allstate Ins. Co.* **supra**, 33 Cal.4th at p. 809). Disallowing ecovery of *Brandt* fees incurred by assignees would also t nd to discourage assignment of bad faith claims against insu rance companies, contrary to public policy favoring transfer bility of causes of action. (38 Cal.4th 1265).

329

IV.   CONCLUSION

[5]   We conclude that an insured's assignment of a cause of action against an insurance company for tortious breach of the covenant of good faith and fair dealing by wrongfully denying benefits due under an insurance policy carries with it the right to recover *Brandt* fees that the assignee incurs to recover the policy benefits in the lawsuit against the insurance company. (fn. 4)

The Court of Appeal's judgment is affirmed.

George C.J., Baxter J., Werdegar J., Chin J., Moreno J., and Corrigan J.,   concurred.

(FN 1) Not before us is the validity of the underlying assignment. Therefore, for purposes of analysis, we assume its validity.

(FN. 2) The assignment states: "Luis Sanchez, dba L.A. Machinery Movers ("Assignor') conveys and assigns to Five Star Dye House, Inc., ("Assignee"), all of its rights, remedies, titles and/or interest in and to any and all claims and/or causes of action against Essex Insurance Company ("Essex"), arising from the facts and circumstances regarding the lawsuit filed in the Superior Court of the State of California for the County of Los Angeles, bearing Case No. BC 119424, entitled *Five Star Dye House, Inc. v. Rosco Machine Company,* et al., ("Five Star Lawsuit") including, but not limited to, claims and/or causes of action for Breach of Contract, Breach of the Covenant of Good Faith and Fair Dealing, Fraud and Declaratory Relief arising from Essex' failure to provide a defense or indemnity to Assignor arising from the Five Star Lawsuit....In exchange for this assignment, Assignee agrees to defer collection of the judgment against Assignor until such time as all efforts to collect the judgment against Essex and/or any insurance broker and/or agent....have been exhausted."

(FN. 3) Unless otherwise stated, all further statutory references as to the Civil Code.

(FN. 4) *Xebec Development Partners, Ltd. V. National Union Fire Ins. Co.,* **supra**, 12 Cal.App.4th 501, is disapproved insofar as it is inconsistent with this conclusion.

PUBLISHED ARTICLE BY HERBERT DODELL

LOS ANGELES LAWYER MAGAZINE
JULY/AUGUST 2002 ISSUE

"USING THE APPRAISAL PROCESS TO RE-SOLVE INSURANCE DISPUTES"

The key to virtually every appraisal is the neutral appraiser or umpire

Currently every fire insurance policy issued in California requires that certain disputes be submitted to a process known as appraisal if demanded by either party to the policy. Many other types of policies, including earthquake policies, require the use of the appraisal process in certain circumstances. Insurance Code Section 2070 mandates the use of a statutory form for all fire insurance policies in California. Section 2071 contains the form and all the forms of the insurance agreement, including the appraisal process. On October 5, 2001, Governor Gray Davis signed SB 658, a law that is effective for all policies issued or renewed after January 1, 2002. The new legislation amended Section 2071 and codified the appraisal process in certain particulars.

Insurers and insureds and their counsel should understand the specific procedures that are involved in the appraisal process. The parties must address a variety of issues, including:

- The composition of the appraisal panel, including the selection of an appraiser by each party and the selection of a neutral appraiser o "umpire" (the standard form fire insurance p licy's term for a third party or neutral apprais r and a term that appears in other types of insi rance policies).

- The bases for objecting to the selectior of an appraiser.
- Whether the appraisal will be formal or nformal.
- The powers of the appraisers.
- The grounds for attacking an unfavoral e appraisal award.

Case law often uses the words "arbitrator" an "appraiser" interchangeably, but there are substantial diffe ences as well as similarities between the terms. Although n appraisal proceeding is a form of arbitration and is goveri ed by the general rules of arbitrations, including Code of Civ l procedure Sections 1280 *et seq.* and case law, an appraiser as far greater leeway than an arbitrator in evaluating a matte

Typically, an insurance policy requires each pa ty to select one appraiser, who is termed a "party" appraiser. Jnder the old law, which governs all policies issued before Ja iuary 1, 2002, and not renewed after that date, when th two appraisers are unable to reach agreement regarding lo s and damage, they must jointly select a third person, the n utral appraiser or umpire. The new law eliminates the re [uirement of disagreement between the appraisers as a con ition to the selection or appointment of a neutral arbitrator. Jnder amended Section 2071, party appraisers must select a i umpire, and the parties can seek court intervention solely in the basis of the parties' inability to agree on the selectior of an umpire.

[T]he appraisers shall first select a competent ai d disinterested umpire, and failing for 15 days to agree up n the umpire, then, on request of the insured or [the insurance] company, the umpire shall be selected by a judge of a court of record in the state in which the property covered is located.

The proceedings can be formal or informal, at the option of either of the parties. However, under amended Section 2071, for policies issued or renewed effective January 1, 2002, the proceedings must be informal unless the parties mutually agree to the contract. "Informal" means that no formal discovery can be conducted, including depositions, interrogatories, requests for admissions, or other forms of formal civil discovery. A court reporter cannot be used to record the proceedings. The appraisal panel may not consider coverage issues or causation, but the parties can agree to expand the panel's authority to enable it to make those decisions as well. Expansion of the scope of the appraisal, however, is very risky because a successful appeal from an appraisal award is unlikely, unless a showing of "corruption, fraud, or undue means," or other specified grounds according to the arbitration statutes are established.

For the most part, an informal appraisal is a free-for-all with the appraisal panel members doing just about anything they want to do. No formal rules of evidence may be applied. The only real benefit of an informal appraisal is the reduced cost and a speedier resolution of the dispute.

Formal proceedings involve the taking of evidence, including the examination of witnesses, and a record can be made by a court reporter for use in subsequent proceedings, such as a bad faith action. A formal appraisal is akin to a minitrial, with the usual costs and expenses. The benefit of a formal appraisal is that it serves as prelitigation discovery and can provide a written record of proceedings in which the opposing party has offered evidence that may or may not be accepted by the trier of fact.

Practitioners should consider two recent cases, *Fraley v. Allstate* and *Guehara v. Allstate*, in deciding whether to use the appraisal process in anticipation of a bad faith case resulting

Herbert L. Dodell

from an insurer's unwillingness to pay the full value of a claim. The two cases hold that if there is a "genuine dispute," including reasonable reliance on experts, bad faith is not present as a matter of law. However, the failure to conduct a thorough and timely investigation is not included in the genuine dispute category. Therefore, the use of an appraisal process in which evidence can be developed that reflects delays and a failure to thoroughly investigate can counter an argument that there was a genuine dispute and that a claim for bad faith was thereby negated. The reasonableness of the experts also can be tested in a prelitigation setting by probing the relationship between an expert and the insurer as well as the depth and quality of the evaluation.

Selection of the Appraisers

Appraisers are required to be both "competent and disinterested," words specifically mentioned in Insurance Code Section 2071 and in case law. Most of the cases dealing with the selection process arise from the question of disinterest rather than competence. The reason is simple: An appraiser may be anyone selected by the parties, as long as the appraiser is capable of understanding the proceedings. This would include non-lawyers with special expertise in a particular field. Even if the appraiser does not hold a contractor's license, a law degree, or an adjuster's license, he or she is still likely to be found competent.

The more interesting question occurs when the issue of disinterest is raised. What constitutes sufficient interest to disqualify an appraiser? Cases throughout the United States are all over the map on this issue. In some jurisdictions, the definition is broadly construed, and in others the opposite is true. Interestingly enough, however, an appraiser is universally held to a higher standard of impartiality than an arbitrator, who, in turn, is held to a higher standard of impartiality than a judge. This is because of the tremendous latitude given to an appraiser in performing his or her function.

Further, even though California's contractual obligation statutes may differentiate between a party appraiser and the neutral appraiser selected by the two-party appraisers, the courts have held that all must adhere to the same "competent and disinterested" standard. In *Gebers v. State Farm General Insurance Company*, the court stated that the duties imposed on appraisers generally, coupled with the insurer's duty of good faith and fair dealing, required that all appraisers, even the party appraisers, be disinterested.

Despite this lofty language, many insurers have their favorite appraisers who are regularly hired because they can be relied upon to express opinions favorable to the insurers. Opposing parties should make an effort to disqualify these appraisers, even though the reality is that an appraiser will probably remain on the case unless a strong showing can be made of bias in accordance with the standards set forth in case law.

To the extent that a party anticipates filing a bad faith suit in a matter, either because of a lowball offer or other improper conduct, the selection of an appraiser subject to objection will be another example of tortious conduct, even though the appraiser may be able to withstand a challenge. While the admissibility of such conduct is subject to the vagaries of a court ruling, there is nothing to lose by making the challenge. It is imperative that an objection to an appraiser be made at the time of the appraiser's selection or at the time of the required disclosure of the identity of a party's appraiser, or the objection may be considered to be waived.

While many clings to the ideal that appraisers should be neutral and disinterested, this is unlikely in the real world. The insurer selects a known quantity, someone expected to be partial, and the insured does likewise. It is difficult for some appraisers to be non-biased because they have been selected by a party and are being paid by that party. Since compromises often occur, the strength of the party appraiser's advocacy is important. Certainly, an opposing party does not want an appraiser who is well known as a forceful advocate for the party selecting him or her.

The key to virtually every appraisal is therefore the neutral appraiser or umpire. An award can be rendered by any two appraisers, including a selected party appraiser and the neutral appraiser. Occasionally, the two-party appraisers agree, but it is far more common for the selected neutral appraiser to side with one or the other party's appraiser in rendering an award. Obviously, if the insurer's selected appraiser and the neutral appraiser agree to an award, the opinion of the insured's selected appraiser is meaningless. It is also common for the neutral appraiser to pressure one of the appraisers to agree, thereby allowing for the entry of an award. The dynamics vary from case to case. One thing, however, is absolutely certain, careful attention should be paid to the selection of the neutral appraiser.

If the two appraisers are unable to agree on a neutral appraiser, the parties have the right to petition the court for the appointment of a neutral appraiser. When that happens, both parties face the risk of a neutral appraiser they may not want. For policies issued or renewed after January 1, 2002, the statute and the standard fire insurance policy mandates submission to the state court in which the property is located for appointment of an umpire if the two appraisers cannot agree within 15 days after the effort is first made to select the umpire. Either party may petition the court to make the appointment at the expiration of this 15-day period.

Disinterested and Disclosure

What happens when there is some indication of a relationship between an appraiser or the supposedly neutral appraiser and someone else, a party or an attorney, in the proceeding? Cases vary from jurisdiction to jurisdiction regarding the degree and nature of the relationship used to determine whether or not an appraiser is truly disinterested. Some jurisdictions permit a member of the same country club and even a social friend to qualify as an appraiser, and do not find this type of relationship to rise to the level of interest. Indeed, the majority of the cases focus on a financial interest in the outcome.

Does an appraiser who has been selected by a party in the past qualify, or should that appraiser be disqualified? The leading case on the subject is *Commonwealth Coatings Company v. Continental Casualty Corporation*, a 1968 U.S. Supreme Court case regarding federal law that was adopted into California law in 1970 in *Johnston v. Security Insurance Company*. In *Commonwealth Coatings*, the Supreme Court interpreted the Federal Arbitration Act regarding the issue of disinterest. The Court held that it is sufficient to prove interest when the relationship between the arbitrator and one of the parties is "of such a nature as to give clear grounds for suspicion of the proceedings" and "render it unlikely that the proceedings constituted the fair and impartial tribunal to which the other party is entitled."

Last year, in *Michael v. Aetna Insurance Company*, the California Court of Appeal held that the standard under *Commonwealth Coatings* was identical to that imposed by state law. Appraisers are required to disclose to the parties any reason that might cause a person aware of the facts to reasonably entertain a doubt that the appraiser would be able to be impartial, and the failure to do so constituted evidence of "corruption," which was sufficient to vacate an award.

Although this standard appears to make sense, its application to a particular set of facts is not always certain. The standard does not give sufficient guidance regarding the nature of the relationship that should be disclosed. "Suspicion" is a fairly nebulous word without a concrete and universal definition. The court was clear on one point: The remedy for this problem is not for appraisers to sever themselves from the marketplace, but instead to disclose their relationships. It is the duty of the appraiser to reveal facts that might create the impression of bias; the parties need not engage in discovery on the issue.

In determining whether to disqualify an appraiser, it is not necessary to establish actual fraud, bias, or any improper motive on the part of the appraiser. Rather, it is sufficient to establish merely an" impression of possible bias." Under that standard, the issue is whether a reasonable person would objectively entertain doubts about that appraiser's neutrality based upon the appraiser's history and past actions.

In California, the older cases provided standards for determining whether an appraiser was truly disinterested, but they were not particularly concrete. By the mid-1990s, the arbitration statutes were amended to require detailed disclosure from a neutral arbitrator. Thus, under Code of Civil Procedure Section 1281.9, within 10 days of service of notice of the proposed nomination, the proposed neutral appraiser must disclose all of the following for the preceding five years:

- The names of the parties to all prior or pending cases in which the neutral appraiser is or was acting as a party appraiser or neutral appraiser;
- Any prior attorney-client relationship between the neutral appraiser and any party or attorney involved in the pending appraisal;
- Any professional or significant personal relationship between the neutral appraiser or the neutral appraiser's spouse and any party or attorney for a party.

Generally, if a party wishes to object to the selection of a neutral appraiser because the disclosure raises the impression of possible bias, the objection should be raised at the earliest opportunity if a party elects to refrain from unveiling their knowledge of bias in order to later attack an unfavorable award, the courts will bend over backwards to find that the right to object was waived by not asserting that right on a timely basis. The statute does not affect a party's right to seek to vacate an award for "undue means," under Code of Civil Procedure Section 1286.2. Objections based on information appearing on the face of the disclosure statement should be made immediately, but if the disclosure itself is inadequate, all rights should be reserved until after the award.

These objections and disqualification procedures apply only to the neutral appraiser rather than to the party appraisers. However, case law standards remain crucial for parties seeking to ensure the disinterest of a party appraiser. A motion to disqualify a selected party appraiser may become necessary if disclosure patently provides a reasonable basis for disqualification, and the party objecting does not want to wait for the outcome of the appraisal to seek relief. The failure of a party appraiser to disclose information that might be relevant to the question of competence and disinterest may provide a basis for attacking an award. Cases involving the disqualification of an appraiser are very fact-intensive, and the waiver cases are extremely tricky; therefore, there is no hard-and-fast rule.

Despite the disclosure requirements, the outcome of a challenge is based on many unpredictable variables. When there is a request for an adjudication of whether there has been a proper disclosure, if there is a question of interest, or if there is a basis sufficient to rise to the level of the "impression of possible bias," test outlined in *Commonwealth Coatings*, much depends on the interpretation of the circumstances given by a particular judge deciding the issue. The problem is that every case will be viewed differently by the reviewing judicial officer. Therefore, there is no certainty.

A question remains whether the specific disclosure statutes replace or add to the general "impression of possible bias" test set forth in *Commonwealth Coatings*. What would happen if, for example, a neutral appraiser had a twin brother who had a significant personal relationship with the insurer's attorney, and the relationship is not disclosed? If an insurer later argues that an award for the insurer cannot be set aside because the relationship did not have to be disclosed, what is the likely result? There is no case yet on point. It is far better to make a disclosure than to subject an award to later attack for failure to disclose.

Although there is no time period provided by statute regarding the disqualification of a party appraiser, a party seeking to disqualify the neutral appraiser has 15 calendar days to serve a notice of disqualification. Under no circumstances can a notice of disqualification be served after an award has been rendered. The remedy in that instance is an attack on the award itself.

Conduct of the Appraisers

In California, the appraisal process is limited to determining one factual question only, the amount of the loss, or the actual cash value of the insured item. The appraisal panel may not consider anything else. On the other hand, an arbitration can be used to decide any dispute the parties agree to submit.

Safeco Insurance Company v. Sharma illustrates this principle. In *Sharma*, the insured claimed theft of a matched set of 36 paintings. The insured and the insurer began the appraisal process. The appraisal panel found that the stolen paintings were not a matched set and thus were of lesser value than the insured's claim. The appellate court reversed confirmation of the appraisal award, stating: "In no authority is it suggested that an appraisal panel is empowered to determine whether an insured lost what he claimed to have lost or something different." Thus, although the question decided in *Sharma* obviously affected the value of the paintings, it was held to be beyond the scope of the appraisal. While an insurer is free to litigate questions of the insured's misrepresentations in a courtroom, the insurer cannot raise those questions in an appraisal setting. Courts may use various terms, such as "amount of loss," "actual cash value," or "total loss," but they all mean the same thing.

Unetco Industries v. Homestead Insurance Company also illustrates the limited power of the appraisal panel. In *Unetco*, the earthquake policy in question tied the deductible to the replacement cost. The court held that the insurer was entitled to an appraisal of the actual cash value of an earthquake loss for the purpose of determining the amount of the loss, but was not entitled to an appraisal to determine the replacement cost for the purpose of determining the amount of the deductible.

The appraisal process cannot be used to decide coverage issues unless the parties stipulate to empower the appraiser panel to do so. If the insured and insurer are debating whether a fire loss was caused by a covered windstorm or uncovered arson, neither party can demand appraisal of that issue. As a practical matter, this means if the insurer is demanding an appraisal the insured should understand that the parties are only arguing over dollars and cents; at least there is no coverage battle to fight.

Appraisers have one power that judges do not. Appraisers are free to make their own independent investigation, while a judge is limited to deciding only the issues that are presented by the parties based on admissible evidence. The appraisal panel must give notice to the parties that it is considering evidence outside the hearing, although such notice rarely occurs. Code of Civil Procedure Section 1282.2(g) provides: "If a neutral arbitrator intends to base an award upon information not obtained at the hearing, he shall disclose the information to all parties to the arbitration and give the parties an opportunity to meet it." In *Sapp v. Barenfeld*, the California Supreme Court definitively stated: Arbitrators may inform themselves further by privately consulting price lists, examining materials, and receiving cost estimates. This procedure may be ex parte, without notice or hearing to the parties. It is entirely proper for arbitrators, in a case requiring it, to obtain from disinterested persons of acknowl edged skills such information and advice in reference to tec nical questions submitted to them, as may be necessary to nable them to come to correct conclusions, provided that the ward is the result of their own judgment after obtaining such nformation.

If an insurer is claiming that, for example, a va uable Persian rug can be replaced with a rug of like kind and q ality for $99 at the local swap meet, the appraisers are free to do their own pricing of Persian rugs. It is risky to automa cally assume that the appraisers will conduct their own inv stigation, and if they do, almost anything can be valued on e-bay at garage sale prices. Thus, the insured should produce competent evidence of the proper valuation of expensive P rsian rugs.

The court in *Griffith Company v. San Diego for* V 'omen permitted one arbitrator, acting alone, to consult with a disinterested attorney about legal conclusions. Althou h the case is somewhat obscure, it appears that the consul ation was well known to the other party arbitrator and the n utral arbitrator, because the other party's arbitrator filed a le gthy declaration in support of a motion to set aside the ward. (There is no requirement that all three arbitrators ac as a body).

Although there are no cases addressing the is ue of an appraiser who communicates with an interested p rson, such as a party or the party's attorney, it would seem l gical that such an ex parte communication would represent ndue means, thereby allowing for the vacating of the awar . One big problem for parties is that the deliberations of t e appraisers are confidential and not subject to discovery. herefore, there is little that can be done to monitor the ap raisal panel's conduct without conducting ex parte comm nications with the party's selected appraiser or inquiring f the neutral appraiser, and practitioners' options here are li ited. While certain ex parte communications, such as reque ts for a status report are proper, anything beyond the request would likely be held improper and may subject an award to attack. Moreover, the neutral appraiser is under no obligation to reply to inquiries from any party unless there is a specific request for a particular action to take place.

Challenges to the Award

After the panel of competent and disinterested appraisers has been selected, has listened to or reviewed the evidence, and has made its own independent investigation, the panel will render an award, which can be confirmed, vacated, or corrected. The parties have 100 days in which to seek to correct or vacate the award and four years to confirm it – a clear indication of the courts' bias toward confirmation.

If the insured suspects improper conduct and bad faith in the appraisal process, the time to respond is while the proceedings are incomplete and before an award is determined. It is far more preferable to deal with the appraisal process before the award is rendered than seek to attack it afterwards. The courts view the latter as akin to sour grapes. In addition, the courts follow the judicial principle that a proceeding under attack was conducted properly unless there is substantial evidence to the contrary. Overturning an award or obtaining relief during the proceedings are both difficult.

In California, an appraisal award may be confirmed by filing a petition with the superior court. Once confirmed, the award becomes a judgment and can be enforced in the same way as any civil judgment.

An appraisal award can be corrected only if there is an obvious mathematical error. It cannot be corrected to fix an error of fact or law, even if the error is obvious on the face of the document.

According to Code of Civil Procedure Section 1286.2, an appraisal award can be vacated only if one of the following six grounds is present:

1.   The award was obtained through corruption, fraud or undue means.

2.   There was corruption on the part of any of the appraisers.

3.   The rights of a party were substantially prejudiced by the misconduct of a neutral appraiser.

4.   The award exceeded the powers of the appraisers.

5.   The rights of a party were substantially prejudiced by the refusal of the appraisers to postpone the hearing upon sufficient cause being shown or by the refusal of the appraisers to hear evidence material to the controversy or by other conduct of the appraisers contrary to the provisions of law.

6.   A neutral appraiser who was subject to disqualification failed, upon receipt of a timely demand, to disqualify himself or herself.

While ground four might sound like fertile ground for attacking appraisal awards, it has been virtually eliminated by the decision in *Moncharsh v. Heily & Blasé*. In *Moncharsh*, the employee-attorney signed an employment agreement regarding the handling of fee disputes if the attorney left the employer law firm. The agreement had both an arbitration clause and a fee-splitting clause that seemed to violate professional legal ethics. The arbitrator upheld the validity of the fee-splitting arrangement when rendering the award. On appeal, the state supreme court specifically emphasized the need for finality in arbitration agreements, even when a clear error in law exists. The court did not disturb the erroneous award. In short, courts do not want to retry the merits of any arbitrated dispute.

Thus, the most successful attacks on an appraisal award focus on whether the award was obtained through undue means. This ground for attack arises if an appraiser fails to make adequate disclosures or is not disinterested. Undue means also includes ex parte communications between a party appraiser or neutral appraiser and one of the parties or attorneys. Attacks based on undue means have met with success if evidence provided to the court shows the failure of the neutral appraiser to grant a continuance for the purpose of the introduction of new evidence.

A party seeking to vacate an unfavorable award should carefully examine the adequacy of the disclosure statements. Again, as with other aspects of appraisal disputes, each case, including those involving vacating an award based on undue means, is decided on its facts.

From a practical perspective, almost everything in an appraisal will depend on the motive of the neutral appraiser. With retired judges, financial considerations should not be ignored. The likelihood that a retired judge will be called upon to serve as a neutral appraiser by an insurer in the future is far greater than the likelihood that the retired judge will be selected again by the insured or the insured's counsel. For that reason alone, a careful evaluation should be made of the proposed neutral appraiser before proceeding. It is unlikely that a party appraiser will be disqualified, and a neutral appraiser selected by the court is generally unknown to the parties. Therefore, uncertainty and unpredictability loom large in any appraisal.

To attack an award via a petition to vacate is difficult. The courts are loathe to set aside any award without the clearest of evidence of fraud, corruption, or undue means. Confirmation of an award, however, generally occurs unless the facts are so egregious that the judge ruling on the petition to vacate cannot reconcile the conduct with the award.

Herbert L. Dodell

418. Presumption of Negligence *per se*

[Insert citation to statute, regulation, or ordinance] **stat s:**

_____.

If you decide

    1.   That *[name of plaintiff/defendant]* violat d the law and

    2.   That the violation was a substantial fac or in bringing about the   harm,

then you must find that *[name of plaintiff/defendant]* was legligent
[unless you also find that the violation was excused].

If you find that *[name of plaintiff/defendant]* did not viola e this law or that the violation was not a substantial factor in ring-ing about the harm (or if you find the violation was exc ised), then you must still decide whether *[name of plaintiff/ fend-ant]* was negligent in light of the other instructions.

SUPERIOR COURT OF CALIFORNIA
COUNTY OF LOS ANGELES

Date: 7-21-16   Dept. F51

                              Deputy Clerk

        G. HERNANDEZ

Honorable   Judge

Honorable HERBERT DODELL   Judge Pro Tem

                              Court Administrator

        C. CORDOBA   Deputy Sheriff

            S. NUNEZ 9514   Reporter

3:00 pm   PS018376

        Counsel for

        Petitioner:

        Counsel for

        Respondent:

Nature of Proceedings: PETITIONER'S REQUEST FOR A RESTRAINING
ORDER
(FILED 06/30/2016)

The matter is called for hearing.

The Petitioner addresses the Court regarding the un-availability of his attorney of record,   , and the specially appearing attorney from July 20, 2016.

The Court inquires with Petitioner's counsel of record who is appearing telephonically.

The Court inquires with Respondent's counsel regarding his position.

Respondent's counsel makes a request to dismiss the case.

The Court orders the case Dismissed Without Prejudice for Failure to Prosecute and the Temporary Restraining Order is Dissolved.

If Petitioner files a new request for a Tempora y Restraining Order, he is to give notice to Respondent.

The Court further orders sanctions against Peti ioner
and Petitioner's counsel, jointly and severally to pay o Respondent's counsel,   , the sum of $1,000.00, p yable
within 30 days directly to counsel.

Respondent's counsel is to give notice.

DEPT. F51   Minutes Entered

07-21-16

County Clerk

SUPERIOR COURT OF CALIFORNIA
COUNTY OF LOS ANGELES

SUPERIOR COURT OF CALIFORNIA
COUNTY OF LOS ANGELES

Date: 7-21-16   Dept. F51

Deputy Clerk

G. HERNANDEZ

Honorable   Judge

Honorable HERBERT DODELL   Judge Pro Tem

Court Administrator

C. CORDOBA   Deputy Sheriff

S. NUNEZ 9514   Reporter

3:00 pm   PS018376

Counsel for
Petitioner: (telephonically)

Counsel for
Respondent:
Off the record: The Court orders 1 original tran cript
with the Court to bear the costs.

Court's Order Nunc Pro Tunc:

Petitioner had an attorney,   , appear for him on July 20, 2016. His attorney of record,   , did not appear. The Court heard testimony with   , he emailed a copy of an email from

, counsel of record to her to the court. In speaking with Petitioner's counsel of record, she provided no legitimate excuse for her non-appearance. The Court considered the email which states that Petitioner did not want to spend more money to complete the hearing.

Counsel for Respondent has requested a copy of the aforementioned email. After consideration, the Court believes that he is entitled to a copy because it is considered by the Court. A copy will be provided to   , counsel for Respondent.

DEPT. F51   Minutes Entered   County Clerk
07-21-16

IN THE COURT OF APPEAL
OF THE STATE OF CALIFORNIA
SECOND APPELLATE DISTRICT
DIVISION FOUR

CITY OF LOS ANGELES,   B258980
     Plaintiff and Respondent ,
v.   (Los Angeles County)
            Super.Ct.No. BS150139
ROBERT GARBER,
     Defendant and Appellant

Appeal from an order of the Superior Court of L s Angeles County, Herbert Dodell, Judge. Affirmed.

Robert Garber, in pro per for Defendant and Appe lant.

Michael N. Feuer, City Attorney, Vivienne A. Swa ligan, Assistant City Attorney, and Jennifer M. Handzliik, D puty City Attorney, for Plaintiff and Respondent.

Robert Garber (Garber) appeals from the su erior court's granting of a three-year Workplace Violence Re :raining Order against him under Code of Civil Procedure s ction 527.8, obtained by the Los Angeles City Attorney's Offic e (the City Attorney) on behalf of its employee, Deputy City Attorney Geoffrey Plowden (Plowden). We affirm.

BACKGROUND

On August 5, 2014, the City Attorney filed a petition for a restraining order on Plowden's behalf under section 527.8. According to Plowden's declaration in support of the petition, Plowden was assigned to the Police Litigation Unit of the City Attorney's Office, and had recently opposed Garber, who was representing himself, in Garber's suit in federal district court alleging excessive force by police officers. Plowden stated that "during the trial, Mr. Garber was fixated on myself, the judge and the court clerk [sic], irrationally claiming [that] we "fixed" the case to Mr. Garber's detriment...Mr. Garber aggressively approached me within a few inches, yelling at me in front of the judge and jury."

According to Plowden, on July 30, 2014, the district court judge dismissed Garber's suit in the middle of trial. Garber became enraged, pointed at Plowden about 15 feet away, and "angrily yelled, this is not over!" Plowden believed that "this threat was clearly not about filing an appeal or pursuing further litigation in the case." Four security personnel immediately escorted Garber out of the courthouse. However, Garber returned and was detained by six security personnel.

Plowden has litigated two cases against Garber, and Garber has lost both. Garber "has filed [a] pleading saying [Plowden is] corrupt...and perjure[s] himself] despite [Garber's] knowledge to the contrary." Plowden was "aware of at least three of Mr. Garber's prior arrests for assaultive behavior in the last seven years, wherein Mr. Garber brandished a machete, a gun, and stabbed another man." Based on Garber's "bizarre and threatening behavior," Plowden was afraid for his safety and that of his family and fellow employees.

The superior court issued a temporary restraining order on August 5, 2014, and scheduled a hearing on a permanent restraining order for August 26, 2014.

Garber filed a written opposition to the petition for

a restraining order. In a declaration supporting his opposition, Garber accused Plowden of committing a "fraud on [the] court" in his recently dismissed federal civil rights lawsuit. According to Garber, Plowden presented a "tampered" version of a video of the event in question, as well as perjured testimony by a police officer. After the video was played, the district court judge "abruptly ordered the jurors out of the courtroom and dismissed [the] case by stating that [Garber] was "out of control." Garber accused Plowden of perjury in Plowden's declaration in support of the petition for a restraining order. In particular, referring to Plowden's statement regarding Garber's prior arrests, Garber stated that after his arrest for brandishing a gun he had been acquitted of the charge by a jury (he attached a copy of a minute order reflecting this fact). With respect to his arrest for stabbing someone else, he stated that he had also been stabbed and that no charges were filed against him because of the complaining witnesses' inability to identify him. As to the machete incident, Garber stated that he had no knowledge of any machete. Garber accused Plowden of seeking a restraining order "to continue harassing me by sending the LAPD to come to my trailer, by day or night, throw all my belongings out of the trailer and legally, but unlawfully, "search for an imaginary weapon."

On August 24, 2014, the superior court held a hearing on the petition for a restraining order. Both Plowden and Garber testified. The hearing was not reported and no settled or agreed statement is included in the record on appeal. The court granted the petition, and issued a restraining order against Garber which precludes him from, inter alia, harassing or threatening Plowden, and directs that he stays at least 100 yards away from him, his home, workplace and vehicle. The order expires on August 26, 2017.

DISCUSSION

Section 527.8, subdivision (a) provides in relevant

part: "Any employer, whose employee has suffered....a credible threat of violence from any individual, that can reasonably be construed to be carried out or to have been carried out at the workplace, may seek a temporary restraining order and an injunction on behalf of the employee." A credible threat of violence means "a knowing and willful statement or course of conduct that would place a reasonable person in fear for his or her safety, or the safety of his or her immediate family, and that serves no legitimate purpose." [Section 527.8, subd. (b)(2)].

Garber contends that the evidence does not support the issuance of the three-year restraining order, because the City Attorney failed to prove that he engaged in a credible threat of violence. However, he has failed to provide a record sufficient to consider the claim. Before issuing the order, the superior court heard testimony from Plowden and Garber. No reporter was present, and Garber has failed to provide the court with an agreed or settled statement. (See Cal. Rules of Court, rules 8.130(h), 8.137). Thus, we do not have a record of the testimony upon which the court granted the order.

Generally, appellants in ordinary civil appeals must provide a reporter's transcript at their own expense. [Citation]. In lieu of a reporter's transcript, an appellant may submit an agreed or settled statement. [Citations]. [¶] In numerous situations, appellate courts have refused to reach the merits of an appellant's claims because no reporter's transcript of a pertinent proceeding or a suitable substitute was provided. [Citations]. [¶] The reason for this follows from the cardinal rule of appellate review that a judgment or order of the trial court is presumed correct and prejudicial error must be affirmatively shown. [Citation]. In the absence of a contrary showing in the record, all presumptions in favor of the trial court's action will be made by the appellate court. [I]f any matters could have been presented to the court below which would have authorized the order complained of, it will be presumed that such matters were presented. [Citation].

This general principle of appellate practice is an asp ct of the constitutional doctrine of reversible error. [Citati ɔn]. A necessary corollary to this rule is that if the record is inadequate for meaningful review, the appellant defaults a d the decision of the trial court should be affirmed. [Citation Consequently, [appellant] has the burden of providing an ade quate record. [Citation]. Failure to provide an adequate reco rd on an issue requires that the issue be resolved against [ppellant]. [Citation]. *Foust v. San Jose Construction Co., Inc.* (2011) 198 Cal.App.4th 181. 186-187; see also *Estate of Fain* (19 9) 75 Cal.App.4th 973, 992 ["Where no reporter's transcript ha been provided and no error is apparent on the face of the ex sting appellate record, the judgment must be *conclusively pre umed correct as to all evidentiary matters*. To put it another wa , it is presumed that the unreported trial testimony would d mon-strate the absence of error. [Citation].

Because Garber has failed to provide an ade quate record, he has forfeited his challenge to the sufficiency ɔf the evidence to prove that he engaged in a credible threat f vio-lence. But even if we were to overlook the inadequacy ɔf the record, we would nonetheless affirm. "Where findings f fact are challenged on a civil appeal, we are bound by the 'el men-tary, but often overlooked principle of law, that....the ɔwer of an appellate court begins and ends with a determinai on as to whether there is any substantial evidence, contradic ed or uncontradicted,' to support the findings below. [Citatio]. We must therefore view the evidence in the light most fav rable to the prevailing party, giving it the benefit of every r ason-able inference and resolving all conflicts in its favor in a cord-ance with the standard of review so long adhered to t / this court. [Citations]." (*Jessup Farms v. Baldwin* [1983] 33 al.3d 639, 660).

The record on appeal contains Plowden's decla ation in support of the petition. According to Plowden, (arber believed that Plowden, the district court judge and court clerk conspired to defeat Garber's federal civil rights la vsuit.

During the trial, Garber behaved aggressively, approaching Plowden within inches and yelling at him. After the judge dismissed the suit, Garber became enraged, pointed at Plowden from about 15 feet away, and angrily yelled, "This is not over!" Four security personnel immediately escorted Garber out of the courthouse. Nonetheless, Garber returned and was detained by six security personnel. Moreover, Plowden was aware that within the last seven years, Garber had been arrested for assaultive conduct. Further, Garber's declaration in support of his opposition to the petition for a restraining order confirmed Plowden's claim that Garber was enraged at Plowden over the dismissal of the lawsuit.

On this evidence, a rational trier of fact could conclude that Garber's loud, angry statement in open court to Plowden – "[t]his is not over!" – after which Garber had to be taken from the courtroom by four security guards (only to return again and be taken away by six security guards) was "a knowing and willful statement," means to convey a threat to Plowden's safety, and that under the circumstances the statement "would place a reasonable person in fear for his or her safety." [Section 527.8 subd. (b)(2))]. To the extent Garber produced evidence challenging Plowden's credibility, or disputing the willfulness or threatening nature of his statement, the superior court was entitled to credit Plowden's version of events and discredit Garber's. In short, the evidence present in the record supports the superior court's order.

DISPOSITION

The order is affirmed. The City Attorney shall recover its costs on appeal.

NOT TO BE PUBLISHED IN THE OFFICIAL REPORTS

WILLHITE J.

Herbert L. Dodell

We concur:
EPSTEIN, P.J.

COLLINS, J.

DUI ADVISEMENT OF RIGHTS, WAIVER AND PLEA FORM
(Vehicle Code § 23152)

INSTRUCTIONS

Fill out this form if you wish to plead guilty or no contest to the charges against you. Initial the box for each applicable item only if you understand it and sign and date the form on page 5. If you have any questions about your case, the possible sentence, or the information on this form, ask your attorney, or the judge.

RIGHT TO AN ATTORNEY

1.   I understand that I have the right to be represented by an attorney throughout the proceedings. I understand that the Court will appoint a free attorney for me if I cannot afford to hire one, but at the end of the case, I may be asked to pay all or part of the cost of that attorney if I can afford to. I understand that there are dangers and disadvantages to giving up my right to an attorney and that it is almost always unwise to represent myself.

NATURE OF THE CHARGES (Initial all items you are charged with)

1.   I understand that I am charged with a violation of Vehicle Code section(s):

2.   23152(a): Driving under the influence of alcohol or drugs, or both.

3.   23152(b): Driving when my blood alcohol level was .08 percent or more.

4.   3152(d):   Driving a commercial vehicle when my blood alcohol level was .04 percent or more

5.   23103, 23103.5: Reckless driving involving alcohol or drugs, or both.

6.   Check if applicable: [ ] 14601   [ ] 14601.1 or [ ] 14601.2 [ ] 14601.5. Driving in knowing violation of a driver's license restriction, suspension or revocation.

7.   Check if applicable: [ ] 14601.3 (Habitual traffic offender). Accumulating a driving record history in knowing violation of a driver's license suspension or revocation.

8.   If applicable – I understand that I am also charged with the following **other offense(s)**

TYPE OF OFFENSE(S) AND SECTION NUMBER(S)

9.   If applicable – I am also charged with having the following **other conviction(s)**

LIST OFFENSE(S); CASE NUMBER(S) AND DATE(S)

10.   If applicable – I am also charged with violating the **probation order(s)** in the following cases(s)

CASE NUMBER(S) AND DATE(S)

11.   I understand the charge(s) against me, and the possible pleas and defenses.

CONSTITUTIONAL RIGHTS/WAIVER OF RIGHTS

12.   **RIGHT TO A JURY TRIAL** – I understand that have the right to a speedy, public trial. At the trial, I would be presumed innocent, and I could not be convicted unless 2 impartial jurors were convinced of my guilt beyond a reasonable doubt.

13.   **RIGHT TO CONFRONT WITNESSES** – I understand that I have the right to confront and cross-examine all witnesses testifying against me.

14.   **RIGHT AGAINST SELF-INCRIMINATION** – I understand that I have the right to remain silent and not incriminate myself, and the right to testify on my own behalf. I understand that by pleading guilty or no contest, or admitting other conviction(s), or probation violation(s), I am incriminating myself.

15.   **RIGHT TO PRODUCE EVIDENCE** – I understand that I have the right to present evidence and to have the Court issue subpoenas to bring into court all witnesses and evidence fa-

vorable to me, at no cost to me.

RIGHTS ON CHARGES OF OTHER CONVICTION(S) AND PROBATION VIOLATION(S)

16.   If applicable – I understand that I have the right to an attorney, the right to a jury trial, the right to confront witnesses, the right against self-incrimination, and the right to produce evidence and witnesses for all charges against me, including other alleged conviction(s) or probation violation(s). However, for a charge of violating probation, I do not have the right to a jury trial, but I do have the right to a hearing before a judge.

WAIVER OF RIGHTS

Understanding all of the above, for all of the charges against me, including any other alleged conviction(s) or probation violations(s):

17.   I give up my right to an attorney, and I choose to represent myself (does not apply if you have an attorney).

18.   I give up my right to a jury trial.

19.   I give up my right to confront and cross-examine witnesses.

20.   I give up my right to remain silent and to not incriminate myself.

21.   I give up my right to produce evidence and witnesses on my own behalf.

CONSEQUENCES OF PLEA OF GUILTY OR NO CONTEST

22.   I understand that if I am not a citizen, a plea of guilty, or no contest (*nolo contendere*) could result in my deportation, exclusion from admission to this country, or denial of naturalization.

23.   I understand that a plea of no contest will have the same effect in this case as a plea of guilty, but it cannot be used against me in a civil lawsuit unless the offense is punishable as a felony.

24.   I understand that any plea entered in this case may be grounds for revoking probation or parole which has previously been granted to me in any other case.

25.   I understand the Department of Motor Vehicles (DMV) may consider any of my other convictions for DUI or reckless driving, **even those that are not charged in this proceeding**, and may impose a more severe license suspension or revocation as a result.

26.   I understand that in addition to the fine, **the Court will add assessments which will significantly increase the amount I must pay**. I will also be ordered to make restitution and to pay a restitution fine up to $1000 (or up to $10,000 if the offense is a felony), unless the Court finds compelling and extraordinary reasons not to do so.

27.   I understand that being under the influence of alcohol or drugs, or both, impairs my ability to safely operate a motor vehicle, and it is extremely dangerous to human life to drive while under the influence of alcohol or drugs, or both. If I continue to drive while under the influence of alcohol or drugs, or both, and as result of my driving, someone is killed, I can be charged with murder.

28.   I understand that if I am the **registered** owner of the vehicle used in the offense:

    A.   The Court will impound my vehicle at my expense for up to 90 days, unless it is in the interests of justice not to do so. The Court may also declare my vehicle to be a nuisance and order it sold following a hearing if I have 2 or more other convictions for DUI, vehicle manslaughter (Penal Code § 191.5 or 192.5(a)), or any combination thereof, in the past 7 years.

    B.   The Court may also require me to install and maintain an ignition interlock device for up to three years. Installation of this device, which prevents the vehicle from starting if I have alcohol in my body, does not authorize me to drive without a valid driver's license.

    C.   If I am convicted of a second or subsequent vio-

lation of driving with a suspended or revoked license (V.C. §
14601 *et seq.*) or driving without a license (V.C. § 12500(a)), my
vehicle will be subject to forfeiture as a nuisance.

SENTENCES FOR DRIVING UNDER THE INFLUENCE OF ALCOHOL AND/OR DRUGS (Section 23152)

First Offense within 10 years (see numbers 29-37).

Minimum & Maximum Sentences when Probation is Granted
(3 to 5 years' Probation Term)

The Court may order a jail term of 48 hours to 6 months in jail.
It will impose a fine of $390 to $1,000 and order me to complete a 3-month alcohol/drug treatment program. If my blood
alcohol content was 20% or more, or if I refused a chemical
test upon my arrest, I must complete a 9-month treatment
program. The DMV will also impose a 6-month driver's license
suspension, or a 10-month license suspension if a 9-month
treatment program is required.

Minimum & Maximum Sentences without Probation

96 hours to 6 months in jail, and a $390 to $1,000 fine. The
DMV will impose a 6-month driver's license suspension.

Second Offense within 10 years (see numbers 29-37).

Minimum & Maximum Sentences when Probation is Granted
(3 to 5 years' Probation Term)

A jail term of either (a) 10 days to 1 year, or (b) 96 hours to 1
year, a $390 to $1,000 fine and completion of an 18-month al-
cohol/drug treatment program. The DMV will impose a 2-year
driver's license suspension.

Minimum & Maximum Sentences without Probation

90 days to 1 year and a $390 to $1,000 fine. The DMV w ll impose a 2-year driver's license suspension.

Third Offense within 10 years (see numbers 29-38)

Minimum & Maximum Sentences when Probation is G anted (3 to 5 years' Probation Term)

120 days to 1 year in jail, a $390 to $1,000 fine and comp etion of an 18-month alcohol/drug program if I have not com leted one before. The DMV will impose a 3-year driver's l cense revocation. The Court may impose a 10-year driver's l cense revocation.

Minimum & Maximum Sentences without Probation

120-days to 1 year in jail and a $390 to $1,000 fine. Th DMV will impose a 3-year driver's license revocation. The Court may impose a 10-year driver's license revocation.

Fourth or subsequent offense within 10 years (see nu nbers 29-38)

Minimum & Maximum Sentences when Probation is G anted (3 to 5 years' Probation Term)

180 days to 1 year in jail, a $390 to $1,000 fine and comp etion of an 18-month alcohol/drug program if I have not com peted one before. The DMV will impose a 4-year driver's l cense revocation. The Court may impose a 10-year driver's l cense revocation.

Minimum & Maximum Sentences without Probation

16 months, or 2 or 3 years imprisonment (or 180-day ; to 1 year in county jail) and a $390 to $1,000 fine. The DM / will impose a 4-year driver's license revocation. The Cour may impose a 10-year driver's license revocation.

ADDITIONAL PENALTIES FOR A VIOLATION OF SECTION 23152

29.	I understand that the DMV may suspend or revoke my driver's license under a civil procedure which is separate from this criminal action. I understand that DMV's action, if any, will be in addition to the Court's sentence and that I must obey.

30.	I understand that the DMV will notify me that I am required to install an ignition interlock device in all vehicles that I own or operate, and it will issue a restricted license if I comply.

31.	I understand that the DMV will not restore my driving privilege following a driver's license suspension or revocation unless I provide the DMV with proof of insurance for 3 years.

32.	I understand that proof of my successful completion of an alcohol/drug program must be received at DMV headquarters for my driving privilege to be reinstated, **even if I am not ordered to attend such a program by the Court**. I also understand that I must surrender my license to the Court.

33.	I understand that the DMV will prohibit me from operating a **commercial** vehicle for one year if I am convicted of a first DUI offense or willful refusal to submit to or complete a chemical test to determine my blood alcohol level, which occurred in any vehicle. The DMV will prohibit me from operating a commercial vehicle ever again if I am convicted of a **second or subsequent** DUI offense or willful refusal to submit to or complete a chemical test in any vehicle.

34.	I understand that the DMV will revoke my driver's license for a period of 4 years if I have a prior felony conviction in the past 10 years of Vehicle Code § 23152, 23153 or Penal Code § 191.5(b), 192(c)(1), or any conviction within 10 years of Penal Code § 191.5(a) or 192.5(a).

35.	I understand that if I was under the age of 21 at the

time of my arrest, my driver's license will also be suspended for 1 year, and I must surrender my license to the Court.

36.   I understand that if my blood alcohol level was .15% or more, or if I refused to submit to a chemical test, the Court will consider this in determining whether to enhance the penalties, grant probation, or impose additional terms of punishment.

37.   I understand that if I am placed on probation, it is unlawful to drive with a blood alcohol level of .01 percent or greater and my license will be suspended by the DMV for up to one year if I do so.

38.   I understand that if I am convicted of a third or subsequent DUI violation, I will be designated as a habitual traffic offender for 3 years after my conviction, and I will receive an enhanced sentence if I drive in vio
lation of my license revocation. If probation is granted I may also request to participate in a 30-month treatment program. If this Court grants my request, I will be sentenced to the county jail for **at least 30 days but not more than 1 year as a** condition of probation.

Nature of Offense Reckless driving reduced from driving under the influence

Minimum & Maximum Sentences

If Probation is granted: A maximum of 90 days in jail, or a $1,000 fine, or both, plus attendance at a treatment program.

Other Consequences

If alcohol or drugs are involved, this conviction will act as a separate DUI conviction if I commit a subsequent DUI offense within 10-years.

Vehicle Code Section 14601

First Offense 5 days to 6 months in jail and a fine of $100 to $1,000.

Second or Subsequent Offense I have one or more prior convictions in the past 5 years of either sections 14601, 14601.1, 14601.2, or 14601.5.

10 days to 1 year in jail and a fine of $500 to $2,000 - 10 days in jail required if probation is imposed.

_____

Vehicle Code Section 14601.1

First Offense Up to 6 months in jail, or a fine of $300 to $1,000, or both.

Second or Subsequent Offense I have one or more prior convictions in the past 5 years of either sections 14601, 14601.1, 14601.2, or 14601.5.

5 days to 1 year in jail and a fine of $500 to $2,000.

_____

Vehicle Code Section 14601.2

First Offense 10 days to 6 months in jail and a fine of $300 to $1,000; 10 days in jail required if probation is imposed. (If I have been designated as a habitual traffic offender within 3 years of this conviction, in addition to the penalties above, I will be sentenced to serve 180 days in jail and to pay a $2,000 fine.

Second or Subsequent Offense I have one or more prior convictions in the past 5 years of either sections 14601, 14601.1, 14601.2, or 14601.5.

30 days to 1 year in jail and a fine of $500 to $2,000; 30 days in jail required if probation is imposed.

Vehicle Code Section 14601.5

First Offense up to 6 months in jail or a fine of $$3)0 to $1,000, or both.

Second or Subsequent Offense I have one or more prio con-victions in the past 5 years of either sections 14601, 14 01.1, 14601.2, or 14601.5.

10 days to 1 year in jail and a fine of $500 to $2,000. **Note** - sec-tion 14601.3 constitutes a prior conviction for this offe ise.

Vehicle Code Section 14601.3

First Offense 30 days in jail an a fine of $1,000

Second or Subsequent Offense prior conviction(s) in ast 7 years of section 14601.3

180 days in jail and a fine of $2,000

| 14601.3 | 30 days in jail and a fine of $1000 | 180 days in jail and fine of $2000 |

ADDITIONAL PENALTY FOR A VIOLATION OF SEC IONS 14601.1, 14601.2 or 14601.5

39.   If applicable – I understand that if I am convict d of a violation of Vehicle Code § 14601.2, or if the charge wa for a violation of that section but I am pleading to section 1 4601, 14601.1 or 14601.5, the Court will order me to install an ig-nition interlock device (ID) on any vehicle that I own r op-erate for up to three years. Installation of this device, vhich prevents the vehicle from starting if I have alcohol n my body, does not authorize me to drive without a valid d iver's

license.

40.   I have read and understood the applicable charts on pages 3 and 4 which list the minimum and maximum penalties for the offense(s) I am charged with. (See No. 1 for the offenses not listed in the charts).

41.   If applicable – I understand that the possible consequences for the offense(s) charged, which are not listed on the penalty charts on pages 3 and 4, include other consequences.

PLEA(S)

42.   I hereby freely and voluntarily plead Guilty or No Contest to the following.

LIST CHARGES

43.   If applicable – I freely and voluntarily admit the other conviction(s) that I listed on this form, and I understand that this admission will increase the penalties which are imposed on me.

44.   If applicable – I freely and voluntarily admit the probation violation(s) that I listed on this form and give up my right to a hearing before a judge regarding the probation violation(s).

45.   I understand that I have the right to a delay of from 6 hours to 5 days prior to being sentenced for a misdemeanor, and the right to a delay of up to 20 days for a felony. I give up this right and agree to be sentenced at this time.

46.   If applicable – I understand that I have the right to enter my plea before, and to be sentenced by a judge. I give up this right and agree to enter my plea before, and to be sentenced by:

       Temporary Judge's Name

DEFENDANT'S SIGNATURE _____

DATE: _____